SECRETS
of
SPECIAL OPS LEADERSHIP

SECRETS of SPECIAL OPS LEADERSHIP

Dare the Impossible—
Achieve the Extraordinary

William A. Cohen, Ph.D.
Major General, USAFR, Ret.
Former Air Commando

AMACOM

American Management Association

New York • Atlanta • Brussels • Chicago • Mexico City • San Francisco
Shanghai • Tokyo • Toronto • Washington, D.C.

Special discounts on bulk quantities of AMACOM books are
available to corporations, professional associations, and other
organizations. For details, contact Special Sales Department,
AMACOM, a division of American Management Association,
1601 Broadway, New York, NY 10019.
Tel.: 212-903-8316. Fax: 212-903-8083.
Web site: www. amacombooks.org

This publication is designed to provide accurate and authoritative
information in regard to the subject matter covered. It is sold with
the understanding that the publisher is not engaged in rendering
legal, accounting, or other professional service. If legal advice or
other expert assistance is required, the services of a competent
professional person should be sought.

Library of Congress Cataloging-in-Publication Data

Cohen, William A., 1937-
    Secrets of special ops leadership : dare the impossible, achieve the
extraordinary / William A. Cohen.
    p.   cm.
    Includes bibliographical references and index.
    ISBN 0-8144-0840-0
    1. Leadership.   2. Management.   I. Title.

HD57.7.C643 2005
658.4'092—dc22   2005010447

Printing number

10   9   8   7   6   5   4   3   2   1

For Nurit

CONTENTS

AUTHOR'S NOTE

W H E N W E W E N T to title this book my editor and I found ourselves at odds as to how best to describe the type of unique leadership I had written about. In the United States we now have a major command with components from all the military services known as Special Operations Command, or "SOCOM." In current parlance, what these different types of special military forces do is known collectively as "special operations," or "special ops" for short, and individual practitioners are sometimes referred to as "special operators." However, not too long ago many of us who performed these duties were known as "commandos." I am proud to say that I was once a member of the 609th Air Commando Squadron of the 56th Air Commando Wing before the designations were changed, and the organization of our former members is still known as the Air Commando Association. Many of us grew accustomed to the commando designation.

The term "commando" came from the British in World War II. They got it from the "Afrikaners" when they fought them in South Africa at the turn of the century. As you will see in the book, "commando" or "special operations" go way back in our own history, but we frequently called them by a different name. We used the term "rangers" even before American independence. This term is still used to describe some elite units of the U.S. Army. There have always been these special, unique units in warfare, even in biblical times. In this book, I have used the terms special ops, special operations, and commando interchangeably to describe all units, whether of American, foreign, or historical origin, that are led with the leadership philosophy of daring to do the impossible to achieve the extraordinary.

PRINCIPLES

WHY ARE SPECIAL OPS SPECIAL?

THE FIRST TIME I personally heard about commandos was when I was a five-year-old during World War II. Commandos were the superheroes of the day. They eagerly accepted death-defying missions and routinely accomplished what others considered impossible. They operated behind enemy lines and wrecked havoc with enemy lines of communication. They attacked the enemy even when he was unreachable by conventional forces or aircraft. They raided enemy strongholds and captured high-ranking officers. They provided on-the-ground reconnaissance and intelligence that spelled the difference between victory and defeat. My dream was one day to become a commando.

Air Commandos in the U.S. Military

When I became an Air Force officer in 1959, I didn't hear much about commandos. Yet during World War II, air commandos existed and supported Britain's General Orde Wingate and his "Chindits" in battles against the Japanese in the China-Burma-India theater of operations. In fact, one famous air commando leader, Colonel Philip Cochran, was the basis of the "Flip Corkin" character in Milton Caniff's very popular *Terry and the Pirates* comic strip of the day.

Of course, by 1959, the U.S. Army did have its Special Forces or "Green Berets" unit, and although Ranger units had been mostly deactivated, infantry officers were encouraged to volunteer for Ranger training and to become "Ranger qualified," which entitled them to wear the coveted "Ranger tab" on their uniforms. The U.S. Navy had its underwater demolition teams or "frogmen." Their role in an age of nuclear weapons was unclear. Marine Corps commando units were no longer in existence. All of this was soon to change.

The new air commandos came into existence about the same time that I completed flying school. President John F. Kennedy recognized a growing threat of communist guerrillas subverting a country through armed insurgency, as had already happened in Eastern Europe, although in some countries, such attempts had been defeated. In most cases it was some sort of "special forces," not regular military units, that defeated them. This was the primary mission of the new commandos: nonregular warriors who trained the local populace, lived off the land, put down insurgents, were capable of harassing an occupying force if necessary, and could also operate in their more traditional roles of raiding and operating behind enemy lines with little or no direct support. Later, the missions of the new American commandos in all services were to be greatly expanded.

It took something special to do this kind of work, and President Kennedy asked his armed forces to develop new units or expand what they had to do the job. The military services responded. The Navy converted its "frogmen" underwater demolition teams into the Navy SEALs. "SEAL" is actually an acronym standing for sea, air, and land, the three bases from which Navy SEALs operate. The U.S. Air Force reactivated the Air Commandos, which had been dormant since World War II. Both the Army and Marines increased their commando capability. Those conducting special operations were singled out from all other military organizations. They were special. They did what conventional units and their members were unable to do. I wanted to be an air commando, and I tried hard to become one.

My Struggle to Become an Air Commando

At the time, I was a navigator-bombardier on a B-52 nuclear bomber. In 1963, Strategic Air Command, or SAC, owned the B-52s and had the important mission of deterring nuclear war. Seeking these new and unique warriors, the commandos asked for volunteers from the regular squadrons. I submitted my paperwork and volunteered. However, my volunteer statement and application for the commandos was stopped at SAC headquarters. I was told that the nuclear deterrent mission had a higher priority and that I should forget the commandos. I saluted smartly and went about my business.

However, by 1965 the war in Vietnam had heated up considerably. The air commandos were engaged and badly need qualified people.

Even the B-52 nuclear bomber was being refitted to drop conventional bombs in support of the Vietnam mission. I decided to try and get to the commandos by volunteering for combat duty in Vietnam. That would not mean reassignment to another B-52 squadron, but an entirely different airplane. In fact, the Air Force rules at the time were that if you volunteered for combat duty in Vietnam, you got to pick what airplane you would fly. I planned on volunteering for the A-26A "Counter Invader." This was a modified version of a World War II attack plane. It flew like a fighter, but could carry the bomb load of a World War II B-17. Moreover, it had been fitted with all the modern bells and whistles in avionics: antiskid brakes for use on short runways, tip tanks, and props that could be autofeathered in an emergency. The A-26A could operate in the field out of relatively short airstrips and was flown exclusively by the air commandos.

Alas, the Vietnam mission might have gained in importance, but SAC still had precedence in retaining its highly trained aircrews. My volunteer application for combat duty in Vietnam was again stopped at SAC headquarters.

As a last resort, I decided to try family influence. Almost twenty years earlier, my father, an Air Force officer, was assigned to Hickam Air Force Base in Hawaii. His best friend was a colorful young captain by the name of Harry Coleman. Captain Coleman had a remarkable career. Before the United States entered World War II, Coleman had volunteered and flown with England's Royal Air Force. Then, after the United States entered the war, he had been incorporated into the U.S. Army Air Force. After the war's end, he was offered a regular commission, which he accepted. Much to everyone's surprise, when Captain Coleman became eligible for promotion to major, the Air Force failed to promote him! Now this sometimes happens, and usually an officer gets several opportunities in successive years. Captain Coleman was very discouraged and considered resigning his commission for a much higher-paying airline job. After all, he had his family to consider. It was my father who helped persuade Captain Coleman to remain in the Air Force and give it another shot. Then my father was reassigned and left Hawaii. We lost track of Captain Coleman and his family.

Ten years later, my father ran into Coleman in Washington. The only thing was, he was no longer "Captain" Coleman. Now he was Colonel Coleman, a pretty high ranking officer. Moreover, I knew he was assigned to Tactical Air Command, which was closely involved with the commandos. I called Colonel Coleman and explained my situation. He said something like, "I'm sure there's been a mistake. We're assigning all our best young officers who volunteer for combat in Vietnam to whatever airplane they want. What unit are you in now?"

I told him. "Great," he responded. "I've known one of the generals in your command more than twenty years and was in flying school with him. I'll see what I can find out and get back with you."

Two weeks later he called. He was apologetic. "I would never have believed it," he told me. "He said, 'Harry, if we let that young officer go out of SAC, they'll all want to go.'" At that point, I just about gave up.

However, a year later a new opportunity came up. There was a big push in the Air Force for advanced education, and when I first joined up, I was asked if I had any interest in going to graduate school. Almost carelessly, I said "yes." My academic record at West Point was hardly one that would permit advanced academic training and I never gave it another thought. Nevertheless, after five years of flying duty I was eligible and was contacted to confirm whether I was still interested. The logic of sending folks into combat after graduate school rather than before escaped me. Nevertheless, on my completion of my MBA from the University of Chicago in 1967, I finally was assigned to A-26s as an air commando (although not before having to struggle one last time with Air Force personnel). Over the next two years, flying 174 combat missions in A-26s and one in an A-1, I was proud to be one of these unique warriors called an air commando.

Unique Warriors Equal Unique Accomplishments

In my study of commandos and special operations, I discovered that it makes little difference how these unique warriors are designated or from what country or service they operate. In the United States today we classify them under the general category of special operations (or special ops) because the operations assigned to them are sometimes so difficult as to be termed "impossible" by any rational analysis, making these operations indeed "special." They are still commandos.

For example, during Operation Desert Storm, an eight-man Special Forces team was secretly transported 150 miles behind enemy lines by Black Hawk helicopters of the U.S. Army's 160th Special Operations Aviation Regiment. Thousands of armed Iraqis were between these eight special ops soldiers and friendly forces. Their mission was essential. It was to learn if the enemy had spotted General Norman Schwarzkopf's risky "Hail Mary" maneuver. If they had, Iraqi units could destroy the U.S. VII Corps and the XVIII Airborne Corps individually before they could link up. It could have turned a successful campaign into a disaster and Saddam Hussein could have won the war. General Schwarzkopf had to know the answer, and satellites, useful in many situations, could not have provided precise information. Landing after dark, the eight men built a hidden bunker at the side of the road, right next to the enemy. Before the sun rose, these and other special operators were able to provide critical intelligence to Schwarzkopf from right in the middle of the Iraqi Army. They saved thousands of lives by enabling Schwarzkopf's calculated gamble to pay off—and potentially saving the entire campaign had the two American corps been spotted before they could link up.

America's elite special operations units are at the forefront of the war on terror—and have played crucial roles in the U.S. invasions of both Afghanistan and Iraq. Whether they are called Air Commandos, Navy SEALs, Army Green Berets, Delta Force, Rangers, or Special Operations–Capable Marines, their achievements are remarkable, but still mostly secret. What we do know is that a handful of these unique fighting men won high praise for helping to pave the way for U.S. military victories in both campaigns.

Here are a few of their accomplishments in these environments that we know about:

- In Afghanistan, they were called the "primary instruments" on the ground. There were only between 200 and 300 special ops troops, but they hit the ground before anyone else and by many estimates did the work of a hundred times their number.

- Their work with the Northern Alliance in Afghanistan saved hundreds of lives. Special operators working with CIA teams organized offensive operations by the Afghan resistance, even taking the fight to the Taliban on horseback, although the U.S. Army hadn't used horses in battle since before World War I.

- A handful of special operators turned around a demoralized Northern Alliance in days—winning the confidence of the anti-Taliban force, which was a primary concern of American commanders and politicians.

- In Iraq, operating in units of twelve men or fewer, they met secretly with indigenous peoples hundreds of miles beyond friendly lines. Alone with natives they did not know, they identified tribal leaders willing to pledge allegiance to the United States. Using high-technology lasers and getting up close, they precisely identified enemy military targets for U.S. warplanes, minimizing incidents of friendly fire.

- They seized oil infrastructure, took control of airfields and other key sites in southwestern Iraq, and prevented dams from being blown; they worked with the Kurds up north and helped target and capture Iraqi leadership in key cities.

- They plucked PFC Jessica Lynch from the center of an enemy-controlled area and got her to safety before the Iraqis even realized she was gone.

- They nabbed the terrorist Abu Abbas, who years earlier had hijacked an Italian cruise ship and murdered an American invalid.

- They cleared the way and prepared the ground for the largest military parachute landing since World War II.

- They led two of three battlefronts in the war in Iraq, and in Operation Viking Hammer they took on thirteen Iraqi divisions and captured a camp believed to be harboring Al Qaeda and foreign terrorists.

- They led the forces that went in and dragged Saddam Hussein from his spider-hole hideout.

And American commandos didn't just fight enemies. They proved to be strong friends of countries that had been severely critical of America. When the tsunami hit, commando air crews flew to severely damaged areas of all tsunami-affected countries and under all conditions. Sometimes it was highly hazardous, since they were without ground control and the weather wasn't always perfect. Still, they delivered vital supplies and medical personnel, saving tens of thousands from disease and starvation. Throughout early January of 2005, they delivered forty-four tons of medicine, blankets, food, and water to Aceh, Indonesia, alone.

According to the latest information, U.S. Special Operations forces were deployed in 148 countries and territories,[1] and *U.S. News and World Report* documented 7,648 special operations deployments in fifty-four countries in one week in 2004.[2]

The personnel in all special ops units are especially selected and specially trained. The standards demanded of them are unbelievably high. The risks and hardships they face in their "work" are supreme. The workload is probably more difficult and significantly greater than in any other profession, military or otherwise. Yet, these special people volunteer, take immense risks, and willingly do the impossible for pay and benefits that are almost trivial considering the effort required and the potential payoff.

Clearly, such individuals cannot be led in a routine fashion, and they are not. Special leadership techniques are required. Often they are not the same used in leading regular troops. For example, in one unit, officers and enlisted personnel are on a first-name basis. Yet standards of discipline are so high that disobedience of an order is never considered.

Although these techniques and concepts frequently cross geographic, political, and cultural lines and are to be found in foreign commando units as well as our own, they are not always appreciated by their own armed forces. As one senior four-star general told me, "You special ops guys are all alike; once you have been in special ops you think there are no rules and that you can do anything."

There may be some truth in this statement. However, the fact is that to do what they do, commandos do sometimes need to violate the rules. And just to attempt some of these things, they need to think that they can accomplish anything. The leadership secrets outlined in this book enable special ops units to accomplish what many other military organizations cannot, and they will enable any organization to do the same—provided business leaders understand them and are willing to make the commitment to adapt these leadership lessons to their organizations.

Why Special Ops Leadership Techniques Are Important for Business

Can commando techniques work in business? My research shows they can. If you can select, develop, and motivate your employees to peak performance, they will accomplish dramatic, almost fantastic feats for you—just as fighting commandos do in uniform.

For example, in late December 2004, Donald Trump signaled the second season end of his successful television series *The Apprentice* by announcing "You're hired!" to the winner of the competition. After starting with more than a million applicants and ending with eighteen candidate finalists who, over the season, had competed by leading fellow contestants in various business projects, one individual had emerged the winner. This was Kelly Perdew, a West Pointer and former Army officer who had completed Ranger training. Perdew's winning performance was leading his team in a charity fund-raising celebrity polo match, during which he had to overcome problems ranging from uncooperative weather to an uncooperative team made up of former contestants who had already been eliminated. Trump declared Perdew the winner of the reality show over the other finalist, a Phi Beta Kappa graduate of Princeton who also had a degree from Harvard Law School. According to *The New York Sun*:

> Mr. Trump wasn't just being patriotic—it seemed like Mr. Perdew's military training was actually good preparation for the teamwork, competition, and improvisation needed to complete the tasks that were part of the reality show. Better preparation, even, than the training some of the other contestants had received at Ivy League universities.[3]

One Ranger made this statement regarding the use of these concepts in achieving impossible results in the civilian sector: ". . . [T]hey can succeed because of their will to succeed and the confidence that they can accomplish a mission, in an ethical way, no matter what it takes, whether it takes long hours, innovative thinking, or motivating people to do extraordinary things. That attitude translates to success regardless of what business you are in. . . ."[4]

How This Book Is Different

There are many books attempting to show the application of special operations (also known as spec ops or commando) techniques and especially leadership concepts to business. They have made a contribution to business thinking. And well they might. When an organization can successfully win out against other organizations many times its size with many times its resources, it's worthwhile examining how this achievement was done.

However, what these books have offered is incomplete. There is a theory of special operations on which commando leadership is based. The notion that special ops leadership techniques can be indiscriminately applied to all business organizations is just as erroneous as attempting to apply them to all military organizations. It won't work. The military is very careful about what techniques to use and what to omit in its regular military formations. So, it is important to understand the principles on which commando operations are based, and the opportunities and limitations in applying these powerful concepts.

Also, other books look only at the individual commando organizations with which a particular author is familiar. They show only how this particular organization's leadership techniques may be incorporated in a civilian setting. For example, an author may focus on the Rangers, Green Berets, Navy SEALs, or Delta Force, to name just a few. However, as good as each of these organizations is, each has a very specialized mission and all are American commando organizations. Yet, there is much to be gained from analyzing the commando organizations of foreign countries. Moreover, there are a few organizations that are only nominally special ops organizations, yet they operate that way. Two flying organizations come to mind: the American Volunteer Group's Flying Tigers and the Marine Corps' Black Sheep Squadron, both of which operated during World War II. This confirms the important fact that commando units aren't new and that valuable lessons would be excluded if we do not include in our analysis commando organizations that once existed, but have since become a part of history.

This book takes a comprehensive approach. There is a commonality in how individuals are led in all successful commando units. This book synthesizes these techniques. It covers the essential methods that commando leaders in the British Special Air Service (SAS), Israeli Sayeret Mat'kal, and our own commando units employ. But it also covers techniques that have been used by commando units throughout thousands of years of history to accomplish extremely challenging tasks against vastly superior forces.

Beginning with the principles of special operations, this book is about special ops leadership and how you can apply it to your business or project or any situation where leadership is important, so that you can beat the odds and accomplish the seemingly impossible.

This book reaches across national and military service boundaries into history to explain the background and the premise behind special operations leadership techniques. With that knowledge, you'll understand which of these frequently different yet very powerful leadership techniques can be applied to your organization, when to use them, and when they should be avoided. Commando leadership techniques pay off, and they can pay off for your organization or business.

The Principles of Special Ops Leadership

"There's a way to do it better—find it!"
—Thomas A. Edison

"What he greatly thought he nobly dared."
—Homer

THE WORD *commando* originated during the Boer War in South Africa in the late nineteenth century when the Boers fought for their independence from the British Empire. "Commando" was the Boer word to describe the mobile columns of fighting men that struck suddenly, did the maximum damage, and were gone before superior British forces could react. Through forced marches, ambuscades, and night raids, the Boer commandos created a living hell for the well-trained, well-armed regular British Army.

The British forces didn't much like them, but they respected their ability on the battlefield and the Boers in turn won a worldwide reputation for their accomplishments. However, they were not the first to be organized and perform in this fashion. Commandos throughout history have won acclaim for their abilities to accomplish the impossible or near impossible. As a result, the concept of business commandos, who could accomplish similar feats for business organizations, has always been very attractive.

In his 1996 book *Accidental Empires,* Robert X. Cringely said that business commandos were out in front in new businesses, working hard, fast, and at low expense "to do lots of damage with surprise and teamwork, establishing a beachhead before the enemy is even aware that they exist." Rob Landley further amplified Cringely's thoughts in an article in which he wrote: "Simply put, they create something out of nothing, turning an idea into a product. [Commandos] can literally do the work of a hundred normal employees when they've got the right problems to work on. A start-up without commandos has nothing to sell."[1]

Unfortunately, neither author explained much more about business commandos or how to develop and use them in business. To understand how to accomplish success with business commandos, we must first delve into the history of battle commandos and the theory of commando operations.

Gideon's Trumpets

The bible gives us an early lesson in the employment of commando operations. Around 1100 B.C., ancient Israel was under the domination of the Midianites. According to the bible, God selected Gideon as his special ops leader. Gideon's orders were to attack a vastly superior number of well-trained, battle-experienced Midianites in a fortified encampment. He didn't have much raw material from which to draw, just a ragged assortment of mostly untrained soldiers who had previously been defeated by the enemy. As he screened the men, Gideon first said that anyone who wanted could leave. Twenty-two thousand of his soldiers, two-thirds of his army, packed up and immediately departed for home.

Through various techniques he further screened the remaining volunteers to just 300 commandos. He gave each of the 300 men a trumpet, a torch, and an empty pitcher, then he divided them into three companies. That night the three companies of commandos surrounded the Midianite camp. The empty pitchers covered their torches. On Gideon's signal, they broke the pitchers and blew their trumpets. Then they shouted: "The sword of the Lord, and of Gideon."

In those days, each torch represented at least a full company of men, so the Midianites thought they were under surprise attack by 30,000 Hebrews. The bible (Judges 7:22) tells us that ". . . the Lord set every man's sword against his fellow, even throughout all the host: and the host fled to Beth-shittah in Zererath, and to the border of Abelmeholah, unto Tabbath." This special operation force was so successful that even today the Israeli Army considers Gideon's raid the model for its commando operations.

Early Commando Operations in America

The first rigorous application of the commando concept on the American continent was in the seventeenth century, when American forces, British colonists all, fought. Rangers under the command of Captain Benjamin Church brought the Indian conflict known as King Philip's War to a successful conclusion in 1675.[2] This was a war fought in the Plymouth Colony against the Indians, who were led by an Indian chief known as "King Philip."[3] These Rangers came into existence in response to challenges resulting from the ruggedness of the terrain and the nature of the colonist's opponents, which were far different from those faced in Europe.

In 1756, the American colonies were heavily embroiled in the French and Indian War. Of course, the colonists, English all, fought on the side of the mother country. George Washington, then a young militia officer, received his baptism of fire during this war.

Major Robert Rogers formed the best-known Ranger unit of those early days, using tactics that regular colonial and British redcoats could not. Rogers' Rangers mirrored the Boer commandos of more than a century later, in the same way that modern-day "special operators" do today. They moved fast and fearlessly to attack an enemy where he least expected it and where they could do the most damage. Then, like ghosts, they were gone. Like other commandos, Rogers' dramatic victories won him acclaim from friend and foe alike.

Now we jump ahead another twenty years to America's War of Independence. Right from the start, the colonists began using commando tactics against the regular British forces that opposed them. In "the shot heard round the world" that began the war, the British commander, Lieutenant General Thomas Gage, sent troops to seize a concentration of colonists' arms at Lexington and Concord. Warned through the efforts of patriots like Paul Revere, colonial troops were on hand to fight, and though opposed by more than 700 British regulars, they were able to foil British aims at the cost of only eight killed.

As the British made their way back to the safety of Boston, colonists repeatedly attacked them. The British were trained to fight in tight formations, as if on parade. The colonists used the commando tactics of hit and run. They attacked suddenly from off-road positions, from behind trees. When the British troops stopped and formed their ranks to pursue them, they dispersed, only to repeat the process several miles down the road. Despite being the acknowledged "best army in the world," the British suffered seventy-three killed and 173 wounded.[4] That is, the British suffered almost 32 percent casualties by the time they arrived in Boston. Because of this and other reverses, Gage was relieved of command before the first year of war was out.

After the American Revolution, the United States always had some sort of special operations force in war. During our Civil War, the best known was probably that of Confederate Colonel John S. Mosby. Mosby's Rangers were mounted and operated behind Union lines south of the Potomac River. Mosby employed aggressive action and surprise assaults to force Union forces to be on guard everywhere. He located weak points behind Union lines and then, concentrating superior forces against these positions, attacked, accomplished his objective, and disappeared. He tied down huge numbers of federal forces attempting to deter his raids.

Mosby usually raided with only twenty to fifty of his men in a single operation. But sometimes, he used even fewer with marked success. With inspired leadership and derring-do, he once attacked and routed an entire Union regiment in its bivouac with only nine men. On another occasion, he ruined the career of Edwin H. Stoughton, an up-and-coming Union brigadier general, by routing the sleeping commander from his bed almost in the shadow of the federal capitol. He captured the officer in his nightclothes, awakening him with the flat of a sword to his behind. He also captured the general's staff and forty horses purchased for Union stores. On being informed of this disaster the following morning, President Lincoln was said to have commented: "That's terrible! It's easy to promote and replace a general, but I don't know how we'll replace those forty horses".[5]

Commando Operations in World War II

World War II saw commandos in all American services in numerous operations and in foreign countries as well. The British developed commandos to provide small-scale raiding units that could launch assaults on the German-held and fortified coast of Europe. Later they were used to spearhead seaborne landings and other operations in both Europe and the Far East.

The Royal Marines reorganized their battalions to form Royal Marine Commando units. In North Africa, a Scotsman by the name of David Stirling formed the famous SAS. To disguise the unit's mission and give the impression that the British had flown additional air rein-forcements to the area, the unit was called the Special Air Service, thus the initials by which this unit is known even today. Operating hundreds of miles behind enemy lines, the SAS attacked German airfields, oil depots, and headquarters units. By some accounts, they destroyed more enemy aircraft than did the Royal Air Force. The SBS, or Special Boat Service, soon joined the SAS and echoed the older forces remarkable achievements. Both commando units exist in the British armed forces today.

On the German side, the most well known command unit was led by Colonel Otto Skorzeny. On the direct orders of Adolf Hitler, Skorzeny rescued Italian dictator Benito Mussolini from his captivity on an inaccessible Italian mountaintop, landing his assault force in gliders. With typical commando-style leadership, and despite the risks, Skorzeny personally led the raid and brought Mussolini to Hitler.

All of these operations have a common theoretical basis, and it is important that we understand it before we can understand the substantial differences in the way business commandos must be led from regular employees.

Why Special Operations Are Different

The basis of all strategy is to concentrate superior resources at the decisive point. This is true in commando operations as it is in any other situation, on the battlefield, in the boardroom, or in any competitive human endeavor. The differences in special operations have to do with what resources we're considering. On the battlefield, superior resources usually mean numbers of troops and firepower. Some have termed this combination and other factors "combat power." For business, these resources might be people, money, and know-how. We might call these combined resources superior "business power."

Special operations theory differs in that it defies conventional thinking about what constitutes "superior resources," because on the battlefield, a small force is used to defeat a much larger or well-entrenched adversary.[6] In business, application of special operations principles means that a smaller firm with less financial resources can overcome a stronger competitor that may be already entrenched in the marketplace.

How is this possible? Captain William H. McRaven, a former Navy

SEAL commander currently with the National Security Council committee on counterterrorism, theorized that a small force can defeat an apparently stronger opponent only when the smaller force gains a decisive advantage over its adversary. He called this decisive advantage "relative superiority" and stated that attaining it was essential for the success of any commando operation. Clearly, this concept of a decisive advantage is identical to the terms "competitive advantage" or "differential advantage" commonly used in business.

By analyzing eight historical special operations cases, Captain McRaven derived six principles that the special operations leader could and must control to attain relative superiority. McRaven's principles are: simplicity, security, repetition, surprise, speed, and purpose.[7] It is important to recognize that this relative superiority could not, and need not, be maintained indefinitely. Relative superiority only had to be maintained long enough to achieve the objective.

Previously, my own analysis of business strategy had yielded ten principles.[8] However, these involved business strategy in general and did not focus on the use of special ops techniques. In my further analysis of many additional special ops cases, and numerous other instances in business where smaller organizations intentionally took on and achieved success over larger and more powerful competitors, I confirmed Captain McRaven's principles for what I call "business commando operations." There was some slight variance in these principles, for reasons I will explain shortly. Also, I felt it important to put these principles in their correct order of importance. The principles I confirmed from my expanded study of both history and business operations, in order of importance, are:

- Purpose
- Repetition
- Speed
- Surprise
- Security
- Simplicity

The Principle of Purpose

Having a clear and definite purpose is perhaps the most important principle of strategy, because you can't get there until you know where "there" is! As a leader, you cannot present a clear understanding of what you are going to do if you don't understand it yourself. Peter Drucker says that top management must first answer the question, "What is our business and what should it be?"[9] That's the kind of thing we're talking about. For any specific operation, what exactly is its purpose?

For Colonel Arthur "Bull" Simmons on November 20, 1970, it was clear. Here's what he told his fifty-six handpicked Special Forces assault force prior to the raid at Son Tay during the Vietnam War: "We are going to rescue seventy American prisoners of war, maybe more, from a camp called Son Tay. This is something American prisoners have a right to expect from their fellow soldiers. The target is twenty-three miles west of Hanoi." The purpose was stated absolutely clearly so that there was no doubt. Later, when things began to go amiss (as they always do in any operation to some extent), Simmons's commanders knew exactly what actions to take. One assault helicopter had engine problems. Normally this situation called for landing. The pilot pressed on and completed the mission. When another helicopter tried to land in the compound, it ran into one of the hundreds of high trees on the compound's periphery and, under skilled flying, made a controlled crash. The assault troops it was carrying didn't miss a beat; they proceeded with their assigned duties. In the action, American Special Forces killed fifty prison guards and another hundred enemy soldiers who came running out of their barracks.

Unfortunately, the American prisoners had been moved only a few days before, not because of a security failure but because of an unforeseen happening of nature. A nearby river was overflowing its banks and the Vietnamese feared flooding. Nevertheless, this commando raid was not a complete loss. The raid influenced a positive change in the treatment of American prisoners of war. It also forced the enemy to bring and keep all POWs together in Hanoi to better defend against future attempts to free them.[10]

The Principle of Repetition

McRaven's "repetition" refers to repeated practice of the actions to be accomplished for a particular raid prior to the operation, just like actors practice before a performance of a play. By his definition, repetition is of much less importance for business. This is because business commando operations are usually of much longer duration and, consequently, have numerous additional phases. Employing the principle of repetition as defined by McRaven in, say, the introduction of a new product, through the period of its establishment in the marketplace and over a period of months, is simply not practical and, because of the changes possible during the new product introduction, not particularly useful.

However, repetition does show up in other business and military commando operations in another sense, and that is repetition of a successful method of operating.

Restaurant chains are useful for observing business commando operations and the practice of this principle. If you visit two or more restaurants of the same chain, you can see the same traits of good food, good service, and good atmosphere repeated again and again. The Cheesecake Factory chain provides an excellent example. The Cheesecake Factory's CEO David Overton repeats a successful formula again and again.

One of the outstanding examples of this commando principle in business was that practiced by my old friend E. Joseph Cossman, a true business commando genius. Although Joe introduced product after product, most totally unrelated to one another, he repeated the same success formula time after time. This was:

1. Find a product no one wanted, usually one that had previously failed or gone through its life cycle and was in decline.

2. Analyze the market to make sure the demand was large enough to support a major success with this product.

3. Gain total and exclusive control over the product at the lowest cost possible.

4. Promote the product simultaneously in a variety of new, surprising, and innovative ways and to the maximum extent possible.

5. License the product to someone else after its sales have peaked.

6. Move on to the next project.

Joe followed this formula again and again and was successful almost every time. Over the years he personally made $25 million, which would probably be $50 million today, and yet he never had more than a dozen or so people working for him.

The Principle of Speed

Speed works in two ways. First, the commando can use speed to gain surprise. Speed also allows the commando to achieve his purpose before adversaries can react effectively to counter an attack with their superior resources.

Pursued by a force of 400 of the enemy during the French and Indian War of 1763, Major Robert Rogers led about 100 Rangers at breakneck speed through the northeastern American wilderness. Marching through heavy foliage and crossing numerous swamps, Rogers outdistanced his enemies and wore them out. It was at some cost, because he took casualties merely because of the stress on his own men. He feinted in one direction, then crossed the St. Francis River and struck the French-allied Indian village of St. Francis in a surprise night attack. They killed 200 warriors and captured twenty women and children. They didn't pause to rest, but continued their movement. With their river path blocked by hundreds of French and Indians in both directions, Rogers and his Rangers began a forced march to Coos Meadows, where they expected a British garrison. Almost exhausted and without food, they found the place deserted. They continued on at high speed and without pause to Charlestown, New Hampshire, where Rogers was finally able to escape his pursuers by a water route.[11]

Business commandos must be able to react rapidly to changing tactical conditions. When I was associated with a large university, it took a minimum of two years to implement a new academic program. In fact, two years was considered "the fast track," and limited to one such academic program per year in the entire university! At Touro University, where I now hold a professorship, similar programs could be developed and approved in a matter of days, and be ready to go the next period of academic instruction. The commando principle of speed can have a major advantage in successfully winning out over the competition.

The Principle of Surprise

Surprise is one of the commando's greatest weapons in helping to overcome the advantage of a competitor who is stronger in numbers and resources. Even the strongest of corporations cannot be strong everywhere. So the astute commando can select his targets for the effect desired and, with surprise, achieve maximum impact by concentrating resources at that point. The advantage of surprise applies to all fields of human endeavor.

In the 1988 vice presidential debates, Democratic vice presidential hopeful Lloyd Bentsen demolished his Republican opponent Dan Quayle with a now-famous retort. Bentsen knew that Quayle's relative inexperience compared to his own would eventually be called into question. Both men knew that when Democratic President John F. Kennedy assumed office, he was younger than Quayle and had even less experience. Bentsen anticipated that Quayle might attempt to use this fact and prepared. Quayle took the bait and fell right into the trap, comparing himself to Kennedy. Without missing a beat, Bentsen countered with this statement: "Senator, I served with Jack Kennedy. I knew Jack Kennedy. Jack Kennedy was a friend of mine. Senator, you are no Jack Kennedy." Quayle was stunned. He looked as if he had been hit with a baseball bat and was largely ineffectual during the remainder of the debate. It would be an understatement to say he was surprised.

One of the first commando raids of World War II was the successful operation conducted by the British against the Lofoten islands off of the Norwegian coast on March 3–4, 1941. In Operation Claymore, 500 commandos and fifty Norwegian seamen landed on the German-occupied Norwegian coast from ships. The objective was to destroy factories producing glycerin for the German Army. The Germans hardly expected a raid after numerous German successes that had led to a complete British retreat from Europe at Dunkirk the previous year. They were completely surprised and immediately overwhelmed. The commando force was in and out before the Germans could react effectively.

The extent of the Germans' surprise can be somewhat gauged by the fact that a number of British commandos went so far as to commandeer a bus on the spur of the moment, ride to a nearby German seaplane base, and cause further havoc. A young British lieutenant actually sent a telegram to Hitler from a telegraph office in town, chiding Hitler for the lack of preparedness of his troops. The commandos destroyed eleven factories, 800,000 gallons of oil, and five ships. They also returned with 314 volunteers for the Norwegian armed forces in exile in England, sixty Norwegian traitors, and 225 German prisoners of war.[12] Surprise is a major factor in every successful commando operation, military or business.

The Principle of Security

If your competition knows what you are planning or doing, or even what you are capable of doing, he can take action to thwart your efforts. In a business context, if your competitor knows your advertising themes and the vehicles and dates you will be deploying them in advance, he can maximize the effect of his own advertising and minimize yours.

Anyone who is in business faces security problems. For example, those businesses that primarily rely on direct-response marketing to sell their products have a unique challenge, since their success or failure is publicized and available to anyone monitoring their advertising. If a direct-response advertiser is successful with a new promotion, he keeps advertising. If unsuccessful, he stops. That's basic. All that a smaller company needs to do is to track the advertising in his market. If he notices a sudden increase in advertising for a particular promotion from a competitor, he can jump in the market with the same or a similar product. The risks are much lower since the first to market has assumed the biggest risk. If the company seeking to copy the other's success can get the resources, he may even be able to undercut price on the first company through purchase of materials or products in larger quantities or through a better system of distribution.

For a commando organization, any failure in security can be disastrous. That was one of the lessons the British learned in the large Dieppe commando raid made against the French coast in 1942 during World War II. The raid against the city of Dieppe was intended to promote German fears of an attack in the west and compel the Germans to strengthen their English Channel defenses at the expense of other areas they occupied. At a time when the Allies didn't have the strength to sustain a full-fledged land assault against German-occupied Europe, it was an opportunity to "show the flag" and to test new techniques and equipment while preparing for the eventual amphibious assault to win back the European mainland. The immediate objective was simply to occupy the city for a brief period, blow up some radar installations, and withdraw.

Unfortunately, the coast was well defended by the Germans. Moreover, security was compromised early on when the large British commando force actually departed for the French coast only to be forced by bad weather to return to their port. So the Germans knew that the

British would probably try again and they even knew how they were planning to do it.

A month later, the assault was launched a second time. On the second try, the British had the misfortune to run into a German convoy on the way to Dieppe. As a result, this commando mission had neither tactical nor strategic surprise. The results were a fiasco for the British, the fifty American Rangers who took part, and the Canadian troops that made up the bulk of the commando raiders. Of the 4,963 Canadians who embarked for the operation, only 2,210 returned to England, and many of them were wounded. In all, there were 3,367 Allied casualties, including 1,946 left behind as prisoners of war and 907 Canadians who lost their lives.[13]

The Principle of Simplicity

Everything that can go wrong, will go wrong. NASA has had its problems with reliability and failure. Nevertheless, it was once noted that if every single component in a spacecraft were 99 percent reliable, it would fail 50 percent of the time! With so many components involved in a space launch and its vehicle, the chances of something going wrong increases. The point is that commando operations need to be as simple as possible. The fewer elements that can go wrong, the fewer will go wrong.

One of the most well known American commando failures was an attempt to release hostages taken by the Iranians in the American embassy in Tehran in 1979. In the rescue attempt, a complex plan was developed that demanded close coordination, almost perfect conditions, and the involvement of all four U.S. military services. This failure, which resulted in the loss of American lives, eventually led to the establishment of Special Operations Command, which oversees the human and material assets of most special ops units from all four military services today. Simplicity reduces the number of things that can go wrong by reducing the number of elements that must fit together to make the plan successful.

A Cautionary Note About the Use of Commando Techniques

It is important to understand that commando operations in warfare, as well as their application in business, are heavily dependent on achieving and maintaining the relative superiority or competitive advantage mentioned previously. While a commando organization can exist indefinitely, each commando operation has a finite lifespan. Most operations are short-lived, and the longest probably doesn't exceed several months (as you will see in many of the examples cited in this book). While they sometimes accomplish the super-human, commandos are, after all, only human. They can wear out and lose their edge and ultimately their competitive advantage. When that happens, they are unable to continue to achieve the extraordinary goals you may have set and expect them to accomplish.

Many readers may be familiar with the term *tiger teams*. Today, the term refers primarily to inspection teams of one sort or another, but this was not always so. I first heard mention of tiger teams in the aerospace industry, where teams from various disciplines were brought together to accomplish a specific short-term goal or project. Once the goal was achieved or the project completed, the team was disbanded.

For example, a team might be brought together for the sole purpose of bidding a major contract. While the team was working on this objective, they were expected to work after hours, weekends, whatever it took. However, whatever the project, it rarely took more than thirty days. Once the project was done, the team was done. Each member of the tiger team went back to his or her regular organization in the corporation. No one was expected to perform on a tiger team indefinitely, and while it was perceived to be career enhancing, service on a tiger team was not necessarily sought after or thought of as desirable duty. With some exceptions, including team disbandment and the nonvoluntary nature of most tiger teams, the similarity to commando teams is unmistakable. The lesson for using special ops leadership is that while the techniques may be applicable to business, no leadership technique will enable 24/7 continuous performance, ad infinitum, without eventual burnout.

Implementing the Principles Leads to Relative Superiority

As we've seen, the history of commando operations goes all the way back to biblical times. Success, whereby a weaker organization gains victory over a much stronger competitor, depends on only six basic principles of purpose, repetition, speed, surprise, security, and simplicity. Implementing these special ops principles will allow you to achieve relative superiority—a competitive advantage—over your business competition. But how do you actually lead business commandos to implement these principles?

That's where the commando tactics, the subject of this book, become important. In the following chapters, I will show you how and why others have applied these principles through the use of fourteen key strategies:

- Create the Best
- Dare the Impossible
- Throw the Rule Book Away
- Be Where the Action Is
- Commit and Require Total Commitment
- Demand Tough Discipline
- Build a Commando Team
- Inspire Others to Follow Your Vision
- Accept Full Blame; Give Full Credit
- Take Charge!
- Reward Effectively
- Make the Most of What You Have
- Never Give Up
- Fight to Win

By following these strategies, you too can achieve outstanding success in whatever your business or endeavor.

PRACTICES

1   CREATE THE BEST

"Who laid the cornerstone thereof?"
—Job 38:6

"If you would create something, you must be something."
—Goethe

IN LATE 1941, shortly after the United States entered World War II, American and Filipino soldiers fought a desperate battle against overwhelming odds to defend the Bataan peninsula in the Philippines from the Japanese. Finally forced to surrender, they were marched to prison camps in sweltering heat through a mosquito-infested jungle with little or no food or water. Many thousands died or were killed along the way.

By 1944, at the Cabanatuan prisoner-of-war camp, only about 500 men had survived the brutality of their captors and the epidemics of tropical diseases and starvation. General Walter Krueger, commanding U.S. forces in the area, feared that the Japanese would murder their captives before the U.S. Army could liberate the camp. Given only forty-eight hours warning, Krueger sent the 6th Ranger Battalion, reinforced by Filipino guerrillas and another smaller commando unit, the Alamo Scouts, to rescue the prisoners. The Rangers had to cross thirty miles of jungle behind enemy lines to launch their rescue.

On arrival, the 121 Rangers found that they faced not a few dozen guards, but rather 8,000 battle-hardened Japanese soldiers. However, as planned, Filipino guerrillas acted as a blocking force and kept the Japanese from attacking the Rangers during the rescue. Also as planned, a U.S. Air Force P-61 flew over the field and distracted the guards just as the Rangers launched their attack across a flat field, which made them easily visible. As a result of the surprise and the airplane distraction, only two Rangers were killed and all surviving American prisoners were freed from the camp.

Now the problem was how to get their weak, disease-ridden, and starving charges thirty miles through the enemy-held jungles to American lines. There was no way that the freed POWs (whose average weight was ninety pounds) would be able to walk the distance. Fortunately, the Rangers had planned for this situation, too. Again, the Filipinos saved the day, this time with water buffalo carts that were driven by local villagers. They were waiting at the Pampanga River, only one mile from the camp. All 511 surviving Americans made it back, in one of the greatest rescues of the Second World War.[1]

The 6th Battalion Didn't Just Happen—It Was Created

The 6th Battalion was officially activated on September 26, 1944 after Ranger training in New Guinea. Previously, it had been a field artillery battalion, using pack mules as transportation. Lieutenant General Walter Krueger had become commander of the 6th Army. He didn't need a field artillery unit and mules, so he shipped the mules out.

However, General Krueger did need a large Ranger unit trained in stealth and lightning assault. He wanted them for reconnaissance and raider work behind the lines. First, he found his commando leader: Lieutenant Colonel Henry Mucci, a West Pointer, class of 1936, who had volunteered to develop and lead a battalion of Rangers and had trained Rangers in Hawaii. The problem was, the battalion he would lead didn't exist. What did exist were these all-volunteer "mule skinners." They had been especially recruited mostly from American farms for the unusual and hazardous job of convincing mules to carry heavy artillery on their backs in the mountains of New Guinea. Now they were available. It was Mucci's job to turn these unlikely candidates into Rangers.

Mucci personally built and trained the 6th Ranger Battalion in the mountains of New Guinea. Reports were that Mucci's Ranger training bordered on the inhuman. Mucci worked his men in training to the absolute limits of their physical capacities. He personally taught them all aspects of fighting, from hand-to-hand combat to fighting with a knife or bayonet. He taught them to fight with all types of weapons and to be expert marksmen. He led them on hellish marches through tropical New Guinea jungles, across treacherous rivers, and up mountainsides in the sticky and miserable tropical jungle heat. Mucci taught them jungle combat, night combat, and amphibious combat. Mucci took a full year, but at the end of this year, he had the team he needed. Recalled one of Mucci's commandos:

> I thought he was going to kill us. "I'm going to make you so d——— mean, you will kill your own grandmother," he told us. I wondered why he was putting us through so much, but before it was over, there was no question about it, I knew why. And once he got us trained and picked out, he loved us to death. And there wasn't anything too good for us. . . . He *knew* what he was doing when he was training us."[2]

Why Do You Need Business Commandos?

Just as commandos are needed for special tasks in battle, commandos are needed for special tasks in business. There may be situations where time is important, when resources are low or insufficient, where you are challenging conventional wisdom or established competitors for a turnaround, or where the state of affairs is so critical that if you don't get a cash flow going soon, you won't have a company.

Usually, all these circumstances should be addressed in a planned and organized fashion. So it's important to understand the formalized steps. However, sometimes you'll need to create commandos under fire, under the pressures of time, the competition, the government regulators, or your investors. In that case, you'll need to create your commandos on the spot. In this chapter, we'll look first at more typical situations, where you have the luxury of time and thorough planning. Then we'll see how this job of creating business commandos is done in a crisis situation as well.

Qualities of Special People

You need special people to do special things. You need the best. If you think you can just call some of your regular employees together and give them a pep talk and an impossible task to do, you're wrong. It won't work. Your first task as a commando leader is to create commandos. You can't do much until you have these very special people, these business commandos.

A business commando is an extraordinary employee, a special person. This is an individual who won't quit until the job is done, no matter what. I don't care what obstacles or problems exist, the business commando accepts the challenge and looks for and finds ways (or sometimes the one single way) to accomplish the task. Once engaged, the business commando doesn't rest until success is ensured. The business commando is simply unstoppable. Knock him down and he gets right back up. Put an obstacle in her path and she goes over it, around it, under it, or right through it. The business commando hates to lose, loves to win, and thinks of overcoming tough tasks as a game. The more difficult the job is, the better. He may be laid-back or a hard-charger—quiet and unassuming or a loud mouth and a braggart. It doesn't matter. Business commandos come in all shapes and sizes and physical appearances. They may be male or female. They come from all ethnic groups and belief systems. The only way to stop a business commando from achieving his goal is to eliminate him from the game. And believe you me, that's no easy task for a competitor to do. So business commandos must be created.

How to Create Business Commandos

To create business commandos, first you have to recruit them. Then, you have to train them. Throughout the process and afterward, they need to be kept highly motivated to achieve the organization's goals. Do it in three stages:

- Locate and recruit
- Screen and select the best
- Train and motivate

Locate and Recruit—But Use Only Volunteers

In a sense, candidate commandos must find themselves—that is, they must be volunteers. This step isn't as difficult as it sounds. Once you put the word out that you have a tough job for special people, you'll get more volunteers than you'll know what to do with. However, for several reasons, you don't want to hire them all.

But let's begin in the beginning. Henry Mucci was a volunteer. Mucci was a professional U.S. Army officer; moreover, as a Ranger, he was a volunteer. No one made him do it. Now you may think that because someone voluntarily came to work for you, that makes her a commando-type volunteer, but that's not true. Most come only for a job, an opportunity, a paycheck. If you told them that the job was difficult, required long hours under difficult working conditions with only fifteen minutes for lunch, how many would accept a job with your company? Few? Maybe, but those are the ones that make business commandos.

Max De Pree was chairman and CEO of Herman Miller, Inc. when *Fortune* magazine named the company one of the ten "best managed" and "most innovative" furniture makers in the United States. If that weren't enough, it was also chosen as one of the hundred best companies to work for in America. In his book, *Leadership Is an Art,* De Pree said: "The best people working for organizations are like volunteers. Since they could probably find good jobs in any number of groups, they choose to work somewhere for reasons less tangible than salary or position. Volunteers do not need contracts, they need covenants."[3] The bottom line is this: You can and must get people to volunteer to become business commandos.

There are two stages to recruiting business commandos:

- Find them.
- Enlist them.

In the finding stage, we advertise for what we want. This advertising can be done by word of mouth, by taking out print ads or posting positions with Internet recruiters, by seeking recommendations from others within or from outside the company, or even through the use of consultants or headhunters to find candidates.

It is important to document exactly what you are looking for first. You're going to want to write down the characteristics not only of the job, but of the group. What exactly do you want your business commando organization to do? Only after you've described the organization do you start describing the various positions needed within it. Only then you are in a position to write your ad. If it is a print advertisement, it could read something like this:

WANTED: BUSINESS COMMANDOS
We are developing a small elite group of degreed business professionals from all disciplines and functional areas to work on difficult, demanding, important assignments that will require long hours of work and possible worldwide travel to a variety of countries. While not physically dangerous, assignments will be mentally and physically

challenging due to short time requirements. This group will report to top management.

Requirements include:

- An earned degree from any discipline; advanced degrees a plus.
- Five to ten years of business experience, in any industry.
- Ability to work and get along with others on a team.
- Excellent health.

In addition to standard benefits and a competitive salary, successful candidates will:

- Be cross-trained in other functional areas.
- Be able to develop themselves further in their specialty.
- Have direct access to top management.
- Be considered for future management opportunities in the company.

Verbal versions of the same advertisement can also be passed around to in-house managers and others. Many of your best commandos may already be in your organization, but you must identify them and form them into a special team the way Henry Mucci did. Once you are face-to-face with a potential candidate, you can let him in on more of the specifics. Such an advertisement will probably result in more candidates than you can handle. Most will want to know more about the work. Since you'll have real information, you'll be able to say more.

Regarding compensation, you have to think things through carefully ahead of time. While you don't have to pay some outlandish amount, you do want to pay competitively so your commandos know that they are special. Money, by itself, may not be all it's cracked up to be as a motivator. Still, it's a sign of appreciation and achievement, and most people welcome higher compensation to pay the bills and afford luxuries that make their lives more enjoyable. Compensation can be structured so that documented performance means higher pay. That's what successful sales organizations do. However, you are also offering training and experience with access to top management that normally would not be available to regular hires. You also offer the promise of special consideration for promotion to management in the future.

In the enlistment stage, you want to confirm that your potential commandos made the right decision and that joining your organization is the best, most powerful career move they can make in life. Don't tell them how easy they're going to have it. Tell them how tough it's going to be, but that it is worthwhile.

Screen and Select the Best

Screen your candidates carefully. Fully interview only the best. Have them meet all senior managers. The manager you have selected to lead this group should have final say. You can also give various personnel tests that can assist in making your decision. You want the best. The more screening you do, the better the commando group you can put together. Also, the difficulty of the screening process itself helps to add to the mystique and eliteness of the group. (You want to work carefully with your human resources people to ensure you are not violating any laws against discrimination.) All candidates should be treated with respect, and those not tendered offers should be tactfully rejected.

In your interviews with candidates, make no bones about the fact that the work will not be easy and may frequently require overtime and work on weekends.

Train and Motivate

Arrange to start your new business commandos on about the same date so that training can be started at the same time. The training given depends on what you want your commandos to do and needs to be worked out ahead of time and approved by your commando manager. For example, if you are going to cross-train across functional areas (as described in the sample advertisement), then there needs to be coordination among all those who will give the training, again with the approval of your commando manager.

What motivates people to become commandos and remain commandos is most important. Motivation is necessary at every stage of the process of creating business commandos, and motivation must be a prime factor in maintaining them, too. Why would anyone volunteer for commando assignments when they have to go through extremely tough and harsh training (which they may not even complete successfully), then spend unpaid extra hours to maintain themselves at the highest professional standards, and then continue to risk their lives to perform at incredible standards to accomplish almost impossible feats? What motivates these individuals? There isn't one single reason (though we'll soon look at the most important motivator for most people). But first, let's examine what, in general, doesn't work very well and what does.

What Do People Consider Most Important About Their Jobs?

Social scientists have studied many industries to determine what factors employees consider most important in their jobs. My psychologist-wife tells me that hundreds of thousands of workers have been surveyed over the past fifty years. The results have been known for some time. They are not secret. Yet few organizations really act on them.

One of these studies was done by the Public Agenda Foundation and reported on by John Naisbitt and Patricia Aburdene in their popular book *Reinventing the Corporation.*[4] Before I show you these results, maybe you would like to take the survey yourself. I've given it to thousands of leaders in my seminars. All you need to do is rank the following factors in the order of importance you think your employees or any worker would put them. Take a couple of minutes to do this exercise. There are thirteen factors. Rank each factor in its order of importance to those who work for you, with "1" being most important, "2" being second most important, and so on.

Exercise: What Motivates Employees?

Rank the following motivators from most important to least important:

1. Work with people who treat me with respect
2. Interesting work
3. Recognition for good work
4. Chance to develop skills
5. Working for people who listen if you have ideas about how to do things better
6. A chance to think for myself rather than just carry out instructions
7. Seeing the end results of my work
8. Working for efficient managers
9. A job that is not too easy
10. Feeling well informed about what is going on
11. Job security
12. High pay
13. Good benefits

Don't turn the page until you are sure you have these factors in their order of importance to *your employees.* Then turn the page for the answers.

Job Security, High Pay, and Good Benefits Not Important?

That's right, the factors are exactly in their correct order as listed. Remember, these are the results after interviewing hundreds of thousands of employees. How many did you get right? Ninety percent of leaders I have surveyed put job security, high pay, and good benefits in the top five. That is, they think that these factors are most important to their employees. But these three factors are usually far down the list. Even when teams of leaders take the survey in my seminars, a team rarely ranks the actual top three in their top three.

I'm not saying that job security, high pay, and good benefits aren't important. They are. But other factors are usually more important—with one caveat. Job security, high pay, and good benefits can be used to reinforce recognition for good work, which is one of the top-three motivators. For example, when I was active as an air commando, the hazardous-duty pay differential, even combined with additional pay for combat duty, was a fraction of the standard pay that everyone else re-

The Answers
1. Work with people who treat me with respect
2. Interesting work
3. Recognition for good work
4. Chance to develop skills
5. Working for people who listen if you have ideas about how to do things better
6. A chance to think for myself rather than just carry out someone else's instructions
7. Seeing the end results of my work
8. Working for efficient managers
9. A job that is not too easy
10. Feeling well informed about what is going on
11. Job security
12. High pay
13. Good benefits

ceived—at most 15 percent additional of the total pay package, by my estimate. Certainly not enough to compensate for the additional risk and work.

What Are the Prime Motivators for Commandos?

If high pay, job security, good benefits, and as we have already seen, pleasant working conditions aren't the answer, what is? Captain Ronald E. Yeaw, a naval officer who spent his career in the Navy SEALs, with plenty of combat thrown in, says this about what motivates SEAL commandos:

> They want to go to the Grim Reaper, get right up next to him, and punch him out—do it three or four times a day. That's what they really want to do.[5]

In other words, according to Yeaw, commandos are motivated in large part by danger and risk. They get a feeling of satisfaction from putting their lives in jeopardy and surviving while accomplishing the mission. In business commando terms, it is like the entrepreneur who willingly "bets the farm" and risks bankruptcy repeatedly, which he justifies by stating that this risk taking is what helped his company to grow.

So, commandos are motivated by risk taking. But what else? General Maxwell Taylor, who became President John F. Kennedy's favorite general during the Cold War, was known as a highly intellectual officer. Among his academic accomplishments was his fluency in several foreign languages. However, during World War II he didn't exactly have the most intellectual of assignments. He commanded the 101st Airborne Division during the Normandy Invasion and the Western European campaigns in combat. In those days, "airborne division" meant the elite paratroops.

A newsman once asked him why he liked to jump out of airplanes. "I don't," he answered, "but I like to be around men who do."

General Taylor and others enjoy the reputation of being a commando and the things that come along with it—such as being expected to accomplish difficult or near-impossible tasks, being part of an elite force, being given special pay and privileges, even if the pay and privileges don't amount to very much in practical terms. Thus the U.S. Army Special Forces units are proud of their distinctive Green Berets, which no other soldiers are allowed to wear. Army Rangers have their unique shoulder tab; Navy SEALs their Trident, Anchor, Eagle, and Flintlock badge. Uniform distinctions worn by other commando organizations are equally prized because they denote membership in an association of special individuals who must accomplish extremely difficult tasks under extremely difficult conditions. Several years ago, U.S. Army Rangers almost rebelled when the then–Army Chief of Staff mandated that all soldiers would wear a black beret as a morale booster. Formerly only Rangers were permitted to wear a black beret. They were only slightly mollified when he ordered khaki berets be reserved solely for Rangers.

Some years ago I was a guest, along with a couple dozen other academics from universities around the country, of Mary Kay Ash, the founder, and at the time CEO, of Mary Kay Cosmetics, the billion-dollar corporation most famous for awarding pink Cadillac automobiles to its most successful saleswomen. We were invited to participate in one of the corporation's annual sales meetings, called seminars, at which almost 10,000 women were in attendance.

I was amazed at the commando-type techniques and various forms of recognition used to motivate these already highly motivated saleswomen. Groups of saleswomen belonged to units that also competed for recognition and prizes. These units had self-selected, colorful names like "The Gentle Tigers" or "The Beauty Team." Different clothing and adornments were worn by different units and signified different levels of accomplishment. All were tied to the corporation, and everything was done to confirm that if you belonged to the Mary Kay organization, you were special.

Another motivation for commandos is the challenge. Training is tough, and not everyone is able to complete it. Navy SEALs have "Hell Week," which culminates training. Army Rangers must pass four difficult phases of training, each lasting about ten days, during which they get little sleep and food while they alternately are assigned leadership roles in Ranger-type missions—urban, mountain, jungle, and desert—before they graduate. During the Vietnam era, they ran to a cadence:

I want to be an Airborne Ranger
I want to live a life of danger.

"Airborne" referred to the fact that many Rangers were also qualified as parachutists. One former Ranger who fought in the Vietnam
War said he volunteered because ". . . something was missing in my
life. Life was too easy; there was no challenge."[6]

Creating Commandos Under Fire

As mentioned at the outset of this chapter, you must sometimes create
commandos under fire, under the least favorable conditions. The need
to create commandos under fire can occur in any organization. Fortunately, there is usually "people gold" in your organization that you may
not have considered previously.

Finding the Gold You Need for Commandos[7]

There is an old saying in the military that in a good army, every soldier
has a marshal's baton in his backpack. This is a way of saying that
even the most junior employee in an organization should be prepared
to assume higher responsibilities. It also says that there may be top-
management talent lower down in your organization that is immensely
valuable, though currently unrecognized and untapped.

Jim Carroll, one of my doctoral classmates at Claremont Graduate
University back in 1978, was a stock boy with only a high school education when hired by his company. Over a seven-year period, he rose
from his initial hourly position to the presidency of that firm. During
the same period, he went back to college and earned a bachelor's and
then a master's degree at night school. Jim may have been a stockboy,
but he carried a marshal's baton in his backpack..

Unfortunately, for a variety of reasons, talent exists but goes unrecognized. Historically, one of the greatest examples that comes to mind
is Ulysses S. Grant. During the Civil War, Grant was eventually selected
as general-in-chief of all Union forces. He was the only commander
who was able to defeat Confederate General Robert E. Lee and end the
war. Before the war, Grant had been an unsuccessful dry-goods clerk in
Galena, Illinois, working for his younger brother, who hired him only
because he couldn't get a job anywhere else. He had been kicked out of
the army for drunkenness. Despite being a West Point graduate and
having a strong military background, including awards for bravery and
leadership during the Mexican War, Grant was turned down for relatively junior commands until, almost by accident, the governor of Illi-

nois commissioned him a brigadier general of volunteers from his state. He proved to be the outstanding commander of federal forces during the Civil War. And, of course, Grant went on to become our eighteenth president.

Why does this gold in organizations go unnoticed? The most common reason is that these individuals are currently in assignments where others do not perceive their potential. General Grant may have been a so-so clerk, but he was an outstanding general and he was capable of functioning as a U.S. president. Only four years separated the clerk from the president!

What all this means is that there may well be valuable commandos in your organization already, only they are performing some very mundane and overlooked jobs, or else they have not yet become motivated to become commandos. Your responsibility is to identify these individuals and then put them to work where they can do the most good. This responsibility becomes all the more important when you must create commandos under fire. Here is an example from academia. It is particularly noteworthy because the academic setting limits many of the normal motivation and "command and control" methods available both in business and the military.

Academia: Unusual Organizations with Unusual Power Structures

I never associated academia much with commando operations until I became an academic myself and was able to observe close up how these environments operate.

At most U.S. colleges and universities, the organization is considered "a community of scholars." The "scholars" teach and do research in their respective disciplines. They are also expected to serve the academic organization, their academic disciplines, and the community at large. These responsibilities include serving on committees to ensure educational programs are up to par; examining the records of colleagues and making recommendations regarding their advancement in academic rank; organizing and serving as officers in academic associations; helping local, state, or national governments with problems in which they have expertise; and more.

Upon receiving his doctorate degree, in the United States a new professor is hired at the lowest rank of assistant professor. Given a record of achievement in the areas noted above, the professor may be promoted to the rank of associate professor and awarded tenure. Having tenure means that this individual cannot be fired without extreme cause, the most common being "moral turpitude." It usually takes six years to acquire tenure and the rank of associate professor. This promotion is not automatic, and in some universities, the percentage of eligible professors attaining it may be as low as 10 percent. Failing to achieve this milestone requires that the assistant professor leave the university and find employment elsewhere.

Given a continuing record of accomplishment, the final promotion to full professor may be considered after another six years. Again, this is far from automatic and in some cases may never be awarded. However, having attained tenure, a professor may remain an associate professor, without promotion, until retirement. He cannot be easily discharged.

Each professor is considered almost semi-independent, with no "boss" and minimum supervision. Still, a department chairman heads each discipline and is responsible for his department and the professors in it. Although the department chair reports to the dean of the college or school, the rewards (monetary or otherwise) may be small. In many schools, the duties of the department chair are rotated every few years.

The dean, in turn, reports to the head of the university, usually termed the president, although sometimes an intermediary is imposed between a dean and the highest official in a university, usually titled a provost. This position corresponds roughly to a VP of Operations. In the parlance of academia, positions of dean or higher are termed "administrators" and considered management. The department chair may or may not be in this category, depending on the school.

Administrators generally receive greater compensation than professors, but not always. There are some cases where professors receive higher compensation than the president of their university. Administration is considered a separate career track from being a professor, and a professor who happens to be a good manager or leader may or may not seek to become an administrator.

As a result, in most academic units, the power of the chain of command is much more limited than in most other organizations. While each administrator may serve at the pleasure of his superior, individual professors, once tenured, cannot be discharged. This is designed to protect the special freedom of expression granted an academic in the classroom.

An Academic Department Has Problems

Because the position of department chair is not necessarily highly desired or sought after, some universities find difficulty in even filling the position. This was the case in one public university. The serving chair was not necessarily the best qualified or the best manager; rather, the dean would duly appoint the only professor willing to assume these duties. One particular chair served adequately for several years. In this twelve-member department, there were ten tenured full professors, the department had a history of accomplishment, and few demands were made. However, the environment eventually changed and the department became much more difficult to lead.

First, budget cuts were initiated by the state, which meant fewer resources for teaching, travel to academic conferences, and equipment for professors. Budgets were based on the number of students in each discipline. As academic programs within the department aged without revision and professors allocated more time to their individual projects rather than those likely to help the department, the number of students began to decline. In academia, students equate to sales. Over a three-year period, the numbers of students choosing to pursue a bachelor's or master's degree in this discipline declined by almost 40 percent. There was no money to hire adjunct professors any longer, so they were all but eliminated. Several professors retired. They were not replaced.

Then, publication became an accreditation issue. Major accrediting bodies within the United States oversee all academic programs and periodically visit the colleges and universities they accredit to ensure standards are being maintained. A major shift of emphasis by the accrediting body in this discipline required that the university's professors publish significantly, but only in peer-reviewed, scientific journals (whereas previously, publications had been focused on other outlets). This chairman was unable to change the publishing habits of the department's members.

Moreover, the department membership was blissfully unaware of the extent of the decline in the number of students and of the absolute necessity of publishing in academic journals. Professors observed only the increasingly bizarre behavior of their department chair—and the increasing lack of available resources. While morale plummeted, their response was to work increasingly on their own projects and to ignore the needs of the department.

Things reached a crisis when the department chair suffered a personal tragedy of major proportions that led to a nervous breakdown. As other problems, including financial mismanagement, were uncovered, the dean persuaded this chair to resign rather than face dismissal. A former department chairman was asked to assume the position. When informed of the actual state of the department he was stunned. This department, once considered preeminent, was now last in almost every measurement when compared with departments of other disciplines in the college.

A Commando Leader Takes Action

The new chair was forced to create commandos under fire. His initial actions deviated from the typical model of location and recruitment, selection and screening, and training and motivation. He had to go with what he had, and he had to do it fast. He had to decide what needed to be done, and then do it. And he had to convince nine other professors of identical rank and the former chair, all his peers, to follow his lead.

Yet he had none of the usual tools to work with. He only had two untenured faculty members; the remainder could not be fired no matter what he did. Even if the number of students declined further, tenured professors were exempt from firing. Salaries were fixed, so he could do little regarding compensation. Resources could not be doled out to motivate. They were too little. However, the chairman did have one advantage. He recognized the gold in the department. He knew where it was buried. He knew the strength and weakness of every potential commando.

This commando leader decided that he had to focus on three tasks that needed to be turned around immediately. These were:

- Student enrollment in the discipline
- Publication in peer-reviewed journals
- Department morale

He further recognized that the first two goals were heavily dependent on morale. He knew that under these circumstances, motivation was critical yet extremely difficult.

The new chairman developed a plan and called a department meeting. He laid everything out, explaining exactly where the department ranked and what had happened. He told them what they could do to turn the situation around and how they could do it. He got agreement from every department member. He appointed teams to work on various aspects of every issue—including promotion and bringing in additional students—with a responsible leader for each. The teams utilized the strengths and interests of every member of the department. He got all groups to agree to take additional students, up to the limits of seating in each class. More students would enable additional resources. He established awards to recognize accomplishments in teaching quality, which helped to attract additional students and research. For every accomplishment he issued a letter of appreciation and delivered a copy to the dean and the professor's file.

Within one year, the numbers of students rose by 36 percent. Whereas in the previous year only two professors had submitted articles to peer-reviewed publications and were published, all but one professor had submitted articles to scientific journals, and half had received notification of acceptance. The number of adjunct professors increased from two to nineteen. It was an outstanding example of creating commandos under fire, under extreme circumstances and limitations.

Do "Special People" Stay That Way?

Through the steps of recruiting, selecting, training, and motivating, you've made a hefty investment in individuals with almost amazing capabilities in order to build the very best team possible. The question is, do they retain these capabilities or do they disappear?

Both my research and personal experience indicates that these capabilities can be retained, but this retention is not automatic.

As proof that they can be retained, one need only look at the alumni of commando units in Israel. One of the best known and most elite is the Sayeret Mat'kal, reporting directly to the Chief of the General Staff of the Israeli Defense Forces. Former members of this relatively small unit include two former prime ministers, a former minister of defense, two former Chiefs of the General Staff (corresponding roughly to our Chairman of the Joint Chiefs of Staff, but with command responsibilities), and members of the Knesset (the Israeli Congress) from both major political parties. If one were to include all Israeli commando units, then the list of those who went on to top business and government positions would be even longer. In fact, Moshe Dayan, one of the most famous generals and politicians in modern Israel's history, led a commando unit as a young major during Israel's War of Independence in 1948–1949.

There is recent evidence in our own country as well of special ops forces producing capable leaders. Two generals from special operations have reached the top outside of special operations in the armed forces, and many have become generals or admirals in commanding special operation organizations. One of these is General Hugh Shelton, a general from special operations, who became Chairman of the Joint Chiefs of Staff, the highest military office in the U.S. Armed Forces. As another example, General Pete Schoomaker was once commander of Special Operations Command (SOCOM), the top commando job in the United States. He was recalled from retirement in 2003 by Secretary of Defense Donald Rumsfeld to become the thirty-fifth Chief of Staff of the Army, the highest office in that branch of the armed forces. The Navy SEALs achieved its first vice (i.e., three-star) admiral in the person of Eric Olson, as deputy commander of SOCOM. Clearly, the trend is positive.

Although few have looked at business in quite this way, I'd be willing to wager that leaders who can create commandos, especially under extreme difficulty, like the academic department chairman or others described in this book, are well respected and poised to reach the top in their industries, too.

Commando Notes

Business commandos aren't born. They must be created. And, as a commando leader, this is part of your job. The process of creating a business commando involves three stages. Potential business commandos must be:

- Located and recruited
- Screened and selected
- Trained

And, most of all, your business commandos must be motivated. There are times when business commandos must be created under conditions that do not allow for formal recruiting, screening, and training procedures. As commando leader, you may have to go with what you've got. Finally, there most certainly is a need for the care and feeding of business commandos. This aspect cannot be ignored. To accomplish proper "care and feeding," you need to consider why individuals become and remain commandos, and build your retention of commandos around these facts.

2 DARE THE IMPOSSIBLE

"Consider nothing, before it has come to pass, to be impossible."
—Cicero

"Who dares, wins."
—British SAS motto

IT WAS JULY 4, 1976. As the United States celebrated its bicentennial, the national news networks suddenly interrupted radio and TV programming in progress to make an incredible announcement. Israeli commandos had flown 2,200 miles across Africa and Lake Victoria to land in Uganda and free more than a hundred Jewish and Israeli hostages threatened with death by their terrorist captives. Not only was this an amazing feat, but it came after a long series of aircraft hijackings by various groups seeking to gain publicity through terror in the sky. Israel's commando operation demonstrated that the world need not put up with these threats and what could be done to stop them by those who dared.

This particular hijacking had started several days earlier, on June 27, 1976. Air France Flight 139, with 246 passengers traveling from Ben Gurion Airport in Israel to Paris via Athens, was hijacked by terrorists who boarded during the stopover. Armed with guns and grenades, the hijackers ordered the plane to divert to Benghazi, Libya for refueling. When the plane took off again, the terrorists ordered it to a predesignated location: Entebbe, Uganda in Africa.

The operation had been carefully planned by Dr. Wadia Hadad's Popular Front for the Liberation of Palestine (PFLP), a branch of the Palestine Liberation Organization (PLO). The landing in Uganda was with the approval and assistance of Ugandan dictator Idi Amin. Though a Muslim, Amin had visited Israel earlier and promised peaceful relations with the Jewish state. He even wore Israeli paratrooper wings on his military uniform after his visit. But now he needed money. Seeking economic aid from other Muslim states, he sought to change his image of being friendly toward the Jewish state.

On landing, the terrorists separated the passengers into two groups: Jews and non-Jews. Non-Jews were released. The French aircrew was also released, but they refused to depart until such time as their Jewish passengers would be released as well.

The terrorists demanded that fifty-three convicted terrorists who were serving sentences in Israel, France, Germany, Switzerland, and Kenya be released. They threatened to execute the remaining 105 Jewish and Israeli hostages if their demands were not met. A forty-eight hour deadline was set before the executions were to begin. Eventually, the deadline was extended until 2:00 A.M. on July 4.

Meanwhile, a plan for Israeli commandos to rescue the hostages was initiated as soon as the hijacking became apparent. The rescue operation was under the overall command of Brigadier General Dan Shomron, who later became Chief of the Israeli General Staff. The plan was complicated by the fact that the aircraft was owned by a foreign carrier and the hostages were held in an unfriendly foreign country several thousand miles away. Furthermore, the Israelis knew that they didn't have very much time to either plan or rehearse the raid. Although the risk was great, they decided to dare to do the impossible.

The plan that evolved was for a night attack by the Sayeret Mat'kal, an Israeli special operations unit reporting directly to the Israeli general staff, along with a few commandos with special skills on loan from the elite Golani infantry brigade. Lieutenant Colonel Jonathan (Yoni) Netanyahu commanded the 200-man assault force. Lieutenant Colonel Netanyahu was the Sayeret Mat'kal's commander and brother of Benjamin Netanyahu, who had earlier served in the same commando unit and later became Israel's prime minister in 1996.

The assault commandos would be airlifted by four C-130 Hercules aircraft. One C-130 included a deception team. To deceive the Ugandan soldiers assisting the hijackers, a black Mercedes limo, identical to the one used by Idi Amin, and Land Rover vehicles typically employed by Amin's army would lead the assault force. A fifth C-130 was to carry the rescued hostages to freedom.

Overhead, an Israeli Air Force Boeing 707 would circle to provide overall command and control of the operation. Another Boeing 707 contained hospital medical teams and landed at nearby Nairobi, Kenya and was prepared to take off for Entebbe at a moment's notice.

Late into the night of July 2, Israeli Air Force pilots practiced landing their C-130 aircraft in the dark. Meanwhile, the deception and assault teams rehearsed their roles. Only when satisfied that the operation could be successfully executed did General Shomron recommend to his superiors that they actually implement the plan.

At 1:20 P.M. on July 3, the assault force took off. They split up on takeoff and flew off in different directions to mislead unfriendly eyes that may have watched the takeoff, since the military airfield was adjacent to Ben Gurion Airport. Out of sight, the attacking armada then headed south at low level to avoid detection by Russian ships and Egyptian radar. They avoided the easy direct route and flew through stormy weather over Lake Victoria to get to Entebbe. For about a third of the route, they were escorted by Israel F-4 fighters, but eventually, the fighters had to break off and returned to base because of fuel limitations. It was thought that aerial refueling would make the procedure unduly complex and could compromise the mission. The Israeli force flew on, arriving at Entebbe about 11:00 P.M.

Although the Israelis had prepared to land in the dark, amazingly, the landing lights at the Entebbe airport were on. Without permission from the control tower, and after a seven hour and forty minute flight, the aircraft landed only one minute off of preplanned schedule. As the aircraft turned onto the taxiway leading to the old airport terminal, the rear cargo ramp of the leading aircraft was lowered and the black Mercedes and two Land Rovers drove out. Ugandan flags flew from the Mercedes and all thirty-five commandos on the deception team were dressed in Ugandan army uniforms.

The team made it past the first Ugandan guards without incident. But then a suspicious guard challenged the force and a firefight broke out. Netanyahu immediately ordered the assault on the old terminal where the hostages were held and guarded by the terrorists. Meanwhile, Israeli armored personnel carriers isolated the airfield from Ugandan reinforcements. Other commandos secured all access to roads to the airport and took over the new terminal and the control tower. Aircrews took fuel pumps off one of their planes in preparation for refueling from Entebbe's own supplies for the return trip.

The assault on the old terminal building was completed within three minutes after the lead plane landed—which was quicker than their practice runs in Israel.

Within seven minutes the hostage passengers and crew of Air France 139 were evacuated onto Israel Defense Forces (IDF) planes. The old terminal building was left deserted except for the dead bodies of the eight hijackers.

As the C-130 with the hostages took off, other commandos destroyed Ugandan MIG fighter aircraft on the ground to prevent any pursuit in the air. The commandos took their own wounded, two wounded hostages, and their single killed in action casualty. They reloaded their vehicles and equipment and the last Israeli plane departed. From landing to departure, the raid lasted only an hour and forty-eight minutes.

Although only one commando was killed in action, it was nevertheless a heavy loss for the Israelis. A sniper had killed Lieutenant Colonel Netanyahu, the commander of the assault force. One hostage could not be rescued. She had been moved earlier to a local hospital. She was later executed on orders of Idi Amin.

The daring raid, with impossible logistics and unbelievably limited preparation time, was launched as a complete surprise, which helped to make this rescue a great success. As noted in one report, "It was a setback for terrorists everywhere since it showed that a determined nation could successfully mount counteroperations to defeat them with no gain for the terrorists at all. The success also weakened the dictator Idi Amin by emboldening Amin's opponents. Sabotage and resistance increased, and by 1979 he was deposed."[1]

Who Dares, Wins

The motto of another extraordinary commando force, the British Special Air Service (SAS), is "Who dares, wins." A young British officer by the name of David Stirling founded the SAS. Although a nonflying unit, it was given this unusual name to disguise its true function and modus operandi.

During the early part of World War II, the SAS attacked hundreds of miles behind enemy lines across the North African desert, traveling by lorry. Out of touch and off-road for long periods of time, they navigated by the stars. During the fifteen months that Stirling was in command of the 1st SAS Regiment, the unit destroyed 250 German aircraft. It also blew up ammunition depots, mined roads, attacked trains, set fire to gasoline storage depots, and generally made life a living hell for thousands of German and Italian soldiers who thought themselves safe far behind the front.[2] By the time the Allies moved into Europe, the actions of the SAS were considered so deadly that in 1944 Adolf Hitler issued an injunction: ". . . These men are highly dangerous . . . they must be ruthlessly exterminated."[3]

The Israelis proved the SAS motto once again at Entebbe. However, this motto isn't limited to military operations. There are business commandos that dare to do the impossible, and as the SAS motto proclaims, more often than you might expect, they are successful.

A Business Commando Who Made a Career of Daring the Impossible

Last year a good friend of mine passed away. He had lived a long and event-filled life, with many business and personal successes. He was born in poverty. He had no money to go to college, and most of his triumphs occurred long before he had any formal education, although he took the time to attend college to earn a master's degree (he never did get a bachelor's degree) after his formal retirement from business. His name was E. Joseph Cossman, and I have documented many of his accomplishments in my books to illustrate various concepts that he followed and that led to his successes.

Joe was unique not because he built a mighty business empire. He didn't. I believe he could have if that was what he wanted to do, but it wasn't what he wanted. He had too much fun being a business commando who operated in a different way.

What Joe did was to introduce new product after new product into the marketplace. Most of these products had little in common with each other. What connection does a toy ant farm have with a medical device for easy identification and treatment of illnesses, or an insect poison with a fishing lure? In every case, Joe would introduce and promote the product, make a bundle of money, and then after a couple of years, sell the product off to someone else. Then he would find another new product and start a brand new business. In some cases these products are still selling profitably today, almost half a century since Joe introduced them.

What these projects did have in common was that in almost every single case, Joe went up against almost impossible odds, such that few people would have though he had much chance for success. Moreover, every time it was the same. Joe only developed a small band of business commandos to help him succeed. Notwithstanding widespread sales and production operations and public relations achievements, including national magazine coverage, an appearance on *The Tonight Show* on NBC, and more, Joe never had more than thirteen commandos in his organization at any one time.

Despite the odds, Joe succeeded almost every time. And they weren't such small successes, either. Joe sold 3.1 million ant farms. That was a toy for children. He sold 310,000 unique self-propelled fishing lures, 317,000 bullfight posters, 1.6 million rubber shrunken heads as a novelty item to hang on your car mirror, 5.8 million cans of solid insect poison, and 208,000 hypnotic kits.

These represent just some of his outstanding successes. In almost every case, he was new to the business and his competitors were well established, had the resources and the contacts, and "knew" what would sell and what would not. Joe had only his business instincts and his self-confidence. As time went on, his financial resources increased, but they never equaled those of the larger companies he competed against. Let's examine one project in detail to derive some lessons from what Joe did.

The Potato Gun Miracle

Cossman didn't stumble into impossible situations; he sought them out. He did so because he felt that the potential for profit was the greatest and the investment lowest in situations that others thought were impossible. His "Spud Gun" provides an excellent example and is typical of how he operated.

Joe found new products by locating products that failed but for which expensive production tooling had already been constructed and was available at low cost. One method Joe used was simply to cold call companies and ask if they had old tooling lying around that they wanted to get rid of. One day someone he called told him that he had tooling for a "Spud Gun" he was willing to sell. Joe didn't know what a Spud Gun was. So he asked.

It turned out that a Spud Gun is a toy gun that a child loads by thrusting the gun barrel into a potato spud. In the process, the open barrel automatically pinches off a small piece of the potato. The piece seals the barrel. Then the child cocks the gun by pulling back a mechanism. When the trigger is pulled, the mechanism compresses air, providing the propellant that shoots the piece of potato about ten feet. It is harmless because potatoes are 90 percent water. The toy company owning the gun had introduced the product ten years earlier. It made expensive tooling and manufactured 10,000 units. Ten years later, as a reminder of their failure, they still had the tooling and most of these 10,000 toy guns in their warehouse. They badly wanted to get rid of it. On the face of it, that should have ended the deal right then and there. The conventional wisdom was that once a product failed, you could not go back and make it a success. The consumer wouldn't want it, and distributors wouldn't want to take the risk. However, Joe wanted to know more before dismissing the product.

Joe asked for several samples. He took the guns and played with them. Then he had his children play with them. It was fun for both. He investigated and confirmed that both the government and consumer's groups considered the product to be safe for children. He called representatives of the potato industry and the U.S. Department of Agriculture. He found that there had been a bumper crop of potatoes in the United States that year. In fact, there was a glut on the market and farmers were hard-pressed to get rid of their potatoes. He investigated the gun's design and the cost to produce it. He made certain of the patent rights. He also researched the campaign that the original toy company had conducted ten years earlier. He thought he understood what it had done wrong and felt certain he could promote it successfully.

After he had conducted a thorough investigation, Joe visited the company that owned the guns. The owner was a successful toy manufacturer. He was disgusted with the whole potato Spud Gun business. He had sunk a lot of money into manufacturing, advertising, and promoting the guns, to no avail. He had lost a lot of money on the project and had long since moved on to other products. However, the guns were taking up valuable warehouse space. As a result, he was only too happy to get rid of them. Joe negotiated a deal whereby he would receive the entire lot of 10,000 guns, plus the tooling, for $500! The tooling alone had cost the toy company more than $20,000.

With the tooling in hand, Joe negotiated with other manufacturers to produce additional guns when required. He called several potato distributors and told each of them that he had a product through which he could also promote the potato. He asked whether they would donate potatoes that he would need for the promotion. They agreed. Joe told them to ship some of their best potatoes to the hotel where he would be staying for the upcoming annual toy show in New York City. This would be the main thrust of his promotion: to toy retailers attending the show looking for new products to sell.

However, Joe didn't leave it at that. He sought means of distribution outside of normal retail toy channels. For example, he negotiated with many supermarkets and food distributors to sell his gun in special promotions. With each sale of his gun, the customer would receive free "ammunition," which consisted of a five-pound bag of potatoes. This cost Joe nothing, not even for the potatoes. Both supermarkets and food distributors were happy to consider the potatoes as promotional expenses.

When Joe arrived at his hotel in New York he was almost arrested. Not only was his room filled with 100-pound sacks of potatoes, but his abundant supply of potatoes extended into the hallway, on both sides, all the way to the elevators. If this weren't enough, Joe needed various city permits to keep food produce in the hotel in these quantities. Not expecting that he would receive so much Spud Gun "ammunition," he hadn't thought these measures necessary. When the United States has a bumper crop, it really has a bumper crop! Joe got his permits, made special arrangements with the hotel, and pressed on. Every commando expects "battle friction." That's what the nineteenth-century German strategist Carl von Clausewitz called unexpected deviations from plans. They always occur, and a commando has to be ready for them.

Actually this "battle friction" worked in Joe's favor. He got all kinds of free publicity and press coverage at which he was able to talk about and promote his product. Furthermore, anyone found with 100-pound bags of potatoes extending out of his room and along hotel hallways is bound to attract a lot of attention from fellow guests. In this situation, these guests were toy retailers: his potential customers.

Joe had hired attractive female models as assistants and he set up a Spud Gun shooting range in his room. His models helped run the promotion. Signs all over the hotel directed convention attendees to Joe's room and announced an opportunity not only to receive a free potato Spud Gun, but also to win "a valuable prize."

Those hotel guests getting out of the elevator on Joe's floor were greeted by a long line of good-humored toy retailers waiting their turn to shoot Joe's Spud Guns. The models handed out soft drinks, Spud Guns, and "valuable prizes," which turned out to be more potatoes. Joe told me that if a shooter hit the target he got a ten-pound sack of potatoes. If he missed the target, he had to take two sacks.

Everyone had a good time, and Joe's Spud Gun was the hit of the show. By daring to do the impossible, Joe eventually sold 1.6 million potato Spud Guns.

If we analyze what Joe did, we can understand his secret and why daring to do the impossible is an essential element of successful special ops leadership in battle or in business. First, Joe didn't wait for things to happen. He aggressively sought out potential opportunities, in this case for abandoned tooling. Next, he didn't go crazy over his product and invest a lot of money before he knew what he was doing. Joe thoroughly investigated the business situation he was facing—he made sure he understood why the product had failed previously and what the current environment was regarding the food "ammunition" the product used.

Once he had satisfied himself that conditions were right for a successful campaign, he decided to take the product on and "dared to do the impossible," even though conventional wisdom was that a past failed product could not succeed. He negotiated a minimal price for the product and its tooling and set up other possibilities for production. He didn't squander his resources needlessly.

However, he didn't let it go at that. He planned and acted carefully but expeditiously. He sought new systems of distribution outside of regular retail toy channels, prepared extraordinary promotion and publicity, and in general did everything he possibly could to set the product up for success. Like many other commandos who dare to do the impossible, after thorough investigation, planning, and action, he was successful.

How a Man Built a Jet Fighter Faster
Than Anyone Thought Possible

Clarence "Kelly" Johnson was the famous business commando leader who built and ran "the Skunk Works" for Lockheed Aircraft Corporation. It started when Johnson was an aircraft designer at Lockheed in 1943. The U.S. Army Air Corps asked Lockheed to pull out all the stops to design and produce a fighter after battle reports that the Nazis had flown their own high-speed jet fighter in the skies over Europe. Johnson was only thirty-three years old when Lockheed's president, Robert E. Gross, gave him the job. But the truth is, few Lockheed engineering managers wanted the job because there was one big catch. Lockheed was supposed to deliver a flyable prototype in only six months!

Johnson got permission to raid other projects for commandos. He quickly built a team of twenty-three engineers and 103 shop mechanics working in a small assembly shed at Lockheed in Burbank. Their situation recalled a story line in Al Capp's *Li'l Abner* comic strip that featured a "skonk works" where Li'l Abner and friends, all Appalachian hillbillies, threw in skunks, old shoes, discarded clothing, and other assorted oddments to brew up a powerful and intoxicating drink called Kickapoo Joy Juice. So Johnson called his project "the Skunk Works."

Johnson and his commando team brewed and delivered a flyable prototype, which eventually became America's first operational jet fighter, in just 143 days, with thirty-seven days to spare.

Johnson and his commando team at the Skunk Works went on to design many outstanding aircraft, including the world's fastest and highest-flying aircraft—the SR-71 Blackbird, which made him a legend both here and abroad. He won many prestigious awards, including being elected to the National Academy of Sciences in 1965 and enshrined in the National Aviation Hall of Fame in 1974.[4]

Commandos Reject Easy Tasks

I noted earlier that one of the reasons that Joe never built a giant corporation was that he liked the challenge of difficult yet unrelated new businesses. Other commandos are quite happy to take on the challenge of building large corporations, and from Microsoft to Wal-Mart, they leave obvious evidence of their struggles and ultimate triumphs. What all commandos share, however, is the love of the good fight, the tough challenge, and the difficult task.

In April 1937, Claire L. Chennault, then a captain in the United States Army Air Corps, retired from active duty. He accepted an offer from Madame Chiang Kai-shek, wife of the Chinese president, for a three-month mission to China. He was to make a confidential survey of the Chinese Air Force. A year later, Madame Chiang asked that he form a new Chinese Air Force on the American model.[5] Chennault founded and led the American Volunteer Group, or AVG, as part of the Chinese Air Force against the Japanese in the early part of World War II. In 1942, when the AVG became part of the U.S. Army Air Forces, Chennault became a major general. General Chennault and his unique commando force always fought against superior numbers of enemy fighters. Yet Chennault's "Flying Tigers" destroyed 297 enemy aircraft and lost only twelve of their own planes in aerial combat. Typical of commandos, one of his squadron commanders once radioed him: "The more hardships, work, and fighting the men have to do the higher our morale goes."[6]

All commandos are like this, and as a commando leader, you have to remember this and give your commandos what they really crave. Do so and dare the impossible and the results will amaze you. The fact is, commandos don't want to be given easy things to do. They want tough things to do. Tough challenges motivate commandos; easy tasks do not. In fact, too small of a job will probably de-motivate a commando.

For a Real Commando, a Job Can Be Too Small

Forty years ago, when I was earning my MBA at the University of Chicago, I had a professor in organizational development by the name of Thomas Whistler. Professor Whistler introduced me to a unique concept. He was lecturing about one of his most brilliant and capable doctoral students who had taken his first job at a major corporation and then failed to perform adequately. As a result, he was fired. His former student then went to another corporation where he had immediately done so well that within six months he had been elevated to the position of vice president. Professor Whistler invited us to speculate about the reason for this amazing personal turnaround.

Our ideas ranged from a personality conflict with his initial superior, to personal problems outside of work, to the job being beyond the capabilities of a new graduate, even one with a Ph.D. None of these theories proved to be correct. "The problem," Professor Whistler told us, "was not that the job was too big, but that the job was too small. The only mistake my former student made was to accept the first job."

I had never heard this line of thinking before. I had always been taught the old saw about there being no small jobs, only small people. A few years later when Dr. Laurence J. Peter introduced his theory of workers rising to their levels of incompetence, popularized as "The Peter Principle," the doctoral student's situation confused me. If this graduated doctoral student had instantly reached his level of incompetence, how could he be so successful at a higher level in a different job?

Over subsequent years I have personally observed numerous individuals who, like Professor Whistler's former student, did a poor or mediocre job at a low level, working on an unimportant task, but rose to great challenges to accomplish the most difficult, even impossible tasks imaginable.

Peak Performance Commandos

Dr. Charles Garfield, a psychologist with degrees in both psychology and mathematics, found this phenomenon was particular true of what he called "peak performance individuals." While working with NASA during the first manned missions to the moon, Dr. Garfield was amazed to discover that many individuals who previously had barely done satisfactory work had suddenly caught fire and were doing things that neither they nor anyone else had even thought possible. Then suddenly, the moon landings had been accomplished, and it was like they fell back to earth. They returned to performing at their previously barely acceptable levels. They and their superiors treated the whole peak performance experience as an aberration.[7] Too bad. The truth was that many of these NASA employees were peak performance commandos. Properly led, they could have continued doing the impossible far into the future.

Difficult Challenges Breed Business Commandos

Some years ago, I heard about a nonunion company called Oberg Industries, a tool-and-die company. Oberg Industries was located right in the middle of union country in western Pennsylvania. Given its non-union status, you might think that working conditions in the company were pleasant. You would be wrong. Oberg Industries had a fifty-hour workweek with only a fifteen-minute break for lunch allowed for both management and labor. Don Oberg, the founder and then president, was no easy touch. INC. magazine called him "the Lord of Discipline."

Not only did employees line up to work at Don Oberg's company, but listen to this: At the time, annual sales for most tool-and-die companies were on the average $2 million a year. At Oberg, sales were $27 million annually. Moreover, average sales per employee were, on average, 30 percent higher than in other tool-and-die companies. Yet 1,600 potential employees applied for only thirty job openings that year! (And it wasn't a recession year that we're talking about.)

Now, why is this? Were Oberg employees well paid? Of course they were. However, there was something far more important than compensation. Don Oberg, the hard taskmaster that he was, had convinced his employees that if you managed to meet Oberg's difficult challenges, you were the best.[8] Clearly his employees were business commandos, a cut above the norm. They probably were the best. By the way, today, Oberg—which has an additional location in Arizona—has annual sales of $100 million.

Ordinary People Ask Why—Commandos Ask "Why Not?"

The difference between a business commando and ordinary individuals is that ordinary people seem to ask why (e.g., Why do we want to attempt this thing?) while commandos ask why not. Let's face it, an ordinary businessperson, even a successful one, would look at the Spud Gun opportunity and ask, "Why attempt it?" An ordinary businessperson might say to Joe Cossman: "Joe, this other company tried exactly what you want to attempt. They've been in business a long time and have the experience and the resources. If anyone could have made this successful, they would have been able to. They couldn't make a go of it. With all their knowledge, experience, and resources in this business, if they couldn't do it, what makes you think you can? Why not find an easier product, with a much higher probability of success?"

The difference is that commandos know that what happened in the past doesn't necessarily equal what's going to happen in the future.

An Air Commando Repeats a Movie Stunt—in Battle

Major Bernie Fisher flew the A-1E/H "Spad" aircraft as a member of the 1st Air Commando Squadron located at Pleiku Air Base, South Vietnam, during the Vietnam War. The A-1E was a single-engine, propeller-driven fighter-bomber that first saw service with the Navy in World War II. It flew low and slow in support of troops on the ground. More than twenty years after World War II, Fisher led a two-ship formation of Skyraiders to the A Shau Valley in support of friendly troops under enemy attack in Vietnam.

Another "Spad" piloted by Major Wayne "Jump" Myers was hit. The airplane couldn't fly, and Myers was too low to bail out. He was forced to crash-land the airplane right then and there, and in the target area. Myers bellied in with wheels up. Surviving the crash, he ran for cover behind a nearby embankment. Unfortunately, while the closest friendly helicopters capable of a pickup were thirty minutes away, the enemy infantry were only 200 yards from Myers, and closing fast. Even if helicopters had been on the scene, how could they hover and make a pickup in plain sight and under enemy fire? Moreover, the weather was beginning to turn sour, which would have also argued against a helicopter pickup.

Air Commando Fisher quickly sized up the situation. He decided that a standard helicopter rescue was impossible. He spotted a makeshift landing strip. No one had actually landed even a World War II fighter in a target area during combat with the intent of rescuing a fellow pilot except in the movies. However, Fisher was a commando, and commandos are attracted to difficult tasks.

Fisher lined up his two-seat A-1E aircraft on what he perceived to be the smoothest part of the old strip. The enemy was right in front of him and shot at him all the way down. He taxied the aircraft to where Myers was hiding and pushed back the canopy. The other commando didn't need to be invited twice. He scrambled up the starboard wing and quickly climbed aboard. He strapped himself into the empty right seat as Fisher revved up the single engine and pushed the stick forward to raise the tail and gain speed. Dodging shell holes, debris, and enemy fire, Major Fisher made it off the ground with everybody and his brother shooting at him. Landing back at the home base, he had only numerous shell holes and Myers as evidence of his amazing exploit. Without the shell holes and his live wingman with him on board, it is unlikely that anyone would have believed his story. But then maybe they would have, because like Cossman, these air commandos routinely dared the impossible.

In Real Battle, Don't Waste Commandos on Less Important Missions

Leon Uris, the famous author, based one of his best novels on his own combat experience in the Marines during World War II. His book, and the later movie, was *Battle Cry*. It was the top-grossing movie of 1955, with Van Heflin playing the role of "High Pockets" Huxley, a career Marine Corps lieutenant colonel who trained his battalion to the peak of combat readiness—the best in the division. Yet every time the Marines invaded an island, Huxley's battalion was relegated to a secondary role. Finally, with the major invasion of Iwo Jima coming up and once again not given the most difficult assignment, Huxley could take it no more. He requested and received an appointment with the commanding general.

In a direct confrontation with his superior, Huxley demanded a beachhead assignment for his battalion. When reminded of his obligation to obey orders, Huxley retorted that he knew when he requested the interview that he was coming back to lead his battalion in a beachhead assignment or he probably would be relieved of his command and wouldn't be coming back at all. "I'm not going back to tell my boys we're going to be in a supporting role again. You don't train a major league team and then throw it away in the minors," he said. His arguments hit home and Huxley got his beachhead.

Uris made a valid point. Once you've got your commandos ready, you can't just throw away their talents on less-than-important tasks. They signed up to dare to do the impossible, and that's what they want to do.

Commando Notes

Commandos exist to take on and perform missions considered impossible by almost everyone else. That's what they are recruited, selected, and trained for, and that's what they are psychologically prepared for. Give them these demanding and important jobs, and the results will blow you away. Give them anything else and not only are you wasting your resources, but your commandos will soon disappear and go somewhere else.

3 THROW THE RULE BOOK AWAY

"Hell, there are no rules here—we're trying to accomplish something."
—Thomas A. Edison

"Innovation is capable of being presented as a discipline, capable of being learned, and capable of being practiced."
—Peter F. Drucker

ON MARCH 3, 1944, Brigadier Sir Bernard Fergusson stood with the First Chindit Brigade of the British Army with a commando force of 3,000 men on the western bank of the Chindwin River in Burma. It was 140 miles and twenty-six days from their departure from the minuscule town of Ledo in India. They had dragged, crawled, clawed, and hacked their way through steaming jungles, up and down and around cold mountains, and fought mosquitoes, snakes, and dangerous animals. Fergusson's brigade was part of Major General Orde Wingate's Chindit commando force. It had an almost impossible mission. The brigade was going to attack superior numbers of its Japanese opponents almost 300 miles from its own home base, well behind Japanese lines. The unit had a nonspecific objective: to get right into the midst of enemy territory and disrupt the Japanese army's communications and supply lines while creating havoc and unrest wherever it could.

After almost a month in the jungle, the Chindits encountered the fast-moving Chindwin River. Despite the obstacles they had overcome to get to this point, they were only at their halfway point in their planned penetration of Japanese occupied Burma. Moreover, the Chindwin River represented an apparent insurmountable obstruction. Because of the river's velocity, they couldn't swim across. There was no bridge, and a pontoon bridge could not be easily constructed even if the materials were available, which they were not. The river even ran too swiftly to be crossed by a boat unless it was engine-powered. To cross the Chindwin River, the Chindits needed powerboats.

Brigadier Fergusson was aware of this fact before his departure. He also knew that there was no way that powerboats to ferry 3,000 men with supporting gear could be carried along through the jungles and over the mountains. It simply couldn't be done. The Japanese knew it, too. The mere existence of the Chindwin River as a barrier lulled the Japanese into a sense of complacency. It represented an impediment that no force on earth could overcome. Or, so it seemed.

However, Fergusson knew a secret that the Japanese, and even his own officers, did not. On orders of President Franklin D. Roosevelt and General Henry "Hap" Arnold, the Chindits were supported by the 1st Air Commando group, commanded by Colonel Philip Cochran. Cochran had come up with a plan. They couldn't parachute the boats in. They were simply too heavy and would be lost or damaged. However, if a landing strip could be cleared by the river, two large CG-4A cargo gliders could be landed in the jungle clearing. Each cargo glider was big enough to carry a single powerboat. However, the gliders were relatively untried and had never been used in the jungle terrain of Burma before. That in itself was an interesting innovation, but there was more.

The possibility of glider use for resupply had been considered by others, but rejected. It was possible for motored C-47 transport aircraft to take off with the gliders in tow. Once over the strip, the gliders could be cut loose and could glide in, and provided the strip cleared in the jungle for them was suitably prepared, it was doable. The problem was, it was a one-way ticket. Gliders had no engines. They could glide in, but they couldn't take off on their own power again to get out. And, of course, if regular airplanes could have landed, they wouldn't have needed gliders in the first place.

However, real commandos innovate, and Colonel Cochran was not only a real commando, but also an original. On schedule, the CG-4A gliders were cut loose from the C-47 transport planes and landed safely. The powerboats were quickly unloaded and within five minutes were in the water with the first contingent of Chindits on the way to the east bank of the river.

Meanwhile, the glider commandos didn't rest on their laurels. As the Chindits put the powerboats to immediate use, the glider pilots began assembling and raising two structures resembling goalposts along the landing strip. Then they played out nylon tow ropes attached to the noses of their gliders. The other end of the rope had a large loop that was suspended between the two poles of each "goalpost." A pickup hook protruded from behind each C-47. Those Chindits awaiting their turn in the boats looked on in amazement. Were the C-47s really going to hook the gliders as they flew by and whisk them into the air? Maybe, but they weren't to see a show that day. The two C-47s were scared off by what they thought was the approach of enemy aircraft. However, the following day the C-47s swooped down, their hooks snared the nylon loops, and the C-47s with gliders and pilots in tow returned to their base without incident.[1]

Commandos Innovate

Commandos do things differently. They frequently throw the rule book away. They innovate. There is hardly a method that commandos have not used to enter the battle arena in which they will perform their duties and accomplish their tasks: by air assault, jumping out of airplanes; underwater from submarines or on rubber rafts, speedboats, and special underwater vehicles; on land over mountains or through jungle driving jeeps, or over snow on ski, you name it. Commandos are constantly innovating and doing things differently. They are at the forefront of innovation and the use of experimental and cutting-edge equipment.

The glider stunt wasn't Colonel Cochran's only air commando innovation. He was the first to requisition and employ in battle the then-still-secret "hovercraft." In case you're wondering, that's the helicopter's original name, and those that have since employed rotary-winged aircraft in hundreds of roles, both military and civilian, owe a debt of gratitude to air commando leader Cochran for his pioneering work.

How to Innovate

Innovation is not only *not* easy, but frequently, you are likely to get a lot of opposition and only lukewarm support. That is, until you are proved successful. Then the old saying about "victory having many fathers" will be confirmed a thousand times. But as demonstrated in Chapter 2, commandos take risks, and as a commando leader you are going to take risks as well. A great many of these risks will have to do with innovation. However, leading innovation is not difficult. You just need to follow these simple directions:

■ Stay current with what's going on in the world.

■ Encourage innovation in subordinates (which involves sharing clear goals, looking beyond the ordinary, and rewarding successful innovation).

■ Know that there is always a way and find it!

Stay Current with What's Going On in the World

Things are happening every day of every week that alter the competitive situation. In some cases, your ability to make use of this knowledge will give your commandos a tremendous competitive edge. In other cases, you may have lost an advantage that you once possessed. You need to constantly ask yourself how you can apply what's going on to your business or your organization. Knowledge of the latest developments or happenings in the world, and your ability to apply this knowledge in a timely fashion, is critical to commando leadership. Commandos go all the way; they hold nothing back. They expect you, as a special ops leader, to be on top of every new development that can affect your operations. Staying current about what's going on in the world is the only way for you to stay on top. If you do so, you will be able to avoid effects that can have a negative impact on your organization, and you can take advantage of opportunities presented by new developments before your competitors can react—or, like the Chindits, before your adversaries are even aware of the potential.

Technology is changing and advancing all the time. The changes wrought by technological advancement have an almost immediate effect on a company or even an industry. For example, the entire vinyl record industry disappeared within two years after CDs were introduced. That was a huge, $500 billion business, and it was gone in a flash. Now, digital downloads and "memory sticks" may be on the way to making CDs obsolete.

Pickett was once the leading name in slide rule companies. Pickett dominated the market. You may not even be familiar with slide rules. Yet they were once as common and as much a symbol for engineers as the stethoscope still is for doctors. The slide rule performed the same functions as an electronic handheld calculator today, only a slide rule was mechanical. An engineer manipulated a movable slide printed with numbers back and forth between one or more additional stationery rulers that also had numbers imprinted. Reading through a movable cursor, you could rapidly accomplish simple calculations such as addition, subtraction, multiplication, and division, but also advanced mathematical, algebraic, and trigonometric calculations. Pickett sold millions of slide rules every year, some at hefty prices of up to $100 each, depending on the complexity and functions provided.

Then the electronic handheld calculator came on the scene in the early 1970s, and within a few years Pickett went under. Today, people buy and sell Pickett slide rules on the Internet as collectibles.

Pickett had plenty of business commandos on board. That's how the company was able to build such amazing products that stayed far ahead of the competition. However, the leader of these commandos failed to stay current with what was going on in the world, and so his commandos failed him because he failed his commandos.

In the same time period, a commando leader by the name of Joseph Sugarman had access to the identical media as the president of Pickett. However Sugarman realized the potential advantage of handheld calculators over slide rules. So he didn't hesitate. He used this knowledge and introduced an electronic handheld calculator product even before giant Sears, Roebuck and Co., which was one of the first retailers to sell this new invention. Consequently, Sugarman's business commandos helped him to make a fortune. His Northbrook, Illinois, company, JS&A Group, Inc., soon grew to become one of America's largest single sources of space-age products.

Later, Sugarman, the same commando leader, learned about the technology of a new type of tinted polycarbonate that could block harmful blue rays from the sun. When applied to glass lenses, it enabled the wearer to see better and without eyestrain. The only previous users had been the NASA astronauts. Sugarman did his homework and got the name of the manufacturer. He negotiated the rights to sell the sunglasses to the general public and, through his own direct-TV marketing efforts and retail stores, sold 20 million pairs of his BluBlockers brand.[2]

Cossman's Hypnotic Kit

Remember Joe Cossman, selling all those Spud Guns? Joe built this and other successful products simply by keeping his eyes open and applying what he saw. Here's another example.

In 1952, Morey Bernstein, a local businessman and amateur hypnotist in Pueblo, Colorado, hypnotized a woman by the name of Virginia Tighe. While under hypnosis, Bernstein performed an age regression. That is, he suggested to Tighe that she was a certain younger age. He then had her relate her experiences at that age.

This is a fairly common phenomenon under hypnosis. Hypnotic subjects are frequently able to remember small details about their lives at the age to which they have regressed—details they have long since forgotten. When they are regressed to preschool ages, they even begin to talk like toddlers and lose vocabulary.

Bernstein wondered how far back he could regress this subject into early childhood with her memories of that period intact. Bernstein proceeded to regress Tighe into her period as an infant. Then, on the spur of the moment, Bernstein suggested that Tighe had not yet been born. Suddenly his subject began to speak in an Irish brogue. Tighe claimed to be a nineteenth-century woman, Bridey Murphy, who lived in Cork, Ireland.

Over several months, Bernstein conducted numerous sessions with his subject. Based on a number of regressions with Virginia Tighe, Bernstein wrote a book four years later. Bernstein's 1956 book, *The Search for Bridey Murphy,* became a best-seller and set off a worldwide interest in hypnosis and reincarnation.[3]

When the Bridey Murphy story became public, Cossman didn't miss it. As an entrepreneur leading the thirteen business commandos in his small company, Cossman asked himself a very important question: Could he somehow apply this information in a business environment and if so, how? Cossman couldn't answer these questions immediately. He decided to seek additional information. He wanted to talk to Bernstein, but so did everyone else in the world, and he couldn't get through to him. No one knew Virginia Tighe's real name in those days. In the book, her name was disguised as "Ruth Simmons," so he couldn't talk to her, either.

The first thing Cossman did was to go to the public library. Cossman spent an entire day there searching for and finding out all he could about hypnosis and reincarnation. Although reincarnation was pretty far off the mainstream, he was surprised to learn that hypnosis was a common phenomenon and not infrequently employed by psychologists, psychiatrists, doctors, dentists, and even law enforcement. Cossman decided that his next step was to learn how to induce a hypnotic trance and to practice hypnosis himself.

Cossman located Gil Boyne, a stage hypnotist who had a school of hypnotism in Glendale, California. (In 1985, before I heard Cossman's story, I attended Boyne's school myself to learn hypnotism.) After learning the basics and actually hypnotizing a number of subjects, Cossman put his hypnotic kit together. It consisted of a short booklet of instruction, a 78 rpm record (remember, these were "the old days") of a hypnotic induction, and a piece of inexpensive costume jewelry, which, as I recall, Cossman called a "hypnotic crystal." The idea was that the crystal would provide a point of fixation to assist subjects being induced into a hypnotic trance. Cossman and his commando team sold 208,000 hypnotic kits, which represented over $1 million in sales. As a college student, I was one of Cossman's customers. I can't say it helped me in my studies, but since I graduated, it probably didn't hurt any, either. This kind of sales volume is not bad for someone simply paying attention to events in the world and asking a few simple questions. Commandos expect their leaders to be on top of current events, and real commandos innovate by doing exactly that.

Encourage Innovation in Others

No special ops leader is omnipotent, and smart ones know that the only way they can succeed over the long haul is to make use of the brainpower of others. Frank Jewett, a one-time vice president of research and development at AT&T, once noted that: "The real creative ideas originate hither and yon in the individual members of the staff, and no one can tell in advance what they will be or where they will crop up."[4] The truth is, the final innovative idea to complete the cycle may originate with someone not on staff.

Silly Innovations Can Be Accidental and Worth Millions

During World War II, most rubber came from rubber trees grown in areas that had been captured by the Japanese. In 1943, General Electric engineer James Wright was attempting to create a synthetic rubber made by mixing boric acid and silicone oil. The product bounced like crazy. Moreover, it was impervious to rot and was soft and malleable. It could be stretched many times its length without tearing and could copy the image of any printed material it came in contact with when pressure was applied. In fact, it could do just about anything except act as a substitute for rubber. Wright went on to better things, but General

Electric was intrigued with this strange material with its unusual properties. General Electric had a product without a practical use. Fortunately, they didn't trash it.

A few years later, a very unlikely innovator came on the scene. By varying accounts he was an unemployed marketing consultant, an unemployed advertising executive, or an itinerant salesman. In any case, his name was Peter Hodgson. Hodgson immediately saw the product's potential as a toy, a use overlooked by General Electric, probably because it was outside General Electric's product line. General Electric sold Hodgson the rights and it was Hodgson that named it Silly Putty.

Some fifty years later, I was in China teaching some MBA students about leadership in marketing. No one spoke English. I took some Silly Putty with me to impress my students with American technical acumen. I no sooner took the sample from my briefcase when there was a universal shout in unison in English: "Silly Putty." There could be no finer testimonial to the unknown commando leader at General Electric who knew that he and his team, who developed the stuff, were onto something—though he didn't know exactly what. He maintained his faith in the product until external commando Hodgson came along, unemployed or not, to finish the job.[5]

As leader, you are, in a sense, chief innovator, so to get the best from your business commandos you need to take three actions:

- Encourage a shared vision with clear goals.

- Develop a tolerance for the bizarre, strange, and unusual.

- Reward successful innovation.

Encourage a Shared Vision of Clear Goals

You won't get anywhere until you get your business commandos to agree on where you are going and what you are trying to do. For certain, there is a time for simply giving orders and expecting them to be obeyed. That's usually important when time is short, it is an emergency, and you don't have the luxury of explaining your reasons or your thinking. However, that isn't the case when innovation is critical. In fact, even in a situation where time is critical, the need for innovation may outweigh the need for usual "command and control" leadership.

How Innovation Saved Apollo 13

On April 13, 1970, Apollo 13 was on its way to the moon with a crew of three. Without warning, the understated declaration, "Houston, we have a problem," was broadcast from 200,000 miles in space to Houston, Texas, where the NASA command post was located.

A faulty oxygen tank had exploded, causing the craft to lose oxygen, with shrapnel from the exploding tank tearing into another tank and causing loss of its oxygen as well. The astronaut commander, Navy Captain James Lovell, was the veteran of three previous missions and 572 hours in space. However, no one had ever planned for or allowed for a situation like this. In another typical understatement, Lovell said, "To get Apollo 13 home would require a lot of innovation." And no wonder. The crew could not remain in the command module (CM). There was insufficient oxygen to get them back to earth and they would soon lose all power in the CM if they didn't shut it down. There was oxygen in the lunar module (LM). The problem was, it had no heat shield. On reentry to the earth, it would burn up. So the three-man crew had to electrically shut down the CM and go to the two-man LM to survive until just prior to reentry. Then they had to restart the electrical system in the CM. Completely new procedures had to be written and tested in the simulator in Houston before being passed up to the crew. The navigation problem was also different and new. The crew needed to know when and at what attitude to burn the LM descent engine to return home. The existing system for breathing wouldn't work as it existed. A jury-rig fix of the crew's environmental system had to be designed and then assembled by the crew to reduce the carbon dioxide to an acceptable level. That wasn't all. The spacecraft's attitude had to be controlled from the LM without an attitude indicator.

All of this had to be accomplished in varying critical time periods, some within only minutes, with failure meaning loss of the spacecraft and crew. For a successful return, additional innovations were needed to correct other problems, such as:

■ Insufficient ampere hours in the LM batteries

■ Insufficient water for cooling the electrical system

■ Insufficient lithium hydroxide needed to remove carbon dioxide for breathing

■ Inability to use the sextant for critical navigational alignment because debris from the ruptured service module interfered with visual fixing of the stars

■ Inability to get rid of waste so as not to disturb the established homeward trajectory

■ Lack of procedures for powering up the CM after its extended shut-down

There were many more problems, but you get the general idea. Every single problem required something new, and every single problem was dealt with through an innovation—something that had never been done before. According to Captain Lovell, Apollo 13 was able to successfully return to earth because of innovation made possible through a shared vision of goals. Instead of relying on the direct style of decision making, which is usually exercised in emergencies, NASA decided to share information and authority in space and on the ground.

Through encouraged innovation at light speed, procedures normally taking months to develop and publish took just hours. The Apollo 13 recovery is one of the most outstanding examples of the value of a shared vision encouraging massive and rapid innovation.[6]

Develop a Tolerance for the Bizarre, Strange, and Unusual

By the time ordinary people get to be commandos, they are no longer ordinary. So don't expect them to come up with ordinary ideas, either. Expect the bizarre, strange, and the unusual. That's good because unique ideas that competitors wouldn't dream of are exactly what you are looking for. That's what beats the competition time after time, and your commandos love the innovations and love beating the competition, too.

Consider the ice cream cone. It wasn't invented at the same time as ice cream. At the 1904 World's Fair in St. Louis, Missouri, ice cream vendor Arnold Fomachou invested in more ice cream than he had cups to serve it in to his customers. Desperate, he needed a solution—any solution—fast. There were plenty of vendors selling ice cream at the fair, and no one had an extra supply of cups or plates. Fellow fair vendor Ernest Hamwi had a booth nearby. He was selling waffles. He suggested rolling Fomachou's ice cream into his waffles and selling the ice cream that way. Is that weird or what? The product caught on right away. They called it the World's Fair Cornucopia. The popularity of the ice cream cone continued, and Hamwi took his waffle oven and opened the Cornucopia Waffle Company to make ice cream cones. Eventually he founded the Missouri Cone Company.[7]

If that's not strange enough for you, I like the advertisement someone thought up to promote a new temperature thermometer. The advertisement read something like this: "If you think sticking a thermometer in the ear to take body temperature is unusual, what do you think they said about where they stuck that other type of thermometer?"

Reward Successful Innovation

When your business commandos are successful, let them know by celebrating their success. In 1942, the United States was still recovering from the shock of the Japanese surprise attack on Pearl Harbor. The enemy was winning everywhere. A U.S. Navy submarine commander proposed that U.S. Army twin-engine bomber aircraft (we had no Air Force then) be launched from an aircraft carrier to attack Tokyo and other Japanese cities. The airplanes would then fly on and land at secret bases in China. Senior commanders agreed that this plan was feasible, and with the approval of President Roosevelt, they proceeded to plan the mission.

The job of commanding the bombers was given to then Lieutenant Colonel Jimmy Doolittle. He not only had an almost unbelievable reputation as a pilot, but he was one of the very few U.S. Army officers to possess a doctorate in aeronautical engineering.

Tolerances were very close. Though it was theoretically possible to fly a heavily laden B-25 bomber from an aircraft carrier, it had never been done before. The crews practiced for weeks. When Doolittle determined them ready, the aircraft were loaded on the aircraft carrier *Hornet* with great secrecy. The attack force departed on the mission with equal secrecy. Even the carrier's commander, Captain Marc Mitscher, didn't know the details of the mission until the sixteen bombers were loaded. The plan was to get 400 miles from the Japanese coastline. In this way, with little margin for error, they had just enough fuel to reach their recovery bases in China. However, on April 18, 1942, enemy picket boats sighted the force more than 600 miles out. A decision was made to strike anyway. Additional cans of fuel were distributed to each crew and carried in the aircraft itself. However, every crew knew that it would require courage, luck, and a great deal of innovation to get back home in one piece. Doolittle promised his men the biggest party ever on their return.

Every airplane successfully reached and bombed its target in Japan. It is noteworthy that while every single aircraft ran out of fuel and had to crash-land, some at night, few crewmembers lost their lives and only a few were captured. Moreover, while intended primarily as a morale booster, the mission had important strategic consequences. The Japanese withdrew forces from the Pacific for home island defense. More-over, concerned with the danger from American aircraft carriers, senior Japanese commanders made major blunders at the Battle of Midway a month and a half later,[8] which was the turning point of the war in the Pacific.

Doolittle kept his promise and rewarded his fliers with a major celebration party. The military wasn't stingy with its rewards, either. All participants were decorated for heroism, and Doolittle was not only awarded the Congressional Medal of Honor, but was bumped up to the rank of brigadier general, skipping the grade of full colonel entirely.

Many business organizations and most sales organizations know how to reward successful selling, and we can learn a lot from them. Mary Kay Cosmetics is renowned for giving away pink Cadillacs to its most successful saleswomen, but it also offers diamond-studded bum-blebee pins, mink coats, and a host of lesser awards for every single success. It's important for us to understand that salespeople innovate every time they make a sales call, because every single sales call is dif-ferent. So the sales model is a good one for all business commandos to follow.

Know There Is Always a Way and Find It!

All commandos have one common belief system: They believe there is always a way. As a special ops leader it is your job to come up with the solution, whether you do it yourself or tap your commandos for ideas. The idea may be far out or right in front of you. So, when the need arises, don't focus on your problem. Instead, focus on the idea that there is always a way and start thinking about various possibilities. Remember that the great inventor Thomas Edison had no college edu-cation and only three months of formal schooling. Yet Edison obtained 1,093 U.S. patents, the most issued to any individual. His inventions, including the lightbulb, phonograph, and motion picture technology, still impact our lives more than 150 years after his birth.

Edison knew that there was always a way. When he was stuck on a problem, his most famous technique was simply to go into a darkened room and think, and he'd remain there until the idea came. It's claimed that he tried more than a thousand different materials before he was finally successful in finding a filament that would actually work with-out burning up in the first lightbulb. Challenged because of his nearly

1000 failures before this eventual success, he retorted: "These were not failures. I have succeeded in discovering almost a thousand filaments which are not the correct ones and will not work."

Commando Notes

As a special ops leader in business, you can't sit on your hands and you can't always go by established rules: You must be an innovator. Your commandos will expect this of you. All you have to do is take three actions. First, stay current about what's going on in the world. That way, you'll see the opportunities and threats in your environment and you'll know what you can apply in your business. Then you need to encourage innovation in your subordinates. You are not all-knowing and all-powerful, no matter what you think. Properly encouraged, your commandos will come up with some amazing innovations. Finally, know that there is always a way. As a special ops leader, part of your job is to persist until you find it.

4 BE WHERE THE ACTION IS

"It is easier to pull a piece of cooked spaghetti in a given direction along a major axis than it is to push it in the same direction."
—General George S. Patton, Jr.

"Follow after me: for the Lord hath delivered your enemies."
—Judges 3:28

THE VIETNAM WAR was a tough, dirty war that was so controversial in the United States that after more than thirty years, it has left psychic wounds that have yet to heal. But the courage and performance demonstrated by American special operations units during this war have never been doubted. On March 14, 1969, the Navy SEALs were in the forefront of some of the toughest action. Lieutenant Joseph R. (Bob) Kerrey was a young naval officer commissioned a few years earlier after graduating from the University of Nebraska. He volunteered for the SEALs and made the grade through its tough training.

Lieutenant Kerrey had already completed many combat operations with his SEAL team when he was ordered to lead a mission to capture important members of the enemy's political cadre known to be located on an island in the bay of Nha Trang. It was going to be a tricky operation. The SEALs would be up against superior numbers, and the objective was not to kill, but to capture these enemy political leaders alive. Kerrey knew the dangers, and as a SEAL team leader, he knew his job was to lead from the front.

Kerrey first led his team up a 350-foot sheer cliff. The operation was dangerous and had to be done in absolute silence. Gaining the summit, he positioned his men above the ledge on which the enemy was encamped. They could look down and clearly see the enemy below. Kerrey split his assault force into two groups. He led one in a stealthy night descent right into the enemy's camp. Almost on top of their objective, they were spotted and the enemy opened up with an intense fire. Just as Kerrey touched down on the ledge, a grenade exploded almost at his feet. He was badly wounded. Although bleeding profusely and in great pain, Kerrey remained out in front and continued to control his group's fire on the enemy. However, with fire from both sides about equal, they were at an impasse. Then Kerrey directed that the other group of his team open fire. The enemy was totally unaware of the other group and was caught by surprise. The enemy was now in a devastating crossfire. Kerrey immediately ordered an assault to overrun the enemy headquarters. The SEALs didn't waste time. They knew who they were after, and they identified and took the right prisoners.

By this time, Kerrey's multiple wounds almost completely immobilized him, but he remained up front where the action was, and completely in charge. On his orders, his team secured and prepared the extraction site so the commandos could get away before the enemy could react with their superior numbers. Kerrey and his SEAL team, with their prisoners, were evacuated by helicopter. The enemy leaders who were captured provided critical intelligence.[1]

Lieutenant Kerrey's wounds were serious, and he lost a leg because of them and was forced to retire disabled from the Navy. However, the principles of his commando service in the SEALs never left Bob Kerrey, not as governor of Nebraska, not as a U.S. Senator, and not as a university president. He remained at the head of those he led, out in front.

Leading from an Air-Conditioned Office Is Not Recommended

If you want to accomplish impossible missions—high-velocity, first-to-market new product introductions with extreme turnarounds, or wildly effective, unexpected competitive strategies against larger and more powerful competitors—you've got to be right on the firing line, regardless of hardship or risk. You cannot lead from an air-conditioned office; you must be out there where things are happening. Actually, it was Tom Peters, the business writer and consultant, who popularized the simple fact of what Napoleon had said in a battle context. Napoleon had recommended that a leader "march toward the sounds of the guns." Peters recommended a leadership technique he called "management by wandering around." However, it was probably the legendary CEO Herb Kelleher of Southwest airlines who knew it best. His philosophy was that employees don't want to be managed, they want to be led—and you can only lead by setting the example.[2] That implies getting out in front.

For business commandos, the key is to be where the action is. That kills two important birds with one stone. First, people can see you sharing their problems, hardships, failures, and successes. Second, being where the action is ensures that you can immediately see what's happening and can take immediate action where necessary. Remember that in business and special operations, everything that can go wrong will go wrong, so it is important to be able to cut through layers of potential miscommunication and talk directly with your commandos who must get the job done.

You Must Be There to Lead and Be Seen

Sometimes, just being there, taking charge and taking action, can have a tremendous effect. One of my first jobs when I left the military was working as director of research and development for Sierra Engineering Company. A larger corporation has since absorbed this company (and was, in turn, itself later absorbed). However, thirty years ago Sierra Engineering Company was well known by its own name in the field of aviation life-support equipment. This is equipment used primarily by aviators for both everyday and emergency use.

A man by the name of Aaron Bloom hired me. He was the company's president and my direct supervisor. The company had a rather dramatic history. It was started just before World War II as a machine shop. Sometime during the war it got into the business of producing breathing masks for military pilots, and by the 1960s it was preeminent in this field. It produced just about every military oxygen mask made for U.S. and allied forces that used U.S. aircraft. Moreover, it not only manufactured oxygen masks used by civilian airline pilots, but it dominated the market for the emergency yellow oxygen masks you see demonstrated before takeoff whenever you fly today.

Years earlier, Bloom had been my predecessor as director of research and development and then had been promoted to vice president of engineering. However, a year after his promotion he had been fired by the then president of the company.

Ever since the advent of jet aircraft, when pilots started wearing protective plastic flight helmets that abutted the oxygen mask, Sierra had wanted to get into the helmet business. It would sell this product as it sold oxygen masks—in large quantities of upwards of 40,000 units to the U.S. government, which made one-time buys every year. A company called Gentex located then, as now, in Carbondale, Pennsylvania, dominated the helmet market for military aviators. After Bloom left the company, Sierra's president decided it was time to pull out all the plugs to break into the helmet market. He entered a bidding war that almost drove both companies into bankruptcy. However, Gentex emerged victorious and prevailed. Sierra, the loser, entered Chapter 11 of the bankruptcy laws. Moreover, the president of Sierra was found to have illegally invested employee retirement funds in his efforts. With this money lost and in disgrace, he committed suicide. Leaderless, Sierra shrank from more than 300 employees to less than fifty.

The bank contacted Bloom and brought him back in to run the company and see if it could be saved. Ten years later when I arrived on the scene, the company had long since fully recovered. The story I heard of how it happened has served me as a tremendous lesson in commando leadership ever since. I verified the story later by talking to Bloom, government customers, and even competitors. However, I heard it first from employees who had been there and gone through the experience. Bloom knew that to save the company, they needed an immediate cash flow. Contracts with the government were pending. If they could deliver the goods, they would receive money, which would buy the company survival time. Materials and machinery were already on hand to produce the helmets. The problem was, there was no longer a workforce to either manufacture or assemble them, or packers to pack the helmets properly or ship them to their destination.

Bloom called everyone together and told them what needed to be done. To save the company, these helmets had to be manufactured, assembled, and shipped. All employees had to work and perform their regular jobs at peak efficiency from eight to five. Then, all of them— senior executives, engineers, secretaries, and janitors—would report to the assembly line and take their orders from the few remaining production supervisors, where they would work for another four hours building the helmets. The company would provide the meals, but they had to continue this all-out work routine until the orders were shipped and fulfilled. Bloom led the way. He was on the production line with his sleeves rolled up every night, working alongside everyone else. They got the helmets out, and with this feat done, Bloom was able to keep things going. After two years, the company had worked itself out of Chapter 11 protection from its creditors. By the time I arrived, company sales were at an all-time high, and the number of employees had returned to normal. The lesson to me was very clear. The centerpiece of Bloom's turnaround was getting out in front and being where the critical action was taking place—in this case, where the helmets were assembled.

The Mystery of Joan of Arc

One of the most amazing of history's mysteries is the story of Joan of Arc during the Hundred Years' War between France and England in the fifteenth century. The English invaded France, and the French king-to-be, Charles, tried desperately, but unsuccessfully, to free his country from the English. Then, from out of nowhere, this eighteen-year-old girl appeared. She announced to the future king that she had been chosen by God to lead the French armies. It is no mystery why the king finally agreed. Even his advisers said essentially, "Give her the command. We've tried everything else." The French were desperate.

The mystery is how, in an age where there were hardly equal rights for women, this young, uneducated girl could have possibly succeeded when seasoned French generals failed. Consider her first battle at Orleans. For eight months, the French Army had strived to break the English siege and had failed utterly. Then Joan took charge of the army and she broke the siege in just eight days! For about ten months, until captured by the English, the French Army, led by Joan, had an almost unbroken string of victories. Many of our greatest generals would like to boast a record like that. How in the world did she do it?

Some years ago, I came across an account written by one of the chroniclers of her age. Yes, the fifteenth-century equivalent of Dan Rather or Tom Brokaw had managed an exclusive one-on-one interview.

"How do you do it?" the interviewer asked. "Do you like to fight? Did you receive special training in swordsmanship or warfare when you were growing up in your village?"

"No," Joan answered. "Personally, I don't know how to fight. But I have a large banner which all of my soldiers recognize. What I do is to look at the battlefield and see where the important action is and where it is crucial that we be in order to win. I ride to that position. My soldiers see my banner and where I have ridden. They follow me, and we win." Mystery solved. Joan got out in front and went where the action was. Even with no military education or experience of any kind, she led her soldiers where they had to be, and she and they won repeatedly.

Attributes of Getting Out in Front

In my analysis of battle and business commandos, I've identified four attributes of getting out in front. These are:

- Be in charge.
- Suffer the hardships.
- Assume the risks.
- Share the defeats and the victories.

Be in Charge of Everything

Herb Kelleher is a keen student of military history. Maybe that's where he learned his commando-style leadership. As founder, part-owner, and later CEO of Southwest Airlines Co., Kelleher built the airline into a team of 30,000 passionate, dedicated, almost fanatical business commandos. Southwest's accomplishments under Kelleher's leadership are awe-inspiring. Frequently number one on *Fortune's* list of best American companies to work for, Southwest Airlines had no layoffs during Kelleher's tenure. In fact, there was only one strike in the airline's history. Financially, Southwest was doing $5.7 billion per year in business with a market capitalization of $14 billion. That was bigger than the combined capitalization of competitors United, American, and Continental at the time. Southwest's customer satisfaction ratings were consistently high. In fact, it led all other competitors in metrics that the Federal Aviation Administration (FAA) used to measure airline performance. When Kelleher gave up the titles of president and CEO in 2001, the airline had been profitable for almost thirty years.[3]

Kelleher was seen to be in charge of everything. He regularly met with employees at all levels. So much so that a senior executive once complained to Kelleher that ordinary employees had better access to him than he did. He met his commandos on the taxiway and runways, on the airplanes, and even after hours in Dallas bars where he knew his employees frequented. He was clearly out in front and in charge of human resources.

Customer service? Kelleher constantly flew on Southwest's planes. He talked with customers as well as his employees. One frequent flyer claimed he sat next to Kelleher three times when he was president. Each time, Kelleher conducted a one-on-one customer survey, asking him and other passengers seated nearby how well Southwest was doing. Kelleher even invited frequent flyers to interview potential Southwest employees.

Kelleher didn't like the fact that competitors charged millions of dollars a year to use travel agents' reservations systems, so he had his commandos develop an electronic, ticketless system. Strategic planning? Kelleher didn't hire experts. He came up with his own methodology. He fought and won legal battles, planned and introduced new routes, and formulated strategy. One day every quarter he carried bags, worked the ticket counter, and served drinks at 25,000 feet.[4]

Yet through it all, Kelleher was not a micromanager. He let others do their jobs the best they could. But I don't think there was a single employee who didn't know that Kelleher was the commando-in-charge.

Suffer the Same Hardships as Those Who Follow

Brigadier General Frank D. Merrill was a West Pointer who had served as General Douglas MacArthur's intelligence officer and then went to work for General "Vinegar Joe" Stillwell in the China-Burma-India theater of operations. Stillwell knew that he could rely on Merrill to get the job done regardless of circumstances, and these circumstances were not good. Totally outnumbered and without logistical support except from the air, Merrill's secretive commando unit of slightly under 3,000 highly trained jungle commandos would fight behind enemy lines with Chinese and Burmese tribesmen and strive to make the lives of the Japanese in Burma so miserable that they would leave. Officially the unit was designated the 5307th Composite Unit (Provisional), but this was such a mouthful that in honor of their leader, the unit would become known simply as "Merrill's Marauders."

Beginning in January 1944, the Marauders were involved in three major operations in Burma. During this period they fought five major battles and thirty smaller ones, not counting the numerous firefights involving small patrols and ambushes. They hacked their way through the jungle. They endured mosquitoes, leeches, and other parasites and contracted malaria. They suffered enormous casualties; marched a thousand miles through hell on foot; and routinely went without food, medical attention, and sleep. The Marauders became the only unit in the United States Army in which every single man was awarded a Bronze Star for heroism.

Frank Merrill was with his commandos every bloody step of the way, suffering every hardship that his men weathered. However, the strain eventually proved too much. On March 28, 1944, General Merrill suffered a heart attack. Even then, he refused to be evacuated until all of his wounded had first been taken out.[5] He survived this heart attack, but years later his heart, weakened by his experiences in Burma, gave out. The sacrifices of Merrill and his Marauder commandos were not in vain. They accomplished their mission.

Assume the Same Risks as Those Who Follow

In 1943, Italian dictator Benito Mussolini, allied with Hitler during World War II, was imprisoned by the new Italian government. Without Mussolini, Hitler knew that Italy would soon be out of the war. Hitler chose Captain Otto Skorzeny to organize a commando raid to rescue Mussolini. Skorzeny had a reputation for bravery in combat and unconventionality. Plans were developed for a rescue attempt, but Mussolini was moved to a secret location before they could be implemented. German radio intercepts eventually found that Mussolini had been moved to the Campo Imperatore Hotel on Gran Sasso d'Italia.

The Gran Sasso is a high peak in the Apennine mountain region eighty miles northeast of Rome. Before the war, it was a winter ski resort. The only access to this hotel was by a cable car that ran up the side of the mountain. From an Italian general friendly to the Germans, Skorzeny had learned that in addition to the location's inaccessibility, Mussolini would be well guarded. It would be a dangerous mission all the way around. Skorzeny conducted an aerial reconnaissance over the Gran Sasso and located a possible landing place for an assault: a small lawn only yards from the front of the hotel.

Skorzeny decided that a parachute assault would not be possible because of the winds and the risk of scattering his commandos. Eventually he decided that only a glider assault was possible. The glider landing would be difficult and dangerous, but not impossible. Simultaneously, other commando elements would capture the cable car station in the valley and a nearby airfield in the valley. Once Mussolini was freed, a light aircraft would be landed and Mussolini flown off the mountain from an airstrip hurriedly put together on the hotel's lawn.

Skorzeny assumed the same risks as his commandos. He would lead the assault force himself. That this mission was not without danger was confirmed when several gliders crashed on landing and many of the commandos were seriously injured. However, the surviving commandos and the Italian general friendly to the Germans were able to convince the guards to surrender and to free Mussolini without a shot being fired. Then a new obstacle arose.

The light aircraft landed, but the conditions were less than favorable for taking off again. The improvised airstrip was strewn with rocks that could not quickly be removed. Moreover, alternative methods of spiriting Mussolini away had already been considered and eliminated. These options included leaving Gran Sasso by the cable car and then taking the road for Rome or flying from the captured airfield. Skorzeny considered both options too risky since he was certain the Italians had already learned of the raid and they were likely to be intercepted. However, the light aircraft pilot hesitated.

Skorzeny decided to assume the risks himself—in fact, add to them somewhat. He would go too, in the plane carrying Mussolini! The risks would be greater because of the additional weight, but there was no doubt in the pilot's mind that Skorzeny was sharing the risk. The plane was held in place by the commandos and only released for takeoff when it was at full power. Pilot, Skorzeny, and the Italian dictator made it safely off of Gran Sasso, and Mussolini was returned to power in Northern Italy.[6] This was not a good thing for the Allies, and it undoubtedly prolonged the war. However, one can admire Skorzeny's special ops leadership and his willingness to get out in front and share the risks. Without it, this operation could not have succeeded.

Share the Defeats and the Victories

No organization, even the commando organization, avoids setbacks. Every organization has defeats as well as victories. To be out in front means that you must share both.

One of the really great stories illustrating this concept is that of Ken Iverson, a great commando leader who passed away in 2002 at the age of 76. Iverson took over a failing business in a declining industry and built it to be the largest steel producer in the world with $6.2 billion in annual sales last year.[7] Iverson's company was Nucor Corporation. Facing bankruptcy in 1964, the company brought F. Kenneth Iverson on board.[8] He soon turned things around and Nucor became the third largest steel company. Those were the good times, and Iverson made sure his commandos shared them. But then, in 1982, times really went south for the steel industry. The total number of steelworkers was cut in half almost overnight. Nucor had to halve production. But unlike other steel companies, Iverson didn't lay off a single steelworker.

How did Iverson do it? Iverson shared the pain, too. Department heads took cuts of up to 40 percent. Senior executives took even bigger cuts. Iverson cut his own salary by 75 percent. "I cut my pay from $450,000 down to $110,000," he said. "It was the only right thing to do."[9] When the smoke cleared, Iverson had managed to hang on to all of his employees, and he turned them into business commandos and left a legacy that points the way for all special ops leaders to be up-front where the action is in both good days and bad.

Commando Summary

A leader leads from the only place you can really lead from: the front. There are four attributes of up-front leadership, and any leader wanting to implement special ops leadership should keep them constantly in mind: Be in charge, share the risks, share the hardships, and share the defeats as well as the victories.

5

COMMIT AND REQUIRE TOTAL COMMITMENT

"It is fatal to enter any war without the will to win it."
—General of the Army Douglas MacArthur

"If you start to take Vienna—take Vienna."
—Napoleon Bonaparte

IN 509 B.C.E., Lars Porsenna, an Etruscan king, led a surprise attack against Rome. Rome was not yet an empire. It was still a city-state. The city was considered almost invulnerable. High walls on three sides and the Tiber River on the remaining side protected it. These obstacles completely surrounded the city proper. However, these defenses had an important vulnerability. This was the existence of the wooden Sublician Bridge over the Tiber. In case of attack, the plan was to burn the bridge, so a special ops unit was assigned permanently to the bridge for this purpose.

The Roman plan of defense was faulty nonetheless. The bridge was valuable. The Romans did not want to destroy it unnecessarily. So the unit whose responsibility it was to destroy the bridge was stationed on the far side and forbidden to cross back to the Roman side while on duty. The idea was that if an unfriendly force approached, the officer in-charge could assess the situation up close and not destroy the bridge unless it was absolutely necessary. He and the unit would retreat across the bridge and then burn it before an enemy could cross. This procedure had never been tested, and in practice, as we will see, it failed.

A young Roman officer by the name of Horatius Cocles captained the special unit that was on duty the day the Etruscans approached.

The Etruscans advanced stealthily. By the time Horatius and his men recognized the threat, the Etruscans were almost on top of them. It was too late to destroy the bridge and withdraw safely. The sudden appearance and rapid advance of the Etruscan attack force caused a near panic and Horatius's men started to run. However, now that he recognized the danger, Horatius was committed to his objective no matter what.

Horatius stopped his men before they could escape without destroying the bridge. He ordered them back to the far side where the Etruscans were almost at the bridge. He persuaded them that their only hope was to set fire to the wooden bridge as rapidly as they could while he and two others delayed the enemy's advance. His personal commitment that he would destroy the bridge and stop the Etruscans, come what may, helped to steady his men for their task.

The Etruscans didn't know what to make of the situation. They were confused that only three men stood between them and the bridge to prevent them from crossing. Their indecision caused a delay that allowed Horatius's men to set fire to the bridge behind Horatius and his two commandos. The bridge finally ablaze, Horatius ordered the two soldiers with him to retreat through the flames to safety at the last minute. The two leaped through the flames without injury. Meanwhile, he continued to hold the Etruscans at bay.

Horatius fought on alone. Behind him he heard the weakened bridge fall into the river. Then, even though he wore heavy armor, Horatius jumped into the river. Some say Horatius survived, some say not. All agree that if it were not for Horatius's commitment to his objective, which he made clear to those he led, the Etruscans would have captured Rome. The story of Horatius was told and retold to generation after generation of Roman schoolchildren, as well as new military recruits. Horatius was used as the greatest example of Roman commitment to duty, strength, and honor.[1] It is an example of commando leadership at its finest.

Special Ops Leaders Must Be Totally Committed

If you aren't totally committed to a project, no one else will be. However, if you are committed, your commandos will follow you even at great disadvantage to themselves. General MacArthur said: "It is fatal to enter any war without the will to win it." Napoleon's admonition said the same thing in a different way: "If you start to take Vienna, take Vienna." What this means in business is not to go after any objective unless you intend to achieve it. You don't lead commandos half-heartedly. You lead commandos to win and to achieve every objective you set. Over time, it becomes a habit and your commandos will know that if you set a certain objective or name a particular goal, you intend to achieve it.

Being totally committed yields dramatic results for two main reasons:

1. It proves that the goal is worthwhile and important.
2. It confirms that the leader isn't going to quit before the objective is achieved.

Strong Commitment Needed for Great Success

The need for the leader to be strongly committed is as true in business as it is on the battlefield. Jim Collins led a research team that analyzed the *Fortune* 500 companies during the period 1965–1995. He published his results in *Good to Great*. Collins looked for *Fortune* 500 companies that had achieved rather unusual results: companies that first had cumulative stock returns at or below the market for fifteen years in a row, but then achieved stock returns of at least three times the market average over the fifteen years following. Out of more than 1,400 companies that Collins and his group analyzed, only eleven companies fell into this unique category.

There were many factors that Collins and his team of researchers were able to identify with a company's incredible leap from *Fortune* 500 "good" to *Fortune* 500 "great." One of the most significant differences was in the leadership of the CEOs of these super-successful companies versus the 1,421 others. It was called a "ferocious fearless resolve." What is a ferocious fearless resolve but total commitment?[2]

Showing Uncommon Commitment to Your Commandos

Here are four ways that special ops leaders show their commitment to what they must achieve:

- Communicate face-to-face.
- Make commitments public.
- Don't stop when the going gets rough.
- Always find a way.

Communicate Face-to-Face

Showing total commitment frequently means communicating face-to-face, even when you don't have to communicate that way. During Israel's War of Independence in 1948–1949, Moshe Dayan, Israel's one-eyed hero, was a major in command of the 89th Raiding Battalion. His battalion was a mixed assortment of highly mobile commandos riding mostly in jeeps mounted with .50-caliber machine guns and a few half-tracked armored vehicles. On July 11, 1948, he ordered an attack on the town of Lydda, which was occupied by superior numbers of the British-officered and trained Jordanian Arab Legion.

Dayan called his officers together and told them: "There is to be no stopping. . . . Keep moving at all costs. Shoot, run over obstacles, but keep moving." Dayan launched his attack at 6:20 P.M. He was in a scout car that led the way behind an armored car that the commandos called "the Tiger." At one point, under heavy fire and approaching an antitank ditch, the Tiger and attack column stopped contrary to Dayan's orders.

With bullets whistling around him, Dayan left his scout car to speak with the driver of the armored car, and then to the driver of each half-track vehicle. He could have used the radio, which all the vehicles were equipped with, but he decided he needed to talk to them face-to-face. He looked into each driver's eyes and repeated his orders to advance no matter what.

The driver of the armored car asked, "What if the road is mined?" "Then you'll be blown sky-high," Dayan replied. Only with the column moving again did Dayan return to his own vehicle. According to Dayan, the attack lasted forty-seven minutes. Then, the legionnaires fled. The city surrendered to the commandos officially the next morning.[3]

David Ben Gurion, then Israeli prime minister, called Dayan's victory "the greatest of our successes" during the war. Today, the city of Lydda is called by its original Hebrew name, Lod, and it is now in the general area of Israel's international airport. Dayan became well known to Ben Gurion because of this battle and was eventually elevated to major general and Chief of Staff of the Israeli Army at the age of thirty-eight. Dayan later served as minister of defense during Israel's Six-Day War in 1967, and in the Yom Kippur War of 1973, and after that as foreign minister, during which he negotiated the peace treaty with Egypt.

This Leader Meets Face-to Face with 3,300 Employees Every Year

There are many ways to show your commitment by communicating face-to-face. Patrick J. McGovern is the founder and chairman of International Data Group (IDG), a $3.1 billion technology-media and research company whose headquarters are in Framingham, Massachusetts. McGovern does face-to-face communication with 3,300 IDG employees across the United States when, every year, he personally delivers hand-signed cards, along with glowing words about the employee's individual achievements during the previous twelve months. Says McGovern: "I found the experience an excellent way to express one-to-one my recognition of employees' role in our business progress and ask their personal opinions on what we could do to improve."[4] His action also demonstrates his uncommon commitment to his business commandos, their mission, and his company. And recognition is an important part of communicating face-to-face to show your commitment as well.

Communication and Recognition Are the Secret

High Point Solutions, Inc. is a leader in the internetworking hardware industry, supplying routers, switches, communications servers, and access devices for *Fortune* 500 companies. Some analysts think that this company is one of the best in the industry. In the five years after its founding, the company grew 29,902 percent, despite big-time competitors like Cisco Systems. *INC.* magazine named High Point to the *INC.* 500 as the number-one company in 2001. Interestingly, neither company president Mike Mendiburu nor his brother, Vice President Tom Mendiburu, went to college. CFO Sandra Curran, who has worked with executives with a lot more education, says that part of the secret lies in communication and recognition. ". . . [T]hey communicate. We get a deal, and Tom comes out and thanks everyone. Little things like that mean a lot." This kind of communication and commitment has yielded sales per employee that is ten times that for the industry.[5] These results are supported by research. In one study, 87 percent of employees who said that they were very satisfied with their company's communications also said that they were very committed to their employer.[6] That's an example of good communications, especially one-on-one communications, demonstrating leader commitment and eliciting an almost automatic strong commitment in return.

Henry V's Face-to-Face Speech

One would be hard-pressed to find a more eloquent example of face-to-face communication than what Shakespeare put in the mouth of Henry V when he exhorted his troops before the Battle of Agincourt on October 25, 1415 during the Hundred Years' War. English forces were weary and ill from a long march of 260 miles over a period of seventeen days. Moreover, the French forces, with between 20,000 and 30,000 men, significantly outnumbered England's approximately 6,000 troops. It looked like the English were doomed. However, according to tradition, Henry rallied his troops prior to battle with some of the most stirring words ever recorded, and it was the English, and not the French, that prevailed. Of course, it was Shakespeare in his play *King Henry V* who actually wrote the words. Shakespeare penned this work nearly 200 years after the Battle of Agincourt. Still, it remains the finest dramatic interpretation of what special ops leadership means. So much so that Laurence Olivier did record the speech, literally, and it was played over the radio in 1944 to boost the morale of British troops during World War II.

Here are Henry V's words, according to Shakespeare:

> If we are mark'd to die, we are enow
> To do our country loss; and if to live,
> The fewer men, the greater share of honour.
> God's will! I pray thee, wish not one man more.
> By Jove, I am not covetous for gold,
> Nor care I who doth feed upon my cost;
> It yearns me not if men my garments wear;
> Such outward things dwell not in my desires.
> But if it be a sin to covet honour,
> I am the most offending soul alive.
> No, faith, my coz, wish not a man from England.
> God's peace! I would not lose so great an honour
> As one man more methinks would share from me
> For the best hope I have. O, do not wish one more!
> Rather proclaim it, Westmoreland, through my host,
> That he which hath no stomach to this fight,
> Let him depart; his passport shall be made,
> And crowns for convoy put into his purse;
> We would not die in that man's company
> That fears his fellowship to die with us.
> This day is call'd the feast of Crispian.
> He that outlives this day, and comes safe home,

Will stand a tip-toe when the day is nam'd,
And rouse him at the name of Crispian.
He that shall live this day, and see old age,
Will yearly on the vigil feast his neighbours,
And say "To-morrow is Saint Crispian:"
Then will he strip his sleeve and show his scars,
And say "These wounds I had on Crispin's day."
Old men forget: yet all shall be forgot,
But he'll remember, with advantages,
What feats he did that day. Then shall our names,
Familiar in his mouth as household words—
Harry the King, Bedford and Exeter,
Warwick and Talbot, Salisbury and Gloucester—
Be in their flowing cups freshly rememb'red.
This story shall the good man teach his son;
And Crispin Crispian shall ne'er go by,
From this day to the ending of the world,
But we in it shall be remember'd—
We few, we happy few, we band of brothers;
For he to-day that sheds his blood with me
Shall be my brother; be he ne'er so vile,
This day shall gentle his condition;
And gentlemen in England now a-bed
Shall think themselves accursed they were not here,
And hold their manhoods cheap whiles any speaks
That fought with us upon Saint Crispin's day.

Make Your Commitment Public

Otherwise good business leaders are frequently afraid to make their commitments public. They are afraid of not reaching their goals, or of being wrong, criticized, embarrassed, or they are just plain afraid. But real special ops leaders know the value of making their commitments public.

On May 25, 1961, President John F. Kennedy stood before a joint session of Congress and declared: "I believe that this nation should commit itself to achieving the goal, before this decade is out, of landing a man on the moon and returning him safely to the earth." His words inspired a nation to do what many believed to be impossible, especially after the Soviet Union had clearly shown the world that it, and not the United States, was preeminent in space exploration. Only eight years later, the country achieved the goal that President Kennedy had set, and the United States leaped into a lead in space that hasn't been questioned since.

Similarly, Winston Churchill stood before the British House of Commons during England's darkest hour, when it was forced to retreat from the continent, managed to escape from the French port of Dunkirk, and stood alone against Hitler (since the United States had not yet entered the war). His speech has been called the greatest call to arms ever made in the English language. Declared Churchill:

> We shall go on to the end, we shall fight in France, we shall fight on the seas and oceans, we shall fight with growing confidence and growing strength in the air, we shall defend our Island, whatever the cost may be, we shall fight on the beaches, we shall fight on the landing grounds, we shall fight in the fields and in the streets, we shall fight in the hills; we shall never surrender . . .

Churchill predicted final victory, and unlikely as it then seemed, his public commitment aroused his nation to fight on until ultimately, with Allied and U.S. help, that victory was his.

Don't Stop When the Going Gets Rough

You show your commitment when the going gets rough. That's when your commandos see exactly what you are made of. They decide then and there whether you are for real or not.

Lord Louis Mountbatten, the commander of the English Combined Operations Command during World War II, wrote: "Of the many and dashing raids carried out by the men of Combined Operations Command, none was more courageous or imaginative than Operation Frankton."

"Operation Frankton" was the name given to the commando raid carried out against German shipping in the port of Bordeaux. In 1955, the story of this raid was made into a movie called *Cockleshell Heroes*. The cockleshells were two-man kayak-type canoes. In them, the commandos traveled secretly, at night, for more than a hundred miles.

In late 1941, Britain was on the defensive, having lost major territories to Axis forces all over the world. With the resources for conventional means of attacking enemy ships unavailable, Prime Minister

Churchill ordered that attacks involving innovative "hit and run" methods be considered.

The cockleshell concept was the brainchild of Lieutenant Colonel (then Major) H. G. "Blondie" Hasler of the Royal Marines.[7] Hasler set about developing a canoe that was light enough for two men to paddle, yet strong enough to carry these men plus 160 pounds of munitions and survive lifting, dragging, sand, and sea. At first, several models failed to meet these specifications. In fact, when fully loaded up and manned, they sank. Hasler was told that no craft as he envisioned it was possible. However, Hasler didn't quit. He persisted and eventually succeeded in developing a suitable craft, despite his several initial failures.

After recruiting and training his commando force, he received orders to attack Axis ships that were running the blockade between France and the Far East. His unusual commando unit was officially named the Royal Marine Boom Patrol Detachment.

The plan was to land six canoes with two men each within nine miles of the Gironde River by submarine. After that, the commandos were on their own. They were to hide by day and travel only at night. It would take several nights, but once they arrived at the harbor, they would place limpet mines on the waterline of the ships they found at Bordeaux and time them to go off hours later. Then they would scuttle their canoes and head for neutral Spain, another hundred miles, on foot. French resistance would help them along the way.[8]

The mission was launched on December 5, 1942 with the drop-off from the submarine scheduled for the night of December 6. Things went awry almost from the start. The submarine hit rough weather, encountered an enemy submarine, and had to get through a minefield. Finally, the weather cleared and the submarine was able to fix its position through the periscope. It surfaced and began to disgorge the commandos and unload their cockleshells. It was a day late. The commandos and their canoes were launched from the submarine on December 7. However, upon being unloaded, one of the canoes became damaged and the disappointed crew had to remain with the sub. The other five canoes proceeded with the mission.

The first night out the canoes ran into strong cross-tides where the water was very rough. One canoe with its crew disappeared completely. Next the survivors encountered five-foot-high waves. One canoe capsized and was lost. The crew hung on to two of the remaining canoes and were dragged to safety. Then the three remaining canoes went on and continued with the mission. The crew without a canoe had to remain behind. At this point, with only half of his commando force left, and still several nights to go to get to the target area, Hasler must have had strong thoughts about abandoning the mission and turning back. However, he told his men that no matter what, they were going to complete their mission.

As they approached a major checkpoint they ran into three enemy frigates in line astern. The commandos lay flat, spread out, and paddled silently. They got through, but one boat disappeared. Now they were down to only two boats. The two remaining crews, including Major Hasler, continued. Finally after nine hours of hard paddling, they made their first resting place at dawn on December 8. The next night they had to manhandle their canoes over a sandbar and then ran into tidewaters running heavily in the wrong direction. It took six hours to get through. They had planned to attack the night of December 10 or December 11, but they were still too far away from Bordeaux, so they camped again at another forward base. The following night, they located their targets and attacked. They affixed their mines to the four target vessels and made off. The mines went off the next morning, heavily damaging all four vessels and sinking at least one ship. The two commando crews scuttled their craft as planned. Because the target vessels were some distance apart, the commando crews made for the recovery area separately.[9]

The problems encountered by Major Hasler and his commandos in the recovery phase were as difficult as the attack. The resistance fighters who were supposed to guide them never showed. While some French helped them, others threatened to turn them into the Germans. Hasler never wavered in his determination or his commitment. It was several months before he and one commando from his crew were finally safe in England.[10] The other crewmen that made the attack were betrayed and picked up by the French police. The Germans shot them. Of the three missing crews, one man's body washed ashore. He had drowned. The others vanished completely. The four commandos of the other two crews were all captured by the Germans and executed.

The Cockleshell Heroes are still celebrated by all who have heard of them. In England and in the Royal Marines, their story will be told and retold forever. They suffered 80 percent losses, but they did not fail. Because of Hasler's leadership and commitment to duty and the great courage of his commandos, even when things got their roughest, their mission was accomplished.[11]

Always Find a Way

For a special ops leader, there is always a way. All you have to do is to find it. Steve Jobs was such a leader when he and Steve Wozniak founded Apple Computer, the company that built an industry.

Contrary to popular opinion, Apple was hardly the first usable small computer. The IBM 5100, the Wang 2200, the Hewlett-Packard 9830 series, and the Datapoint 2200 dominated the professional/business sector of the computer market long before Apple. However, their products were not cheap. They sold for up $20,000 in early 1970 dollars. IBM had 70 percent of the computer market. It's easy to understand why. IBM not only had the resources and marketing clout, but the undisputed best research and development team around. There was also a home market for computers. Commodore, Radio Shack, and National Semiconductor all sold low-priced products from $500 to $1,000. However, for the most part, these machines did simple tasks or were video games. They were not serious programmable personal computers, so they weren't serious competitors for what the two Steves had in mind.

Jobs didn't have money or technical know-how about computers. He didn't have marketing experience, a development team, production facilities to build anything, or distribution for anything he might build. He had no track record and he didn't have a college education. However, Jobs recognized the need for real personal computers that were priced lower and were easy to use, and he was willing to find a way.

First, he formed a partnership with Wozniak, a Hewlett-Packard design engineer and a former high school friend. Jobs's first plan was simple. Build and sell small circuit boards, get some money, and show what they could do. Then he'd get backing from a major computer company to develop the personal computer that he envisioned.

By the spring of 1976, they got the plan off the ground. They were building and selling computer circuit boards successfully. The Apple I was sold in small numbers through retailers. Now it was time to find a big-name sponsor. They approached Atari and Hewlett-Packard about financial backing to build a personal computer. Both companies turned them down. Using the principles of strategy, Jobs looked for another way—and not giving up proved his commitment to the business commandos he led.

Jobs had thought about and planned alternatives should his primary approach fail. Now he sought to implement these alternatives.

The two partners concentrated on raising money and were successful in getting some cash and $10,000 more in parts and credit. However, Jobs realized that this money would be insufficient, so the team went back into the circuit board business. With additional financial resources from the profits they were ready to move ahead. They soon developed the Apple II and sold $200,000 in units while, at the same time, signing distribution agreements with several retailers. They were now in the computer business.

However, Jobs recognized that they didn't have the marketing know-how or even yet the finances to be other than a minor player. Again, he didn't let this fact stop him. He and Wozniak found a very creative solution: They recruited Mike Markkula, marketing manager of Intel Corporation, as a full partner. Markkula made a $250,000 personal investment and helped arrange a credit line with Bank of America. At one stroke, Apple acquired high-powered marketing talent and more than doubled its financial resources. Suddenly, Apple Computer was a force to be reckoned with by potential competitors, and the company was very attractive to venture capitalists.

In just a few months Apple received more than $3 million in investment capital, more than enough to begin major production. The company moved out of the garage and into a plant. Two years later, by March 1977, it had 500 retailers. However, Jobs was committed and he had promised his commandos more. He again found a way. Instead of remaining a minor player, this relatively small company surprised its larger competitors by adding 100,000 square feet of manufacturing capacity to the 22,000 square feet it already had. It expanded through five independent distributors to reach a greatly increased number of retail outlets. Almost immediately, Apple entered the business market.

In 1980, Apple Computer went public. At that time sales were $200 million with $12 million net profit. A year later, Apple became number one in its primary market of desktop publishing and drove most of its smaller direct competitors out of business. Both Apple and Jobs himself made a number of mistakes in subsequent years, but more recently the company once again found a way to move ahead with its iBooks and iPods. And no one can fault Jobs for his special ops leadership in the early days, when he led a small but growing commando team against many larger competitors until he successfully took on and, at least for a time, beat them all.

Kelleher Found a Way to Attract the Best People

Chapter 4 described some of the things Herb Kelleher did as CEO of Southwest Airlines. However, he did a lot more to get the best people and keep them. How do you build commitment in an industry as regulated, troubled, and highly competitive as the airline industry has been over the last twenty years?

Look what Kelleher did with compensation. He paid his executives 30 percent *less*, on average, than their counterparts at other airlines and at companies of similar size in other industries. Then he paid the average employee more. With his executives, he made up the difference with stock options linked to company performance. Moreover, he provided all employees with profit-sharing plans. Said Kelleher: "We want them to have a significant ownership of Southwest Airlines. We want them to share our success."[12] That policy, combined with a history of no layoffs, demonstrated the leader's commitment to the company, its employees, and its mission and earned Kelleher and Southwest the full commitment of its business commandos at all levels.

Commando Notes

If you demonstrate real commitment to your business commandos, they will follow you where you lead and do impossible things. Why do they do it? Because they know that when you show real commitment, you prove that whatever your goal or project at the time, it is important, and they have confidence that you aren't going to quit along the way, leaving them "holding the bag." If you aren't totally committed, none of the people that you lead will be either. But if you are committed and show your commitment, they will be, too.

6 DEMAND TOUGH DISCIPLINE

"The ancients, taught by experience, preferred discipline to numbers."
—Flavius Vegetius, Roman military strategist

"Nothing is more harmful to the service than the neglect of discipline; for that discipline, more than numbers, gives one army superiority over another."
—George Washington

THE APPRENTICE is a hit television show built on a business concept and featuring businessman and billionaire Donald Trump as host and star. In its first season on the air, sixteen candidates were gleaned from more than 215,000 applicants. These ambitious young businesspeople, all previously successful and some with MBAs or doctorates, competed against one another for the honor, glory, and career advantages of becoming Donald Trump's personal apprentice and running one of his companies for a year at a $250,000 annual salary.

Each week the candidates were divided into two teams and assigned identical tasks. The first week's assignment was selling lemonade. The weekly assignments soon progressed to more difficult tasks, from renting upscale apartments to selling high-priced art. Each week, the team that brought in the most money was rewarded. The project leader of the losing team and two members of that team (selected by the project leader) had to meet with Trump and two of his advisers in "the boardroom" and face questioning about the reasons and the dynamics of the loss. Each team member had to articulate why he or she should not be fired. At the end of the meeting Trump permanently eliminated one of the three from the overall competition with the words "You're fired!"

At the end of the show's first season, only two apprentice candidates remained. Kwame Jackson was a Harvard MBA who had left a position as an investment manager at Goldman Sachs to compete. Bill Rancic had founded a multimillion-dollar Internet company selling cigars. Trump assigned each a final task of running a major event. Bill was in charge of the Chrysler Trump Golf Tournament. Kwame ran the Jessica Simpson charity show for Operation Smile at the Trump Taj Mahal in Atlanta. Each candidate selected assistants from the last six candidates to be fired, making alternate selections until both had selected three assistants.

Kwame's first choice was Troy McClain, a successful entrepreneur and proven project leader who had become Kwame's best friend during the competition. This friendship, though somewhat surprising, given their different backgrounds, was real. Kwame was a well-educated African-American from Washington, D.C. Troy was a country boy from Idaho with only a high school education. Kwame was tall. Troy was short. Troy was happily married. Kwame was separated from his wife and a self-avowed "skirt chaser."

Kwame's second choice was more surprising. Omarosa Manigault-Stallworth had been controversial throughout the series. She got along with few of her teammates and had fights and arguments with many. However, Omarosa was well educated, articulate, and bright. She had an MBA and was working toward a doctorate. In addition, she had prior experience in the Clinton administration as an intern. (A journalist later said that he had uncovered the fact that Omarosa had been fired from four different jobs while working for Clinton.) Omarosa's main problem was that she was undisciplined. She seemingly would take orders from no one, including her various elected or appointed project leaders, but would do pretty much as she pleased. By choosing her second, Kwame said he sought Omarosa's goodwill.

Kwame assigned Omarosa the task of ensuring that Jessica Simpson, a celebrity rock star, arrived safely and was taken by limousine to her hotel before the event the following night. While at dinner with the team that night, Omarosa received a telephone call from the director of transportation. Jessica Simpson couldn't be located. Omarosa told the director that she was having dinner and that the director needed to work the problem on her own. Kwame, who only knew that Omarosa had a telephone call, asked her what the call was about. Omarosa answered that it was nothing that he should concern himself with.

The next morning, Kwame received a call from the same director. The celebrity had never shown up at the airport and the limousine was being released. The director told Kwame that Omarosa had refused to take the call regarding the situation the previous night. When confronted by Kwame, Omarosa denied it, although the truth was all caught on videotape.

Jessica Simpson was eventually located. Because no one had coordinated her arrival or met her at the airport, she went right to her hotel suite. Kwame thought his big problem was over. Unfortunately for Kwame, this wasn't true. More issues having to do with Omarosa's failure to carry out her instructions soon became evident. A planned celebrity breakfast wasn't ready because Omarosa had never ensured that the responsible individual knew the time of the event. Though she blamed Troy, who Kwame assigned as a general troubleshooter, it became apparent that Omarosa simply didn't do what she was told, but left the work to others. Then, the evening of the Simpson concert, Trump flew in by helicopter to meet the rock star before she performed. Kwame instructed Omarosa to hold Simpson in the greeting room while he went to get Trump. When Kwame returned with Trump and his entourage, Omarosa and Simpson were both gone. Kwame tried calling Omarosa by cell phone. She didn't pick up. Finally, they decided to go to the star's hotel room, where the illusive star and the nonresponsive Omarosa were located. Despite all these incidences, the concert event was termed a success.

Kwame told the cameraman videotaping the activities, and thus the home audience, that when dealing with competent people, he was accustomed to giving them the task and relying on them to see it through or telling him if there were a problem. He considered Omarosa "a space cadet." Omarosa was also interviewed individually. She berated Kwame for being "too laid back." "This is a difficult situation and he has to show some concern if he is going to be a leader," she said, completely overlooking the fact that she had been given responsibility for the activities that went awry.

Later, with 28 million people watching, Trump declared Bill Rancic the winner with the words, "You're hired." It had been very close, Trump said, but Kwame's failure to discipline Omarosa cost him the victory. "She lied to you twice," he stated. "You should have fired her or got her out of the way where she could have done no damage."[1]

Too bad, Kwame. You cannot depend on the undisciplined, and especially someone, no matter how brilliant or well educated, who is unwilling to follow the orders of those in authority.

Without Discipline You Cannot Succeed

In any critical project, you must be able to rely on subordinates without question. If you cannot trust them to follow the instructions you give, you cannot succeed because you will not know what they are going to do.

As a young student of military history, I was amazed that a Union general who had saved the day and created a victory by disobeying the orders of his commander was relieved of his duties almost immediately after the battle. Here's what happened.

In the Atlanta campaign, Brigadier General George Wagner commanded a brigade in the IV Corps under Union General T. H. Thomas and the Army of the Cumberland. This army was sent to fight Confederate General John B. Hood in Tennessee. On November 30, 1864, a unit of Thomas's division of the IV Corps, of which Wagner's brigade was a part, was a half mile in advance of the main Union position. Thomas sent orders to Wagner to withdraw when it seemed that Hood was about to launch a major assault. Wagner disobeyed his orders and stayed to fight, although heavily outnumbered. The two forward brigades were overrun and fled with Confederates so closely behind that the main line could not even fire on them.

Some Confederate troops did penetrate the Union line, but they were forced back by the Union reserves. Because of Wagner's heroic stand, the Union forces lost no ground. Nevertheless, Wagner was relieved from further duty with the Army of the Cumberland on December 9, 1864, supposedly at his own request. Officially, the reason given was due to the illness of his wife. He was sent to Indianapolis and did serve to the end of the war. He was honorably mustered out of the service on August 24, 1865. But it was clear Wagner had been under a cloud. He was not given the customary brevet of major general for his service.[2]

I could not understand this case. "If it had not been for his disobedience, the battle would have been lost," I exclaimed to the officer-professor conducting the class. "Yes," said my instructor, "but in the future, his commander could never have been sure that this officer would carry out his orders and be where and do what his commander intended."

If you disagree with a superior, the time to dispute his orders is before they are given. Once a decision has been made and orders have been given, you must adopt these orders as your own. Otherwise, there is chaos, and any organization that operates in this fashion is almost certain to fail. There are very rare occasions when disobedience is a correct action. But they are very rare, and the commando is always accountable for his or her decision.

With Discipline George Washington Was Successful

When George Washington's Continental Army entered their encampment at Valley Forge on December 19, 1777, his soldiers were poorly equipped with little military training. They also lacked discipline. As a result, they generally fared poorly in conventional fighting with their enemy.

At Valley Forge, Washington's army faced starvation and illness. That alone cost an estimated 3,000 casualties. However, Washington had acquired the means to a secret weapon in the person of a volunteer to the American cause: Prussian General Friedrich von Steuben. Von Steuben gave the soldiers of the Continental Army the secret weapon, and that weapon was discipline. Von Steuben trained Washington's soldiers and taught them that in combat there was no time to question or debate orders. They needed to be obeyed.

Six months later, when the Continental Army marched out of Valley Forge, it was a different army. Washington sought battle with British General Henry Clinton at Monmouth, New Jersey. With a newborn American spirit, his ragged troops proved equal to British regulars. Though the battle was not a decisive victory (because of blundering by one of Washington's subordinate generals), Clinton was nevertheless forced to retreat from the battlefield in the face of the steadfastness of the Americans. The Battle of Monmouth gave both sides a new perspective on the fighting qualities of the American Army.

Average Soldiers Can Defeat Great Warriors

One of the fascinating mysteries of military history is one generally ignored by most people because they are generally unaware of the facts. American Indians were among the great warriors of history. They were incredibly brave, outstanding marksmen and horsemen, willing to endure great pain and hardship, and able to travel long distances with little food and sleep. One writer called them "the greatest light cavalry in the world."

American Indians were almost always unbeatable when fighting one-on-one against U.S. soldiers. This was partly because the quality of American troops, especially after the Civil War, was not consistent. Some were outstanding soldiers with battle experience. But too many others enlisted in the army because they could find no other work. Some were committed to battle against Indians with little or no formal training. Moreover, alcoholism among the post–Civil War Army of the West was not uncommon.

On the other hand, the American Indian was a true warrior who spent his entire life, day in and day out, fighting and hunting. When not starved, he was in tremendous physical condition and possessed almost unimaginable endurance. Most U.S. soldiers, or soldiers of any other country, for that matter, wouldn't have stood a chance, even though (the thinking goes) U.S. soldiers had the firearms while the Indians were armed with primitive weapons. Even this wasn't always true.

For example, a recent History Channel presentation on the Battle of Little Big Horn stated that up to 25 percent of General George Custer's Indian opponents were better armed for the fight than his Seventh Cavalry. They carried repeating rifles, even the famous Winchester '73, "the gun that won the West." Custer's soldiers were armed with the Model 1870, single-shot "Trapdoor" Springfield. The Springfield had additional problems with expended shell cases expanding and occasionally being trapped in the rifle chamber. They had to be extracted manually with a knife or tool. Not the best task to be engaged in while under fire from hostile Indians. Because of these factors, it was estimated that Custer's opponents could fire seven times to his troops once.

Yet, time after time, the U.S. Army attacked the Indians with inferior numbers and succeeded. How was this possible? American Indian society was one where its members were the freest on the entire planet. Every Indian made his own personal decisions, and his tribe did not punish him for it. Even chiefs had more moral than actual authority over the members of their tribes. This was so contrary to Western thinking that it caused misperceptions again and again. There is no question that the U.S. government broke treaties signed with the American Indians. Part of the justification given for these actions was that treaties signed by Indian chiefs weren't kept. What our nineteenth-century leaders did not understand was that whereas a U.S. president or general could commit the country or troops to the terms of a treaty, an Indian chief had very little authority to do so.

The U.S. Army was organized by companies, troops, and battalions, each headed by a commander with the authority to enforce his orders and an overall commander with authority to enforce discipline and coordinate these subordinate units. American Indian tribes had no such organization and no such authority over discipline. Each Indian took action as he believed correct, according to his own understanding and feeling. So the U.S. Army was able to attack with inferior numbers, and even with inferior weaponry, using surprise and exploiting the Indians' lack of discipline as weapons. Having disciplined organizations against much better individual fighters, they won, as long as the numbers were not too overwhelming. Of course, in situations like where the odds were too heavy against them, these tactics could lead to their own annihilation. Little Big Horn is only the best known, but not the only, example.

Where Self-Discipline Fits In

Discipline is critical for any commando organization, and self-discipline is critical for individual commandos. When the leader is gone, commandos must be able to carry on anyway, no matter the obstacles, difficulty, hard work, or risk. Self-discipline and commitment (see Chapter 5) are closely related. Self-discipline can be developed. And, as a special ops leader, you want to help develop the self-discipline that your commandos already possess so that you'll know your instructions will be carried out and your commandos won't stop until the mission is completed.

From the NFL to Iraq and Afghanistan

You would be hard-pressed to find anyone of greater self-discipline than former NFL player Pat Tillman. At five feet eleven inches, Tillman was undersized for a linebacker at Arizona State. It didn't matter. He was Pac-10's defensive player of the year in 1997. Football demands a lot of time while earning a college degree. Many, maybe even most, players who are good enough to seriously look forward to a career in football go the easy route. They seek an easy degree in an easy field and are satisfied with a gentlemanly "C" average. Not Pat Tillman. He not only got a degree in marketing, but he graduated with honors with a

3.84 grade point average, and he did it in only three and a half years. Clearly, Tillman had the sort of self-discipline demanded by commandos.

Tillman spent four seasons with the Arizona Cardinals. In 2000, he set a franchise record with 224 tackles. The following year, he turned down a $9 million, five-year offer from the Super Bowl champion St. Louis Rams because he felt loyalty to the team that had drafted him out of college. Meanwhile, the Cardinals offered him a $3.6 million three-year contract. However, on September 11, 2001 the United States was attacked. After one more season with the Cardinals, he quit the team and gave up his million-dollar-plus yearly salary. As Tillman saw it his country was in great danger. Never mind that he was a newlywed with a beautiful wife. He put his career on hold and enlisted as a private in the U.S. Army. His new salary was $18,000 a year. His goal was to become a Ranger.

How many of us after 9/11 said: "Well, I'd like to do something, but professionally it's not a good time—any other time." Or "Gee, I'd like to help, but I just got married—next time." Or "I'd certainly do something, but they don't even want to make me an officer, despite my education, unless I sign up for five years—if it wasn't for that . . ." Pat Tillman gave none of these excuses to himself or to anyone else. He went to do what he believed in. He enlisted in the army and volunteered for the Rangers to defend the country he loved and was committed to. Speaking of his self-discipline, one of his Arizona coaches said after he enlisted: "This guy could go live in a foxhole for a year by himself with no food."

On April 23, 2004, the Army announced that Pat Tillman of the 75th Regiment Ranger Battalion had been killed in action in Afghanistan. A U.S. Army spokesman said that Tillman had died during a firefight with anticoalition militia forces about twenty-five miles southwest of a U.S. military base at Khost, which has been the scene of frequent fighting. Two other U.S. soldiers on the combat patrol were injured, and an Afghan soldier fighting alongside the Americans was killed. Afghanistan was not Tillman's only combat tour. Previously, he had also served in Iraq.[3]

Representative J. D. Hayworth of Arizona said: "Where do we get such men as these? Where do we find these people willing to stand up for America? He chose action rather than words. He just wanted to serve his country. He was a remarkable person. He lived the American dream, and he fought to preserve the American dream and our way of life."[4]

Develop Self-Discipline in Commandos, but Don't Try to Create It

Most self-discipline is fixed in the individual by the time you decide to accept any candidate as a business commando. This is true in the military, too, and to ascertain the state of this self-discipline is one of the goals of the rigorous basic training commandos receive. You want to know who has it and who doesn't. That's one reason why Navy SEALs not only have tough training but a "Hell Week," and you can find similar rites of passage for other elite units. As a U.S. Air Force chief master sergeant and the commandant of one school for elite warriors once told me: "I don't care what kind of physical condition the individual is in. I just want to know for sure that when things get rough, as they always do, this guy isn't going to quit on me."

It is true that we aren't born with self-discipline and that individuals can turn themselves around and develop what they lack. Moreover, you can help them to do it. The difference with special ops units as opposed to other organizations that you may lead is that you haven't got the time, and given the critical nature of the work, you can't afford the risk. Commandos either have the basics of self-discipline already or they do not. You can help a commando develop self-discipline further, and you should. However, you not going to be able to turn an Omarosa into a Pat Tillman. As the old saying goes: Don't try to teach a pig to sing. It's a waste of time, and it annoys the pig.

How to Help Your Commandos Develop Self-Discipline

By instigating and maintaining just two policies, you can help the commandos you lead develop their self-discipline. Both techniques fall under the general heading of requiring tough discipline:

- Require obedience to orders at all times, with no exceptions.

- Set the example by obeying rules from above.

Require Obedience to the Rules at All Times, with No Exceptions

The military tries to instill the idea of "instant and unquestioned obedience at all times." I know that sounds pretty harsh, as if its intent is to turn human beings into martinets. It's only partially true.

The military spends hours on the drill field teaching soldiers how to march in formation. What's the big deal about marching? Armies don't fight like that today, and sailors and airmen go through the same thing. Why? By spending the hours listening to and instantly obeying commands given on the drill field, soldiers acquire the habit of obeying those in command. Military operations in combat occur under great risk and adverse conditions. Fear is always present. A soldier must react to orders instantly. If he stops to question them, or argues the point, it may be too late for him or those who depend on his support. So for actions on the battlefield, soldiers are trained in instant and unquestioned obedience. The army knows that if this discipline can be ingrained, it will save lives on the battlefield.

The danger, of course, is that soldiers will become too well trained and will obey ridiculous or unlawful orders. When that happens (as it does), it generally results in tragedy. So instructors walk a thin line. They try to instill discipline at the same time that they conduct exercises that require soldiers to reason and think for themselves. They give instruction so that the soldier understands that he is personally responsible for not carrying out unlawful orders.

The challenge of this problem was played out in the movie *A Few Good Men* starring Jack Nicholson and Tom Cruise. Nicholson is a U.S. Marine Corps colonel who gives, but later denies giving, an illegal order that results in the training death of one of his men. Cruise is a young naval attorney defending enlisted Marines who carried out Nicholson's illegal order. In the end, Cruise proves that Nicholson gave the illegal order. However, although he succeeds in mitigating their sentences, the Marines who obeyed the order are still guilty.

Fortunately, the idea of drill fields and instant and *unquestioned* obedience is a bit silly for business commandos, and it is unnecessary. What is necessary is that legitimate orders be enforced.

A Good Leader Fails the Obedience Test

Here is an excellent example of the implementation of this concept. An entrepreneur started a company that grew rapidly from nothing to more than \$20 million in sales a year over a five-year period. One of the first company employees was a young female high school graduate who was willing to work hard and to learn. She soon demonstrated not only her intelligence, but a talent for leadership as well.

As the company grew it needed more managers, so the company president promoted her to a management position and gave her responsibility for more than a dozen subordinates, including several with college degrees. She did well and was considered indispensable to this company's operations and perhaps even a future vice president.

This young woman possessed yet another talent. She was an outstanding singer and sang frequently as a part-time professional. During one annual vacation, she went to Nashville to audition, but was unsuccessful. One day she approached the company president. There was a special opportunity in Nashville, but she needed to be there to audition. She wanted permission to take a week's leave for this purpose. Unfortunately, that week was a critical one for the company. Without her presence, there was no question but that the company could suffer a major setback in its operations. The president told her that he was sorry, but for the good of the organization, he could not permit this special leave of absence at this time. He had already publicly announced that no leave of absences would be granted during this critical week.

Angrily, she told her group that she was going to Nashville anyway. She told them that the president wouldn't dare to fire her. She left. The president did the right thing and the young woman was fired.

Of course, if the situation permitted it, the president would have allowed her absence. But the point is that if you want to lead a commando organization, you must insist on obedience with no exceptions to the rule.

Set the Example by Obeying Orders from Above

Nature being what it is, you will not always agree with the orders you receive from above and those to whom you are responsible. Sometimes you don't have all the facts. Or maybe you don't appreciate "the big picture." Though what you think should be done is right for your organization, it could be wrong for the overall organization of which your unit is only a part. This is known as suboptimizing. It is something that makes sense or optimizes the subordinate organization at the expense of the organization as a whole. But let's face it—surprise, surprise:

There will be times when you are right and your boss is wrong. It doesn't make any difference which is true. You can privately (and tactfully) try to convince your boss of the errors of his ways, but once a decision is made, that's it. You must support the decision fully as if it were your own. If you do not, you can expect no better from those orders that originate with you. You set the example by obeying orders yourself, no matter how distasteful they are.

Now what if you really cannot support a particular decision? In other words, you believe that what you have been told to do is so wrong that you cannot in good conscience support the decision and require others to do the same. In that case, you must be prepared for the consequences. If possible, you should resign from the organization. Many of our senior commanders in Vietnam have been criticized by today's military commanders for failing to request early retirement rather than fight a war that they knew could not be won given the political and other restrictions placed on their means of fighting. Most stayed because they rationalized to themselves that someone else would just have to do the same thing. Let me give you an example about the kind of thing I am talking about.

How an Air Force General Got Fired for Trying to Save His Men

In the early 1970s a new U.S. Air Force four-star general arrived to take over the air war in Vietnam. Unfortunately, his arrival coincided with the upgrading of North Vietnam's surface-to-air missile (SAM) capability, which had negative consequences not only for the American aviators fighting the war, but for the general himself.

Every war has its own rules of engagement laid down by the civilian leaders who are responsible for everything, including taking us to war in the first place. These rules outline what U.S. military members may and may not do in the course of combat.

The "rules of engagement" in the Vietnam War were uniquely restrictive and frequently resulted in higher risk and American casualties. One of the rules that American airmen had to contend with was that they were forbidden to attack enemy SAM sites until there was an actual "lock on" by enemy SAM radar. A lock-on was achieved just before an enemy fired a missile. Of course, war is not an athletic competition, and the ideal time to attack a SAM site is as it is being built, and continuously thereafter. However, for whatever reason, this restriction was one of the rules and, if disobeyed, it was a serious offense that could result in prison.

While this rule greatly increased the risk to American aircrews and resulted in some unnecessary losses, our technology and airmen were good enough to escape destruction despite giving the enemy this advantage. That is until the enemy suddenly upgraded its SAM radar capability. Now if aircrews didn't take some prior action, their chances of being hit by an enemy SAM increased tremendously, and losses mounted.

The newly arrived general immediately took the problem to his superiors, and it went all the way up to the country's civilian leadership. He requested immediate authority to strike SAM sites as soon as they became aware of American aircraft in their vicinity. His request was denied. He pointed out the daily losses of his airmen and aircraft and again asked for a change in the rules. Again it was denied. He was told to quit bitching and get on with the bombing.

At this point he conceived of a rather innovative solution. He redefined "lock on," which is radar contact prior to firing, to mean whenever the enemy SAM radar acquired the aircraft on their acquisition scopes, in other words, only observed the aircraft. Under those conditions, he told his crews, they had authority to strike the SAM site. Losses immediately dropped dramatically.

However, someone in higher authority soon learned what he had done and the roof fell in. He was relieved of command and was censured. Congress held up all air force promotions of all ranks and conducted a general investigation. The general was forced to retire and leave the air force, and not at the four-star rank that he held, but with only two stars, with commensurate reduced retirement pay and benefits.

Many of us can sympathize with this general. This particular rule of engagement never existed before. Those who flew in World War II and Korea, and I suspect many who have flown in battle in American wars since, would consider this rule not only nonsense, but even criminal, because it was causing the daily loss of lives of American pilots. Still, it was given on the legal authority of those in our government who were empowered to do so. It could not be disobeyed. If the general felt as strongly as he obviously did, his only recourse was to request being relieved of his command and to take an early retirement. Of course, when you've reached the top after more than thirty years of tough work, this is not such an easy thing to kiss off. But for a leader, including special ops leaders, you have no alternative: You adopt the orders that come from above or you get out.

Commando Notes

There is no way around it if you want to be a commando leader. Don't try to be a good guy. Try to be a fair guy. If you want your organization to succeed on a regular basis, you have to insist on self-discipline and enforce tough discipline without blinking—and that goes for unpopular orders that come from on high. You can express your disagreement privately, but once a decision is made, adopt it as your own or get out.

7 BUILD A COMMANDO TEAM

"Individuals don't win, teams do."
—Sam Walton

"An army is a team. It eats, sleeps, lives, and fights as a team. All this stuff you've been hearing about individuality is a bunch of crap."
—General George S. Patton, Jr.

"Four brave men who do not know each other will not dare to attack a lion. Four less brave, but knowing each other well, sure of their reliability and consequently of their mutual aid, will attack resolutely."
—Colonel Charles Ardant du Picq

LIEUTENANT COLONEL Evans F. Carlson was already considered a little odd when he was given command of the 2nd Marine Raider Battalion during World War II. He had enlisted in the Army before he was of legal age and was made a second lieutenant during World War I. Then he was discharged from the Army after the war, so he enlisted in the U.S. Marine Corps as a private. He became a lieutenant again, fought in Nicaragua, and earned a Navy Cross. They sent him to China to observe the methods of the communist 8th Army. Outspoken in favor of the Chinese on his return, he was reprimanded, so he resigned his commission and wrote two books. Convinced that war with Japan was finally coming, he reenlisted a year before the Pearl Harbor attack. Given command of a unit he had helped establish, he really shook things up with his team-building methods.

When he called for volunteers, he got 7,000, though he needed and accepted less than a thousand. His acceptance criteria baffled many, but it came right from Red Army theory. Political views regarding the enemy and attitude toward the war were considered of primary importance. Carlson abolished all traditional officers' privileges. He reorganized his unit around fire teams, the basic idea being that there would be no weapon in the battalion that could not be carried by one man.[1]

He adopted the motto "gung ho" for his Raiders. The literal definition from Chinese confirms the value he put on teamwork. Gung ho means "working together." But to Carlson, it wasn't merely a motto. It was a basic leadership concept. He held open "gung ho talks" with his troops, where everyone was expected to express an opinion. Moreover, Carlson ensured that leaders were recognized by their ability to lead, rather than by their rank.[2] Perhaps his most controversial move was insisting that both officers and enlisted Marines be called by their first names.[3] Interestingly, according to an article in *The New Yorker,* the U.S. Army's super-secret Delta Force of today ". . . called each other by their nicknames and eschewed salutes and all the other traditional trappings of military life. Officers and noncoms in Delta treated each other as equals."[4]

Speaking about Carlson, Cleland E. Early from Pasadena, Texas, later a retired Marine Corps colonel, commented: "He was primarily concerned about the stringent control officers and NCOs [noncommissioned officers] held over enlisted men. He thought you could get more if you acted as a team instead of just issuing orders."[5] Almost everything he did, except fighting, was contrary to traditional U.S. Marine Corps methods.

Carlson's first chance to demonstrate his commandos' teamwork was against the Makin Atoll in the South Pacific. Admiral Chester Nimitz was fighting a close battle with the Japanese 1,000 miles to the southwest in the Solomon Islands. To distract the Japanese resupply effort, Nimitz ordered Carlson's commandos to attack Makin as a diversionary action. He hoped that the Japanese would send more men there and take the pressure off of his actions. Carlson's Raiders were assigned the mission of eliminating an auxiliary seaplane base on the atoll. Two of Carlson's companies would participate. Each company of 100 men was crammed aboard an obsolete submarine in Hawaii for a clandestine ten-day voyage.

As the commandos prepared to land on the atoll on August 17, 1942, the situation turned sour almost immediately. High ocean swells made it extremely difficult to disembark. Although Carlson managed to get his troops into their boats, the ocean conditions were such that he made an on-the-spot decision to head all of his nineteen boats to a single location on the beach instead of two separate landing areas he had previously designated.

The Raiders immediately came under heavy fire. They called for and got fire support from the submarines. As two enemy reinforcement boats approached the shore from another island, Carlson coordinated the fire from one of the submarines. Even though the submarine was firing blindly, it managed to sink both enemy boats. Suddenly, Japanese planes appeared. The submarines immediately submerged. This was a reconnaissance. The Japanese followed with several aerial attacks. The second wave of planes bombed and strafed the island to cover the landing of two large flying boats in the lagoon. Each was filled with troops. With smooth teamwork coming from practice, Carlson's Raiders opened fire and destroyed both planes.

One of Carlson's platoons never got word regarding the change of landing sites during the embarkation from the submarines. Eleven men under the command of a lieutenant found themselves behind enemy lines. But Carlson had trained his commandos for teamwork. He coordinated their activities with his own fight. While most of his force fought against the enemy's front, this platoon attacked against the enemy's rear and then went on a rampage, destroying the enemy's radio station, buildings, and equipment. Under Carlson's orders, they withdrew and made it back to their submarine with only three losses.

By afternoon, Carlson knew he had accomplished his mission. He began a withdrawal back to the boats. Unfortunately, the surf and swells were even higher than in the morning. Many of his boats swamped and he could get only half his men off the island. Major James Roosevelt, Carlson's operations officer and President Franklin Roosevelt's oldest son, got four more boats off the next morning. Those that remained spent the day gathering more intelligence and destroying the remaining enemy installations. Then, with difficulty and under aerial attack, these troops, too, escaped from the island.

Thirty U.S. Marine Raiders were lost in this operation. Nevertheless, the Marine commandos had not only accomplished their mission, but temporarily destroyed the enemy presence on the island.[6] Seven months later; Carlson's Raiders were able to demonstrate their remarkable teamwork to an even greater extent. This was at Guadalcanal. Landed initially to secure a beachhead for army engineers who were going to build an airfield, the Raiders were ordered to penetrate Japanese lines and cause trouble. This they did. They harassed, ambushed, blew up installations, and raised hell all over the island. It was the longest patrol of this type of commando action in the war, lasting thirty-one days, from November 4 through December 4, 1942.[7] Carlson received his third Navy Cross for this exploit. He retired from the U.S. Marine Corps after the war as a brigadier general. Carlson is frequently cited as one of the fathers of U.S. Special Operations forces today.

With Commandos, It's the Team That Counts

In commando organizations, the unit, the team, and teamwork are everything. To replicate this level of teamwork in business, you must build organizational loyalty and a culture that is unique in your company or the industry you serve. However, developing business commandos as a team is not only one of your most important tasks, it is also one of the most difficult. You must work with different personalities with different agendas, different priorities, different motivation, and different ways of approaching any task. As former Navy SEAL Joel M. Hutchins noted in describing SEAL training, "Then each class of candidates is immediately plunged into one of the most basic elements of SEAL life—teamwork."[8]

Over the last fifteen years, there has been a dramatic increase in the use of team structures in companies. Sure, there was total quality management (TQM). But long before the quality movement, teams had already made important contributions in industry, which is the main reason for their increased popularity and growth in business. The fact is, working together efficiently and effectively is a force multiplier. That means you can get more from a team of individuals working synergistically than you get from each working individually.

A Lesson from the Cold War and Nuclear Bombers

Back during the Cold War years, the U.S. Air Force was trying to decide how to best organize its B-47 bomber crews for maximum efficiency. For example, it's a lot more efficient to consider each individual crew member—pilot, copilot, and navigator-bombardier—as an interchangeable part rather than a fixed crew of three. If you could look at each as interchangeable, it allows much more flexibility in flight scheduling, for example. Moreover, from past experience, the Air Force had all sorts of data that showed that total flying time in an aircraft was the most important factor for minimizing accidents and for achieving more accurate bombing, navigation, and aerial refueling. So, the thinking goes, why not organize around flying time instead of crews? Why couldn't you mix crew members as long as you had one particularly experienced aviator? However, when the test was over, the results showed that time spent together flying as a crew was more important than any other factor. In other words, a permanent crew, or team, was critical. Not surprisingly, several years later management guru Tom Peters made a similar observation when he said that "[t]he power of the team is so great that it is often wise to violate apparent common sense and force a team structure on almost anything."[9]

The Importance of Commando Teams Is Almost Universal

Can you begin to see just how powerful and unique a commando or special ops team can be? In fact, teams in industry have had some amazing achievements. One of General Electric's plants in Salisbury, North Carolina, organized teams like Carlson's Raiders and increased its productivity by 250 percent compared to other GE plants making the same product that didn't use teams. General Mills plants that employ commando-like teams are 40 percent more productive than plants without teams. Westinghouse Furniture Systems increased productivity 74 percent in three years with teams. Using teams, Volvo's Kalimar, Sweden, facility reduced defects by 90 percent. In one hospital study of critical care, when patients receiving mechanical ventilation are managed by a multidisciplinary team that proactively oversees the weaning process of removing a tube used for breathing, it takes patients nearly two days less time to become acclimated as compared to the traditional process.[10] Clearly, building commando teams makes sense.

The team structure may be a phenomenon built into all animals for survival. Scientists have observed that when geese flock in a V formation to reach a destination, they are operating as a team. Their common goal is their destination. And by teaming, they extend their range by as much as 71 percent! Flocking also illustrates some other important aspects of effective teaming. One goose doesn't lead all the time. The lead position at the point of the V varies, just as it may in team sports. On different plays, the leadership role varies. Also, at different times, different individuals may assume important leadership roles. In football, for example, at any given time, the head coach, line coach, team captain, quarterback, or someone else may have the most important leadership role on the team.

Getting back to our flock of geese, should a single goose leave formation, it soon returns because of the difficulty in flying against the wind resistance alone. Should a goose fall out of formation because it is injured, other "team members" will drop out and attempt to assist their teammate. You may have thought that the honking noise that geese make in formation serves no useful purpose, but scientists have found that it is part of the teamwork. The honking is the cheering that encourages the leader to maintain the pace. So flocks of geese, football teams, and units of military or business commandos share the following characteristics if they are to be effective:

- They demonstrate coordinated interaction.
- They are more efficient working together than alone.
- They enjoy the process of working together.
- They rotate responsibility either formally or informally.
- There is mutual care, nurturing, and encouragement among team members and especially between leaders and followers.
- There is a high level of trust.
- Everyone is keenly interested in everyone else's success.

As you might expect, when you have a group acting together toward a common goal and showing these characteristics, you see some very positive results. It becomes not just a team, but a winning team. The team members have a degree of understanding and acceptance not found outside the group. They produce a greater numbers of ideas, and these ideas are of higher quality than if they thought up some ideas individually and met to make a list of the total. Such a team has higher motivation and performance levels that offset individual biases and cover each other's "blind spots."

If you saw the movie *Rocky*, you may remember the scene where the brother of Rocky's girlfriend demands to know what Rocky sees in his sister. "She fills spaces," answers Rocky, "spaces in me, spaces in her." With fewer "blind spots" and performing together in such a way as to emphasize each member's strengths and make the individual's weaknesses irrelevant, an effective team is more likely to take risks and innovative action that lead to success.

When a flock of geese becomes a winning team, they get to their destination quicker than other flocks. They get the most protective nesting areas that are located closer to sources of food and water. Their goslings are bigger, stronger, and healthier. They have a much better chance of survival and procreation.

We see the winning football teams every year in the Super Bowl.

Winning commando teams, like Carlson's Raiders, do things in battle that defeat an enemy even against overwhelming odds. And business commando teams rack up high profits, meet impossible deadlines, create unheard-of products, and leave the competition muttering, "How did they ever do that?"

Developing a Commando Team in Stages

Psychologists and researchers in leadership have found that teams progress through four stages of development. Each stage has different characteristics, and members of teams tend to ask themselves different questions in each stage. Partly because the concerns of the team tend to be different in each stage, the leader's focus, actions, and behavior must be different in each stage as well. This is extremely important because what may be the correct actions in one stage would be counterproductive and incorrect in another. For example, in one stage the leader needs to focus on building relationships and facilitating tasks. Later on, the focus shifts to conflict management and examining key work processes to make them better. If you are still working on stage two while your team is in stage three, you may lose your moral authority as leader. One set of now-classic terms for these four stages is forming, storming, norming, and performing, developed by Bruce Tuckman in 1965.[11]

So, as a special ops leader, you must first identify what stage the commando team is in. Then you must pay attention to your focus and take actions to answer the concerns of your team while you help move them toward getting the job done. With this in mind, here are the four stages of team development:

Stage 1   Getting Organized

Stage 2   Fighting It Out

Stage 3   Getting It Together and Making Nice-Nice

Stage 4   Getting the Job Done

Stage 1: Organizing Your Team

When you first get together as a team, you're going to find that many of your commandos may be silent and self-conscious, especially if they haven't known one another previously. This is because they are uncertain. They don't know what is going to happen, and they may be worried about what is expected of them. The questions that they may be asking themselves include: Who are these other guys? Are they going to be friendly, or are they going to challenge me or my way of thinking? What are they going to expect me to do? What's going to happen during this process? Where exactly will we be headed, and how? What are our goals? Where do I fit in? How much work will it involve? Will I be able to do what is required of me?

As the team leader, your primary focus during stage one is to organize the team. Your actions should include making initial introductions; stating the mission of the team; clarifying goals, procedures, rules, and expectations; and answering questions. The idea is to establish a foundation of trust right from the start. You want an atmosphere of openness with, to the maximum extent possible, no secrets. Everyone should have her say, and everyone's opinion should be listened to and considered even at this early stage.

To do this, you must model these expected behaviors yourself. If you aren't open, no one else will be. If you don't treat the opinions of others with respect, neither will anyone else. If you listen carefully, so will everyone else. If you argue and prevent others from introducing their ideas or asking questions, then you'll find those you want to build into a commando team will do the same.

You may be interested in the characteristics of high-performance teams as distinguished from those that performed less well in a number of industries.[12] Keep them in mind as you organize your commandos.

Characteristics of High-Performance Teams

Clear goals	Autonomy
Goals known by all	Performance-based rewards
Goals achieved in small steps	Competition
Standards of excellence	Praise and recognition
Feedback of results	Team commitment
Skills and knowledge of everyone applied	Plans and tactics
Continuous improvement expected	Rules and penalties
Adequate resources provided	Performance measures

In stage one, your principle focus is on getting organized. At the same time, you are laying the foundations of trust and openness for the stages that follow.

Stage 2: Fighting It Out

When you enter stage two, the good news is that if you've done things right, your commandos are now committed to your vision and raring to go. Unfortunately, since individual commandos have so much of themselves invested, team members can become polarized during stage two. They may form cliques, become overly competitive, and could even challenge your authority as leader.

Clearly, you have your work cut out for you. Your focus during this stage must be on what psychologists call "conflict management." The trick is to continue to ensure that everyone gets to express ideas and analyze key work processes to make them better. Then you must get commandos to keep working together rather than against each other and, at the same time, avoid groupthink.

Groupthink and How to Avoid It

Groupthink has to do with adopting some idea or course of action simply because the group seems to want it, not because it is a particularly good idea that has been thoroughly discussed and thought through. The most conspicuous example of groupthink has been popularized as a "trip to Abilene."

This concept to represent groupthink was developed by Dr. Jerry Harvey first in an article in *Organizational Dynamics* and later in a book and video. Harvey's family makes a miserable two-hour trip to Abilene and another two-hour return to a ranch in west Texas. The trip is made in a car without air-conditioning on a hot, humid, summer day on the suggestion of Harvey's father-in-law. All family members agreed on the trip, although later it turns out that they did so simply "to be agreeable," whereupon Harvey's father-in-law states that he didn't want to go, either. He suggested the idea to make conversation. Nevertheless, because of groupthink, they all went to Abilene.

To avoid groupthink, all ideas need to be critically evaluated. You should encourage open discussion of all ideas on a routine basis. Some ideas can be evaluated better by calling in outside experts to listen or even rotating the assignment of a devil's advocate to bring up other ideas against any proposed action. One technique that helps many commando teams to avoid groupthink is a policy of second-chance discussions. With this technique, all decisions taken at a meeting have their implementations deferred until one additional confirmation discussion at a later date. Of course, when decisions need to be taken and implemented without delay, this latter technique is not possible.

During stage two, your commandos will have new questions on their minds: How will we handle disagreements? How do we communicate negative information? Are the right people on this team? How can we make decisions even though there is a lot of disagreement? You may wish that your commandos were not asking themselves these questions. However, rather than be surprised, it is better to be forewarned so that you can deal with these issues.

There are a number of actions you can take to help your commandos bond as a team during this "fighting it out" stage. You can think up ways to reinforce and remotivate commitment to your vision. You can turn your commandos into teachers, so they help each other with problems they may be having. In fact, you should know that using commandos as teachers, or leaders, for particular areas of responsibility helps to generate their commitment. You might think up ways to provide individual recognition. Certificates, lapel pins, coffee cups—any symbol can be established to recognize achievement or the behavior you are trying to encourage. You can look for win-win opportunities and foster win-win thinking, where both sides of an argument or an issue benefit. One way to increase feelings of cohesion in the group is to identify a common "enemy," such as a competitor, on which your team of commandos can focus.

There are plenty of challenges for you as a special ops leader in this stage. Do it right, and your team goes into the final stages looking, acting, and performing like a real winner.

Stage 3: Getting Your Team to Pull Together

In stage three, you have a different challenge. Team members tend to ignore or gloss over disagreements and conform obediently to the group standards and expectations, as well as to your direction as leader. There is heightened interpersonal attraction, and at the end, everyone will be committed to a team vision. Most of this is what you want and to the good.

However, your commandos will still ask themselves questions. What are the team's norms and expectations of them? How much must I give up to conform to the group's ideas? What role can, and will, I perform on this team? Where can I make a contribution? Will I be supported in what I suggest, or will others "put me down"? Where are we headed? How much time and energy will I have to commit?

During this stage, you have several major challenges that are different from the requirements in other stages. In the main, your focus should be on:

- Facilitating role differentiation
- Showing support
- Providing feedback
- Articulating and motivating commitment to a vision

To facilitate role differentiation, you need to continue to build relationships among your commandos. You want them to contribute according to their strengths and where their contributions are most needed. You also want to assist them, as necessary, in areas where they may have difficulty. You can do this by asking about and discovering their strengths and preferences for tasks that need to be done. As they proceed, it is your responsibility to ensure they have the personal and physical resources to do the job. When there are disagreements between commandos, as leader it is your responsibility to resolve the situation. In a task-facilitator role, you may even function in a variety of subroles. At times you may give direction or make suggestions. You are sometimes an information seeker and, at other times, an information giver. You must monitor, coordinate, and oversee everything that is going on.

Avoid taking actions that will prevent others from contributing, and don't let anyone else act as an obstacle, either. People try to block others in a variety of ways. They find fault with them, overanalyze some aspect of their work, reject their contributions out of hand, dominate them, and stall them. They may use some tactics you might never anticipate. Don't let anyone on your team do these things, and don't you, either. It is essential to get the maximum output from every business commando.

You show support for others by building up your commandos every chance you get. Build on their ideas and give the credit to them for being the first to think them up. And as indicated previously, let everyone be heard. Don't let someone who is more articulate, powerful, or popular block the ideas of some other team member who is less outgoing. If you do, you'll not only lose the idea, you'll probably lose the contributions of the ideas of this individual in the future.

Providing effective feedback is not always easy. You must indicate what is going to work and what won't. The real challenge, of course, is to give feedback without offending, so your commando maintains his self-respect and continues to contribute. To best accomplish this, if you must criticize, then talk about behavior, not about personalities. Make observations, not inferences. Be as specific as possible. Share ideas and information. Don't set yourself up as a know-it-all who makes a living by just giving advice or orders. Learn the art of the possible. It is possible to give too much feedback at one time, especially if the feedback is more critical than congratulatory.

Critical feedback can be difficult to deliver and difficult to hear. Try to remove the "sting" of criticism. President Ronald Reagan once gave a small statue of a foot with a hole in it to his secretary of the interior when the secretary made a major public gaff. The statue was the "Shot Yourself in the Foot" award. There was a lot of laughter and good humor as President Reagan presented it. Still, it was criticism. You might establish a pot where people have to put in a couple dollars if they screw things up. In combat, my air commando squadron established a DSOW (dumb shit of the week) award. The "winner" had to provide free beer to the squadron for a week. (I should add that beer was selling for five cents a can then.) Finally, remember why you give feedback. It is because you value and want to improve your commandos . . . not for personal emotional release. It's not to show who's boss or how clever you are.

Finally, you must focus on articulating and motivating commitment to your vision. A vision is a mental picture of the outcome of the mission. We'll talk more about your vision and how to get your commandos to adopt it in Chapter 8.

Stage 4: Getting the Job Done

Your commandos started to get the job done when you first started to organize them. The process continues during all four stages. But if you've done things right, when you get to stage four, you are really on a roll and the focus is on accomplishing the mission. How soon your commandos get to this stage may vary. Clearly, it is to your advantage to get to stage four (or at least be prepared for it) as soon as you can and to spend the bulk of your time working on achieving your goal. During this stage, team members show high mutual trust and unconditional commitment to the team. Moreover, team members tend to be self-sufficient and display a good deal of initiative. By now, the team looks like a disciplined entrepreneurial company. As team leader, your focus during this final stage should be on innovation, continuous improvement, and emphasizing and making the most of what your team does best—its core competencies.

At stage four, your commandos' self-questioning should reflect this striving for high performance. How can we continuously improve? How can we promote innovativeness and creativity? How can we build further on our core competencies? What further improvements can be made to our processes? How can we maintain a high level of contribution to the team?

As leader, your actions are in direct line with these questions. Do everything you can to encourage continuous improvement. Celebrate your team's successes. Keep providing feedback on performance on an ongoing basis. Sponsor and encourage new ideas and expanded roles for team commandos. And most important, help keep your commando team from reverting back to earlier stages. But if this happens, follow the guidelines for the stage they are in.

Anticipating Problems As You Progress

As you progress through the four stages of commando team development, you will occasionally be surprised by commandos you considered first-rate doing things to hurt the team. When that happens, you're going to have to take some kind of action. You might also consider the root cause. Why did this productive commando go wrong? Here are some of the more common reasons that can cause good team members to err:

■ *Inequity.* When one or more commandos fail to work to a certain standard of effort, if you don't take action, you will soon find that others will do likewise. The erring team member thinks, "If this other person isn't working up to snuff, why should I?" This is one reason why you cannot allow one of the team members to goof off and do less than her fair share. You must stop inequity of effort immediately or, better yet, before it happens.

■ *No accountability.* This situation occurs when commandos are allowed to "freewheel" and are given no feedback or criticism of wrong actions. Since no one else seems to care, the team member feels insignificant and unimportant. This in itself can lead to general inequity of effort. It can also lead to all sorts of abuses of power and responsibility. I've said it before and I'll say it again, you must hold your commandos responsible for their actions or inactions.

■ *Identical rewards under all conditions.* Now, in some circumstances, such as when the team does a great job in a group effort, you want to reward everyone equally. However, you must be very careful about individual awards. This situation, too, is related to inequity of effort. The commando team member wonders why he should work harder than others do when everyone, or at least many others, get the same reward. What you want is for everyone to strive to contribute to the maximum extent possible. Identical rewards given for varying efforts can lead to everyone trying to do the minimum. The solution is to set up a reward system, even if the reward is a simple public recognition of an "above the call of duty" or a successful accomplishment.

■ *Coordination problems.* There is no getting around it. The more people involved in an effort, the more coordination is required. It can mean waiting for the work of others or having to get others' approval. For someone who has always worked successfully alone, the inefficiencies and delays are frustrating and painfully obvious. However, as already noted, the loss in efficiency of the individual can be more than made up by the synergistic effect of the team if you do things right. Commandos cannot only help one another, they can cheer each other on and rejoice in each other's success. As leader, you must make certain this happens. You must make it efficient and fun to be part of the commando team. Do this, and all of your commandos will see that they can accomplish more as a team than they ever could individually.

Commando Notes

Commandos don't work as individuals. They perform as a team. Therefore, the time you devote to building your commando team and developing teamwork is well spent. Remember that the development of a team tends to occur in four stages: forming, storming, norming, and performing. Each stage requires a different emphasis or focus. Organizing your efforts in this way leads to the high performance seen in individual commandos and outstanding commando teams in industry.

INSPIRE OTHERS TO FOLLOW YOUR VISION

"To be a leader, you have to make people want to follow you, and nobody wants to follow someone who doesn't know where he is going."
—Joe Namath

"If a man does not know to what port he is steering, no wind is favorable."
—Seneca, 4 B.C.–A.D. 65

ONE OF AMERICA'S outstanding yet strangest commandos was Colonel John S. Mosby of the Fourth Virginia Cavalry, Confederate States of America. For almost four years Mosby made life miserable for Union troops in the Shenandoah Valley of Northern Virginia and around the area of the federal capitol in Washington, D.C. His commandos operated like guerillas. He appeared out of nowhere to strike and disappeared as suddenly as he had first appeared to attack somewhere else. To both sides he was known as "the Gray Ghost," a name given him by President Abraham Lincoln. Many federal officers hated him. They saw his style of fighting as "unfair" and "dishonorable." However, more than one military historian credits him with having a major impact on the war by drawing thousands of Union forces away from where they were most needed, defending the U.S. Capitol, to try and capture him. Yet he never had more than a couple hundred commandos in his entire command.

Before the war, Mosby had attended the University of Virginia, though he was dismissed prior to graduation after shooting a fellow student during a dispute. He joined a law office, passed the bar, and began to practice law. After the war he became a friend of President Ulysses S. Grant, practiced law again, and later yet was appointed U.S. consul to Hong Kong by President Rutherford B. Hayes. The fact that many of his Union adversaries considered him little better than a bush-whacker or horse thief is particularly ironic since Mosby's vision was conceived in his concept of honor.

Mosby's vision, with which he inspired his commandos, was the basis for his victories. This vision was that a commando force, operating with hit-and-run tactics and founded on what he termed "Southern honor," could not be defeated. By his light, a Southerner was committed to the defense of women, children, and his state by any means, violent if required, and not necessarily in the set-piece battles used by the large European armies. In his view, war fought for this purpose of defense was right and ennobling, even if not fought using the conventional tactics of the time. To Mosby, Southern honor encompassed a focus on outward appearance, revenge if demanded, and an adherence to one's word.[1]

Mosby was in his late twenties when Virginia seceded from the Union in 1861. Knowing that invasion of his state was eminent, he rushed to his state's defense and enlisted in the Confederate Army as a private. This was despite the fact that he had publicly opposed both secession and slavery. He first served as a scout at Bull Run, the first major battle of the Civil War. His personal bravery and demeanor were noted by his superiors, and he was promoted to lieutenant.

The new officer carried out several important assignments as an independent cavalry scout. However, he had an idea for a mounted commando force that would operate on a continuous basis behind enemy lines. His scouting experiences taught him that mobility was a key ingredient. Using surprise as a weapon, he believed he could be successful against enemy forces many times the size of his force.

His previous conduct in battle won a hearing for this concept. Though Mosby was physically unimposing at five-feet-eight-inches tall and weighing only 125 pounds,[2] he received authority to form a unit of cavalry commandos reporting to Confederate General Jeb Stuart, but operating independently. His primary charter was to destroy railroad supply lines between Washington and Northern Virginia and to harass the enemy in any way he could.

Mosby was so successful as a commando leader that he was promoted steadily. By war's end, he was a colonel. Often large forces were taken from other vital missions and sent against him, but he always either evaded or defeated them, capturing many of those who sought to capture him. In fact, Robert E. Lee cited Mosby for meritorious service more often than any other Confederate officer during the war.[3]

One of his interesting exploits was the capture of Brigadier General Edwin Stoughton with his entire entourage and forty horses near Fairfax, Virginia, as mentioned in one of the introductory chapters of this book (see "The Principles of Special Ops Leadership"). On another occasion, he easily evaded superior forces sent to entrap him. Having read about President Lincoln's well-known sense of humor, he sent Lincoln a lock of his hair as a consolation prize, believing he would appreciate the joke.[4] But time and time again, it was his vision of mounted commandos, fueled by the ideal of Southern honor, that Mosby followed as a lodestone, and it was this vision that he used to inspire his command.

By this code, violence in the name of self-defense was clearly justified, but deliberate and premeditated murder of prisoners of war was not. On September 22, 1864, Union soldiers acting on orders hanged six of Mosby's men. Murder was outside the bounds of the Southern notion of honor. Revenge killings, however, were not only justified, but required. Within two months, Mosby captured and executed the same number of Union soldiers in retaliation. In a letter to Major General Philip Sheridan, who then commanded Union forces in the Shenandoah Valley, Mosby wrote: "Hereafter any prisoners falling into my hands will be treated with the kindness due to their condition, unless some new act of barbarity shall compel me, reluctantly, to adopt a line of policy repugnant to humanity." The killings of prisoners on both sides stopped.

Mosby was never captured or defeated, nor did he ever surrender. He disbanded his commandos after the fall of the Confederacy.

What Is a Vision?

A vision is an all-encompassing picture of the way you want your organization to look in the future. It is the grand goal that guides all the actions of your organization. Without a vision, your organization is as helpless as a rudderless ship. Seneca's quotation at the beginning of this chapter is aptly descriptive. Without a vision, you'll never get "there," and neither will your organization. Just as Bloody Mary sang in the Rogers and Hammerstein musical *South Pacific,* "You got to have a dream, If you don't have a dream, How you gonna have a dream come true?" Bloody Mary was correct. When Martin Luther King declared "I have a dream," he spelled out a vision that continues to inspire people, in this country and the world, decades after King's death.

Your vision defines the "there"—the place where you want your team to go, the goal that you want to achieve. This vision must be big enough, important enough, and clear enough to be compelling to your commandos. If your "there" has these qualities and you are committed to it, like John Mosby, you cannot fail. Moreover, those who follow you will break their necks to help you and your organization get "there."

The Insect That Teaches Us Leadership

Do you think that you can learn anything about a leader's vision from an insect? Well, I did. It's a great story, and I tell it often. A professor at a large midwestern university was an entomologist. That is, he studied insects and their behavior. He became curious about a strange insect called a processionary caterpillar. What makes this species of caterpillar so unusual is the way it travels. A "team" of these caterpillars moves as a physically connected unit. They actually "hook up," one behind the other, and move in a long, undulating, connected line. The leader in the front has the vision and knows where they are going. The others simply hang on and have a close-up view of the rear end of another processionary caterpillar. The leader-caterpillar makes the decisions when to stop, eat, drink, or rest.

This professor wondered what would happen if there were no leader and hence no vision. So he removed the leader from the procession. The next caterpillar in line then took over as leader. He repeated his action of removing the lead caterpillar several times, and the same thing happened. The professor stopped and thought about what he had observed. Then he designed a little experiment.

The professor took a family of these caterpillars that were connected and hooked the leader up to the caterpillar who was last in line, so that there was really no leader, just a single, unbroken circle of caterpillars. Then, with the aid of assistants, he placed the circle of caterpillars on the rim of a flowerpot whose circumference exactly equaled the length of the circle. He put water and mulberry leaves at the bottom of the flowerpot. Mulberry leaves are the processionary caterpillars' favorite food. He gave the signal, and his assistants allowed the circle of caterpillars to begin to progress around the rim of the flowerpot. Everyone started his stopwatch and watched and waited.

The professor wanted to know whether the caterpillars would recognize that they were now leaderless. He also wanted to know how long the caterpillars would continue to travel around in a circle going nowhere. How long would they continue without a leader and no vision of where they were going before they changed tactics, or at least stopped for a rest and a mulberry and water break? He planned to calculate to the millisecond how long the caterpillars would continue to go around the pot with no idea as to where they were going.

The professor and his assistants never pressed their buttons to stop their chronographs. Why? Because the caterpillars kept going round and round until they fell unconscious from fatigue and lack of sustenance, even though food and water were always only a few inches away. I'm no biblical scholar, but I know that the bible tells us, "Where there is no vision, the people perish . . ." (Proverbs 29:18). That appears to apply to caterpillars also. Nobody can work toward achieving a vision until they know where to go. Motivating people to follow your vision is part of your job as a special ops leader. Now let's look at how best to do it.

How to Inspire Commitment to Your Vision

You can create almost any vision and inspire others to commit to it if you know how. In fact, that's the great danger, because the truth is, you can get others to commit to an evil vision as much as a worthwhile one. Hitler was able to influence millions of Germans to follow his warped vision, causing death and misery on a worldwide scale. Jim Jones influenced a much-smaller following with his warped vision, causing death and misery to "only" several hundred by drinking poisoned Kool-Aid.

The steps to *ethically* achieving your vision with your commandos for a worthy cause are the same. You must:

- Create a clear vision.
- Make your vision compelling.
- Promote your vision.
- Live your vision.

Create a Clear Vision

Once more with feeling: You can't get "there" until you, as the leader, know where "there" is. You must define, in detail, in your own mind, exactly where you want your organization to go and exactly what you want it to be. If you can do that, you are well on the way to inspiring others to follow your vision.

Carlos Slim Helu, a Mexican citizen who is the richest man in Latin America, is the owner of a retail and telecom empire that stretches from the United States to Argentina. *Forbes* magazine's 2005 list of the world's richest people estimates his personal fortune at around $23.8 billion. Yet Helu is hardly a whiz when it comes to computers. It is said that his children once gave him a laptop computer for Christmas and he could barely boot it up. Surfing the Net? Forget it. Helu doesn't know how. However, like special ops leaders that may or may not be able to personally operate each and every piece of equipment used by their commandos, the sixty-four-year-old billionaire and Lebanese immigrant has succeeded because he has a clear vision of how computers and the Internet are transforming the way the world does business.[5]

In Mexico, Helu ran the leading Internet service provider and has become a major computer seller. He took control of Prodigy, Inc. in 1997 and turned it into the number-three ISP in the United States. He's invested on a worldwide basis since then, although more recently he has turned over parts of his empires to his sons. "Technology is going to transform people's lives and society everywhere in the world," he says. "My main task is to understand what's going on and try to see where we can fit in." That's simple, but that's a clear vision, and as a result, it works.[6]

Make Your Vision Compelling

We learned in Chapter 2 that commandos do not take on easy tasks for unimportant reasons. Commandos thrive on the hard-to-accomplish, difficult assignments. The vision you articulate must be compelling, and that means it, too, must be seen as difficult, challenging, and important.

Commandos are incredibly motivated by a challenge because a challenge is compelling. A challenge says, "If you think you are good enough, here's what you must do." Commandos like the idea of accomplishing things that others think are difficult or impossible.

The Famous Message to Garcia

When war was about to break out between Spain and the United States in 1898, it was of extreme importance for the president of the United

States to communicate quickly with General Calixto Garcia, the leader of the insurgents in Cuba. There was much that the president and his senior commanders needed to know. That meant information on the number of Spanish troops on the island, as well as their quality and morale and armament. They wanted to know about the Spanish commanders. They wanted to know about the roads and their condition and the topography of the country and more. Unfortunately, no one knew where General Garcia could be located. It was known that he was somewhere in the mountains of Cuba, but that was about it. Neither mail nor telegraph message could reach him, and he had no representatives in the United States. Yet President William McKinley needed to get in contact with him and get his cooperation and information about Spanish forces in Cuba immediately.

McKinley called his intelligence chief, Colonel Arthur Wagner, who recommended a young West Point lieutenant by the name of Andrew S. Rowan. McKinley told him to offer Lieutenant Rowan the mission. According to Rowan, Wagner told him only:

> Young man . . . you have been selected by the President to communicate with—or rather, to carry a message to—General Garcia, who will be found somewhere in the eastern part of Cuba. Your problem will be to secure from him information of a military character, bring it down to date and arrange it on a working basis. . . . You must plan and act for yourself. The task is yours and yours only. You must get a message to Garcia. Your train leaves at midnight. Good-bye and good luck![7]

Rowan took the letter, left Washington for New York, and departed on a British ship to Jamaica the next day. Four days later he landed by night off the coast of Cuba from an open boat after traversing Jamaica. Because of the risk that he would be hanged as a spy, he crossed by boat to Cuba and disappeared into the Cuban jungle. Three weeks later he emerged on the other side of the island. He immediately embarked again by boat. Eventually, after traversing a hostile country on foot, being attacked and nearly killed by Spanish agents, and braving a storm at sea, he made it to Tampa, Florida and took a train to Washington, D.C. He reported to the secretary of war with the information needed—message delivered, mission accomplished. His extraordinary feat was celebrated in Elbert Hubbard's famous essay "A Message to Garcia," published the following year in Hubbard's magazine *The Philistine*. It has since been published and republished worldwide in many languages. It has become not only a military classic, but a business classic as well. In all, more than 40 million copies have been published.

Now I know that neither President McKinley's nor Colonel Wagner's instructions were a vision in the sense that we normally think of one. But the challenge presented to Rowan in stark simplicity—find Garcia and deliver the message—was enormous. Commando Rowan accepted the challenge out of duty, but also because it was important and was compelling.

Steve Jobs's Challenge to John Sculley

The relationship may have come to a bad end, but I always remember how the young Steve Jobs convinced the older and business-wise senior executive, John Sculley, to leave his secure position as CEO of PepsiCo and become the head of Apple Computer. According to Sculley, Jobs had challenged him with this single sentence, which instantly represented a compelling and powerful vision: "Do you want to spend the rest of your life selling sugared water, or do you want a chance to change the world?"[8]

Two educational researchers, Charles Schwahn and William Spady, came up with a pretty good test to determine whether your organization's vision is "compelling." According to them: "If your staff can't state your compelling purpose in their own words, from memory and with enthusiasm, you don't have one. It's that simple." If you must go to your file, look in your wallet and pull out a printed card, or search for a vision statement behind glass on a wall, you can bet your vision is not as compelling as you might think. This doesn't mean that you shouldn't promote your vision in every way you can, but you can bet that your vision is most certainly not influencing the day-to-day and minute-to-minute challenges of your commando organization.[9]

Consultant Sally Love writes:

> I have had the pleasure of working with some companies and projects in developing and achieving a compelling vision. The people involved successfully created a culture in which people were thrilled to have the opportunity to work. These people were significantly more productive and inwardly rewarded for the job they did. They have left their peers and competition in the dust. These people are proud of the results that they have accomplished and rightfully so. But they couldn't have done any of this without the challenging vision and direction that they created![10]

Promote Your Vision

It is not enough to create a clear, compelling, important, motivating vision. You have to promote it at every opportunity. It's become the norm to promote a vision by having it incorporated into company brochures, mounted in picture frames on the walls, and printed on cards to be carried in wallet or purse. That's all fine and good. However, it barely scratches the surface of possibilities. Short of "walking the talk" and living your vision (which we'll get to in a later section of this chapter), promoting your vision is critical. No matter how compelling, worthwhile, and wonderful your vision is, if your commandos don't know about it, they can't help you to fulfill it.

Here are two ideas used by military commandos that may be adaptable, with a little modification, to promoting your vision in your non-military organization. If nothing else, these ideas should serve to make a connection that will enable you to come up with an entirely new idea that no one has thought of before.

The Organizational Motto

Organizational mottos incorporating vision have been around for hundreds of years. One of the first flags representing the American colonies rebelling against England showed a rattlesnake with the motto: "Don't tread on me!" In a way, this motto was a more dramatic version of "No taxation without representation," which clearly expressed the colonists' vision of what was wrong with the then-current state of affairs.

Or consider the motto of the U.S. Army Special Forces. Initially the Green Berets were conceived of as a force designed to go behind enemy lines to train friendly forces. This vision is clearly evident in their motto: De Oppresso Liber, or "liberator of the oppressed."

When Robert Townsend was president of the Avis Rent-A-Car company in the 1960s, he developed one of the most famous mottos ever conceived to represent a corporate vision in three simple words: "We try harder." This vision was also a wonderful strategy, because it positioned Avis relative to the largest car rental company, Hertz, in a way that took advantage of the very fact that Hertz was larger. Moreover, it was difficult for Hertz to counter. The implication was that Avis had to try harder to get the customer's business because it wasn't top dog. It put Hertz on the horns of a dilemma. Hertz couldn't say it was small, and to promote its larger size only reinforced Avis's position.

Or consider *The New York Times*. The company's core purpose, as stated on its Web site, is to enhance society by creating, collecting, and distributing high-quality news, information, and entertainment. You can see how "All the news that's fit to print" fits right in.

Mottos are an outstanding means of promoting your vision. They can be short, easy to remember, and leave a lasting impression. In fact, many mottos of companies that have long since disappeared from business can still be recalled years later by consumers.

The Challenge Coin

I don't know who actually thought up the idea of the challenge coin.[11] There is some evidence that it actually began with a commando organization, although almost every military organization today and many commanders mint their own personal challenge coins that they give to visitors and guests. The first challenge coins were organizational challenge coins, and they promoted what the organization stood for. They were also used to recognize individuals for outstanding acts, to boost morale, and to build esprit de corps. Thus many challenge coins contain and promote the organization's vision.

Coins are a good choice as a promotional vehicle. For one thing, they last. Coins from ancient Rome, Greece, and China are still around after thousands of years. Moreover, unlike printed cards, coins have an intrinsic value due to their use as money. Most challenge coins are about the size of a silver dollar. With modern technology, they can be even more impressive than silver dollars, being enameled, colored, detailed, and hefty in weight. Yet they are reasonable in cost to reproduce in quantity.

They are called challenge coins for a reason. Once distributed, members of the organization are expected to carry their challenge coin at all times. The challenge comes in a specific way. One member of the group takes out his coin and challenges another member of the organization with the words, "Coin check." If that individual cannot produce her coin, she is required to buy a beverage of choice for the challenging member. If she produces the coin, the challenger must buy the drink.

Live Your Vision

Do you recall Colonel Mosby and the tremendous success he enjoyed by inspiring others with his vision? Mosby never did put his vision in a frame and insist that it go on the walls of his subordinates' offices. Nor did he issue cards to his command that immortalized his concept. His unit didn't have a challenge coin, and to the best of my knowledge, he didn't have a motto, either. Still, he knew the importance of promoting his vision. Moreover, he did the most important thing. He lived his vision on a daily basis. It's no good doing all the promotional things if you aren't serious about your vision. Being serious means that you walk the talk and live your vision and act accordingly every day.

The Prisoner Who Lived His Vision Every Day

I can think of no one who better walked the talk and inspired others to his vision than my West Point classmate, Captain Humbert Roque "Rocky" Versace. Rocky was a Ranger working with South Vietnam troops and the U.S. Army Special Forces during the Vietnam War. The Vietcong captured him two weeks before he was due to return home on October 29, 1963, but they captured him only after he was out of ammunition and grievously wounded.

The enemy spent the next two years torturing and trying to brainwash him to renounce his faith and vision in America. Despite the torture, disease, and horrible conditions, he lived his vision every single day. As senior ranking officer, he assumed command of his fellow prisoners. During this two-year period, he mounted four escape attempts, ridiculed his interrogators, argued with them in English, French, and Vietnamese, and demanded that he and the other prisoners be treated in accordance with the Geneva Convention. He refused to give them any of the military information that they demanded, sticking to name, rank, serial number, and date of birth. According to other American prisoners held with him, he not only didn't break, he never even bent. He deflected much of the torture and mistreatment intended for others on himself. He inspired his imprisoned command to continue to resist their captors, despite the harsh conditions and torture.

Finally, his captors announced they were going to execute him. American prisoners who survived the ordeal of captivity said that Rocky, unbroken, proud, and inspiring to the end, sang "God Bless America" at the top of his lungs from his isolation box all night before he was executed in 1965.

The U.S. Army has a policy of not awarding the Congressional Medal of Honor, the nation's highest decoration, to actions taken while a prisoner of war. It took almost forty years, but the evidence was so compelling and his actions so extraordinary that his classmates, fellow soldiers (those who had been there and others who had heard about what he had done), and Special Operations Command itself mounted a campaign that began in 1969. This campaign on Rocky's behalf finally succeeded in convincing the Army to make an exception. On July 8, 2002, President George W. Bush awarded Captain Rocky Versace the Congressional Medal of Honor posthumously, the award being presented at the White House to Rocky's brother.

Sergeant First Class Dan Pitzer, who served with him both in combat and captivity, had said earlier: "Rocky walked his own path. All of us did, but for that guy, duty, honor, country was a way of life. He was the finest example of an officer I have known . . ."[12]

Commando Notes

Vision is the grand goal that guides all the actions of your team and organization. You not only must have it, you must inspire it in others. You need to know where you are going. That means knowing what your vision is, and getting it down "cold," before you can inspire your commandos or anyone else to follow it. This chapter presented several basic ideas to help you to inspire others to identify with and follow your vision. Most importantly, you must live your vision every day, like Rocky Versace did. Do this, and not only will your commandos help you to achieve the vision, but they will never forget you or what you helped them to achieve.

9

ACCEPT FULL BLAME; GIVE FULL CREDIT

"When you do a deed, then you bear responsibility for it."
—Soviet Marshal Georgi Zhukov

"I neither ask nor desire to know anything of your plans. Take the responsibility and act, and call on me for assistance."
—Abraham Lincoln

IN JULY 1863, General Robert E. Lee saw a chance to win the war for the southern states that had left the Union. England seemed on the verge of recognizing the Confederacy as a legitimate government independent of the United States. Though possessing superior numbers and military equipment and establishing a blockade by sea of the southern states, Union forces had lost battle after battle. A variety of Union commanders had fought Lee and his Army of Northern Virginia, were defeated, and then replaced. President Lincoln had yet to find a general-in-chief that could lead Union forces to victory.

Morale in the North was at an all-time low, and there was much pressure on Lincoln to allow the southern states to secede from the Union and to make peace with them. General Lee had led his army north through Maryland and into Pennsylvania. He thought to encourage border states, such as Maryland, to secede and join the Confederacy. Also, he thought if he could threaten the Capitol and bring enough pressure to bear, the U.S. government would end the war.

Neither the Union Army of the Potomac nor Lee's army intended to fight at Gettysburg. But they had met there by accident on July 1, 1863. Lee's flamboyant cavalry leader, Major General Jeb Stuart, had gone off on his own with Lee's concurrence. But General Stuart had grown careless. Misrouting caused lengthy delays, and there was unexpectedly heavy Union cavalry resistance from a brigade led by a twenty-three-year-old federal brigadier general by the name of George Armstrong Custer. As a result, Lee had very little intelligence about the Union forces he faced or what they were doing until it was too late to avoid a battle he neither sought nor had planned for.

Lee's famous "strong right arm," Lieutenant General Thomas "Stonewall" Jackson, had been killed at the Battle of Chancellorsville two months earlier. Lieutenant General Richard Ewell, who commanded part of Jackson's old corps, could have won the Battle of Gettysburg for Lee the first day. Jackson would have done so. All Ewell had to do was to occupy the almost deserted but strategically important Cemetery Ridge that dominated the Gettysburg battlefield. However, his soldiers had been fighting all day, and he did not understand the strategic significance, so he failed to position his troops. Union troops soon moved in and fortified the position with artillery and the opportunity had passed. Lee had a lot of bad luck, and subordinates had let him down. More was to follow.

The second day of the battle, Lee gave the job of attacking the entrenched federal troops to a very competent corps commander and his second in command, Lieutenant General James "Old Pete" Longstreet. However, for whatever reason, Longstreet was slow in getting his troops into position and late in beginning his attack. Partially as a result of his delay, the attack failed, with heavy losses.[1]

On the third day of battle, Lee thought he had good news. Major General George Pickett and his division, all fresh troops, arrived on the field. Lee decided that he could win the battle decisively, and possibly the war, with a single stroke. He planned to pierce the Union line at its center, where an attack was least expected, using Pickett's division as his main striking force. He thought it was worth the gamble.

Before he could initiate the attack, federal artillery opened up in mass and caused a heavy engagement at another part of the battlefield. If that weren't enough, Pickett's division was in General Longstreet's corps. Longstreet had to actually give the order to attack, and Longstreet strongly opposed doing so. He tried to convince Lee of a different course of action.

Of course, when Lee gave an order, Longstreet obeyed, but in this case, it was without his usual confidence. In fact, when Pickett approached to receive the orders he already knew about, Longstreet, sitting on a log with head bent, said nothing. Pickett had to say: "General, if you want me to make the attack, raise your arm." Longstreet managed to give this minimal signal.

Meanwhile, Lee sent General Stuart, who had returned the previous night, to go behind the lines to divert the federals from the point of attack. But again the young General Custer repulsed Stuart. As a result, when Pickett began his charge, it was not coordinated with a diversionary attack as previously planned. Finally, Lee's artillery did not silence Union artillery as planned, either.

The attack finally got off the ground in the early afternoon. Pickett's troops charged straight into an artillery inferno. If that weren't bad enough, they were fully exposed to the murderous effect of enemy direct fire as they marched right into the holocaust. These men were amazingly brave. They kept going as hundreds of their comrades fell. A few hundred of Pickett's troops even managed to reach Union lines despite everything. However, they were soon overwhelmed, and of the 13,000 Confederates who made the charge, more than 7,500 were left dead or wounded in "no man's land" between the two lines. Pickett's division never fought again.[2]

With the attack clearly failed, the remnants of Pickett's men began straggling back to the Confederate lines. It was a terrible sight that few commanders could have faced. Lee went forward by himself against the protests of his staff to meet the survivors. Lee's subordinate generals, the winners in every previous battle, had made blunder after blunder. Nothing had gone right. Over most of these events, Lee had little control. Nevertheless, Lee took full responsibility without any ifs, ands, or buts, and without exception.

"It was all my fault and no one else's," he said. "You did your best, but it was I who failed you."

In tears, these battle-weary soldiers at Gettysburg shouted: "No! No! You didn't fail, general. It was us." Believe it or not, they asked General Lee to send them back so they could try again![3]

Robert E. Lee is probably the most beloved senior military leader in U.S. history. Not only to the day of his death, but for years afterward, those who knew him or served under him revered his name. Even his former enemies honored him and flocked to visit him after the Civil War. He was at once the most notorious defeated enemy general of the Confederacy, and yet company presidents from New York offered him hundreds of thousands of dollars if he would associate with their companies. He turned them all down. Instead, he accepted a post as president of a small college in Virginia with only forty students. The job paid very little. Today, it is known as Washington and Lee University.

Lee was not a commando leader during the Civil War, although he had served somewhat in this capacity and was recognized for his performance in the war against Mexico in 1846–1848, and his strategies and leadership were always commando-like. In the Civil War, Lee won neither the Battle of Gettysburg nor, ultimately, Southern independence. He was ultimately forced to surrender his Army of Northern Virginia to General Ulysses S. Grant in 1865. The best chance that the Confederacy had to win the Civil War was at Gettysburg in July 1863. Lee had lost this most decisive battle, sometimes called "the high watermark of the Confederacy."

But even when the end came in 1865, his soldiers, though starving, barefooted, and ragged, would have fought on had Lee given the word. General Robert E. Lee always took responsibility for his actions—full responsibility—and his men loved him for it and fought all the harder. As one ragged Texan said shortly before the surrender of his army at Appomattox: "I would charge hell itself for that old man."[4]

You are responsible for everything your commandos do or fail to do, and you cannot escape this responsibility under any circumstances. Obeying this rule will help to make you an outstanding business leader. Ignoring it will ensure your personal failure, regardless of the outcome of the enterprise in which you are engaged.

You Can Delegate Authority, but Not Responsibility

As a special ops leader in business, you can—and must—delegate authority to accomplish certain things to others, because you can never do everything yourself. Lee delegated authority to generals Ewell, Stuart, Longstreet, Pickett, and others. They all failed him at Gettysburg. He held them accountable for these failures. However, regardless of the circumstances, he was responsible for what happened, both to his boss—in this case Jefferson Davis, the president of the Confederacy—and to the men who suffered as a result of his orders. He could not delegate responsibility.

In business, too, a special ops leader may delegate various tasks and authority to subordinates. However, if the project fails, the leader cannot put the blame on either these subordinates or environmental variables. The leader makes the decisions, and if things go awry, regardless of what subordinate leaders or commandos do (or fail to do), the leader is responsible. After all, you selected the leaders and the jobs for their units, or you agreed to them, right?

Take Responsibility for Every Failure

You may think that taking responsibility for every failure like General Lee is a good idea "in theory" but "it doesn't work that way in my company." Oh really. And when your leader refuses to take responsibility and puts the blame for a failure on you, how do you feel about it? Do you want to work hard for that leader? The next time you have to work for the same leader, do you go all out, or do you take care to avoid responsibility whenever possible? Do you think about the good things you can do for the organization, or do you think about leaving as soon as you can for another organization somewhere else?

Do you blame fate, the government, or your commandos when things go wrong? The fact is, you are responsible for every success and failure regardless. In business, those in leadership positions are responsible for everything their organization accomplishes or fails to accomplish, and you can't sidestep the issue. Others know that, and so do your commandos, so you need to accept the reality and proactively grasp that responsibility.

He Took Responsibility and Made a Fortune

Californian Joe Karbo never finished college at the University of Southern California. World War II got in the way, and he dropped out. After the war, he started a number of entrepreneurial efforts, which culminated in a brilliant idea. Nowadays, television goes on all night on many major channels. However, in earlier days, at midnight they'd play our national anthem and the channel would go off the air until 6:00 A.M. the next morning. Joe's idea was to buy the airtime between the time the channel went off and came back on again. Since airtime in the middle of the night was a total loss to the TV station, he was able to buy it relatively inexpensively.

Once he had purchased the time, Joe filled the hours with movies, a talk show hosted by him, and anything else that seemed like a good idea. Then, as his audience base increased, he began to sell advertising to his programs for increasingly greater amounts. To raise capital for this endeavor and maintain operating expenses for his programming,

"Commando Joe" formed a team of investor partners. As his income rose, so did the amounts reinvested. By the early 1960s, Joe was personally making $5,000 a week. This was an extraordinary amount for those days.

Suddenly, the television station was sold to a larger company and Joe found that his contract did not go with the sale. The new owners could do as they pleased, and they did. They decided to run their own late movies and talk shows and sell advertising. This was bad enough, but Joe was caught in a cycle, owing his partners $50,000, which he did not have. Joe's lawyer told him that his only option was to declare bankruptcy. Joe chose to do something entirely different. He took responsibility for his financial dilemma.

Karbo called his partners together and gave them the bad news. He told them the loss was due entirely to his own management mistakes. He told him that his lawyer had advised bankruptcy and estimated that at best they would get ten cents on the dollar. However, Joe proposed another alternative. He said that in "pitching" these various products every night he had learned something about advertising. He had just enough money on hand to begin an advertising campaign based on direct response and print advertising. He showed them a business plan he had prepared. In it, he justified the monthly sales of his proposed product. He showed them that if they didn't sue him and force him into bankruptcy, they would recoup their investment in about two years. Karbo's partners laughed and agreed to his proposal. They accepted it not only because it made sense, but because he had accepted full responsibility for the failure. They laughed because of the product he intended to sell. It was a booklet that he proposed to call "How to Avoid Bankruptcy."

Joe was as good as his word. He went on to sell a number of very successful products through the mail. The most famous was a 156-page book that he advertised with a large display ad on the front page of the classified section in almost every newspaper in the country. The ad read: "The Lazy Man's Way to Riches." This book sold over 10 million copies in thirteen languages. Karbo became the subject of numerous articles and several books, including college textbooks on marketing. His legacy is not only some brilliant tactical marketing methods, but a lesson on just how important it is to accept full responsibility for your actions. That's the sign of a real commando and leader!

Andrew S. Grove, currently chairman of the board at Intel, helped build this major corporation from a small investment with commando methods of leadership. He says: "All of us in management, and in teaching, government, even parenting—men and women, young or old—worry about losing hard-won respect by admitting our mistakes. Yet, in reality, admitting mistakes is a sign of strength, maturity, and fairness."[5]

Insist on Accountability

Taking responsibility doesn't mean not holding others accountable for their actions. For example, General Lee did not overlook his cavalry leader's absence at a critical time. How Lee handled the confrontation with General Stuart was dramatized by famed author Michael Shaara in his best-selling book, *The Killer Angels*. Here is the dialogue, as Shaara envisioned it:

> "You were my eyes. Your mission was to screen this army from the enemy cavalry and to report any movement by the enemy's main body. That mission was not fulfilled."
>
> Stuart stood motionless.
>
> Lee said, "You left this army without word of your movements, or of the movements of the enemy, for several days. We were forced into battle without adequate knowledge of the enemy's position, or strength, without knowledge of the ground. It is only by God's grace that we have escaped disaster."
>
> "General Lee." Stuart was in pain, and the old man felt pity, but this was necessary; it had to be done as a bad tooth has to be pulled, and there was no turning away. Yet even now he felt pity rise, and he wanted to say, it's all right, boy, it's all right; this is only a lesson, just one painful quick moment of learning, over in a moment, hold on, it'll be all right. His voice began to soften. He could not help it.
>
> "It is possible that you misunderstood my orders. It is possible that I did not make myself clear. Yet this must be clear: you with your cavalry are the eyes of the army. Without your cavalry we are blind, and that has happened once but must never happen again."
>
> There was a moment of silence. It was done. Lee wanted to reassure him, but he waited, giving it time to sink in, to take effect, like medicine. Stuart stood breathing audibly. After a moment he reached down and unbuckled his sword, theatrically, and handed it over with high drama in his face. Lee grimaced, annoyed, put his hands behind his back, half turned his face. Stuart [believed] he no longer held the General's trust, but Lee interrupted him with acid vigor.
>
> "I have told you that there is no time for that. There is a fight

tomorrow, and we need you. We need every man, God knows. You must take what I have told you and learn from it, as a man does. There has been a mistake. It will not happen again. I know your quality. You are a good soldier. You are as good a cavalry officer as I have known, and your service to this army has been invaluable. I have learned to rely on your information; all your reports are always accurate. But no report is useful if it does not reach us. And that is what I wanted you to know. Now." He lifted a hand.

"Let us talk no more of this."[6]

A leader cannot condone irresponsibility or overlook major blunders. But in demanding accountability, you must know when to be forgiving, too. The line between demanding accountability and forgiving honest mistakes is a thin one. But this, too, is the responsibility of every leader. The idea is not to demolish the individual and continue to punish him, but to point out the problem, make sure it is understood so that it won't be repeated, and then to move on. Note, too, that General Lee chastised his subordinate general in private. That's why those who have been there say, "Praise in public, but criticize in private."

When I read Shaara's dramatization of Lee's words, I'm struck by the similarity to the advice in another best-selling book, *The One Minute Manager,* by Kenneth Blanchard and Spencer Johnson. Basically what the authors said is that a leader must let the individual know when he is unhappy with something done by a subordinate, and he must hold his subordinates accountable for their mistakes. However, this criticism should take no more than a minute, and then the leader needs to move on. That's good advice.

Demand a High Level of Performance

Part of insisting on accountability is to also demand a high level of performance. I can't think of an organization in the military or in business where the commandos just try and get by. They are doing their absolute best to perform at the highest level at which they are capable, both individually and as a group. They want to win, and they expect that you, as a special ops leader, will demand that high level of performance, like the coach of a winning athletic team. They want you to push them hard, not for your sake, but to get every ounce of performance possible out of them. They want to win, and as their leader, they expect you to help them by demanding their best.

How an American Commando Won a German Award

During the initial phases of Operation Enduring Freedom in Afghanistan, Captain Robert Harward, a Navy SEAL, commanded Combined Joint Special Operations South Afghanistan, known as "Task Force K-Bar." Pundits among his commandos termed the force the "Special Operations Force Olympics" because it included commandos not only from the U.S. Navy, Army, and Air Force, but also from Germany and six other countries.

Safely back in the United States, Harward was presented with the Silver Cross of Honor, Germany's second-highest military medal for his actions as commander. Germany presented Harward with the award not because he had been easy on German commandos in his organization, but because he had demanded high performance without compromising their safety unnecessarily. It was the first time German forces were engaged in combat operations since World War II and the work was extremely dangerous for all. It was a political hot potato, and if the German component had either underperformed or had excessive losses, there would have been a great deal of unfavorable political fallout for German leaders who supported sending the troops to this fight against terrorism.

The K-Bar commando unit was not some kind of symbolic, nonfighting unit. They were the ones who destroyed the Al Qaeda infrastructure in Afghanistan and disrupted its ability to conduct terrorist operations. Captain Harward's commandos meticulously, and at great risk, searched cave and village enclaves in southern and eastern Afghanistan. They not only collected valuable intelligence, but went in and captured suspected Al Qaeda and Taliban prisoners while conducting combat operations. In addition, Task Force K-Bar coordinated extensive strategic reconnaissance, performed combat search and rescue, and even conducted interdiction operations at sea to prevent terrorists from escaping by ship. K-Bar did it all, and in all Harward took responsibility for everything, at the same time he demanded the very best from his commandos.[7]

Give Credit for Every Success

There is an important paradox in special ops leadership that you must understand and act upon if you are to be successful. When things go wrong, you must take full and unconditional responsibility for the mishap. You must do so without rancor, both publicly and privately, and you must do it in every instance. However, when things go right, when your commandos win a victory, you must give full credit and take none for yourself. You must do this unselfishly and without holding anything back, and you must do it in every instance, too. And remember, praise is given primarily in public.

Why is giving credit so important? In the first place, your commandos deserve the credit. They were the ones on the firing line, after all. It was their sweat, commitment, smart actions, and hard work that created the achievement. And they're the ones that you would hold accountable for failure.

Second, this practice is psychologically sound. Good commandos want to know the score. When they screw up, they expect to be held accountable. But at the same time they want recognition for their accomplishments, and the more public the better. Moreover, if someone mistakenly starts giving you all the credit for their success, you had better step forward instantly and set them straight. If you don't, you are going to destroy the guts of your commando organization. Sure, they may keep working and doing their best out of a sense duty, but somewhere deep inside there's going to be a voice saying, "Why work so hard? Why exert yourself so much? Why give up your time? He (or she) is just going to take the credit anyway."

A Tale of Two Professors

I've always had a strong belief that teachers are leaders and that leadership principles are as important for them as for military or business leaders. When I first started teaching, I had an opportunity to personally observe the effect on students of two different professors who taught an identical course, in the same way. The difference was that one professor gave recognition for good work and the other didn't.

This course was in marketing research. It hadn't been taught in several years. One professor set the course up. We'll call him Professor A. Professor B was to teach the identical course to a different group of students the following term.

Professor A talked with his department chairman and they agreed that the course would work best if the students could learn by doing real marketing research, rather than simply learning theory alone.

At the first class meeting, Professor A told his students that one-half of their grade would come from doing actual marketing research.

They would have to recruit a real company or small business and meet with the company's president. During the first ten weeks, the student, or student team of no more than three students, would undertake a particular marketing research project for the firm. On the tenth week, the class would meet at a well-known restaurant. Each student or student team would present results to the group, including the student's client. Part of the deal was that while the company received the research at no charge, at least one company representative had to show up and pay for the expensive dinner for "its" students. On the week following the presentation, the students would take their exam on marketing theory.

Professor A wasn't sure himself how things would turn out. But on the big night, everything was in place, a special room had been reserved, and audiovisuals were set up. The students dressed in their finest to meet with their clients. The results astounded everyone. The presentations were so professional and of such a high caliber that even Professor A was amazed. One client couldn't restrain himself. He had a single student, a Japanese-American, who for some reason went by the name "Tex."

The client jumped up at the end of Tex's presentation and interrupted the proceedings by declaring, "I just have to say something. We were unsure how Tex would do since he is only a student, so we gave him a marketing research project that had already been completed. We paid $50,000 for that study. Tex came up with exactly the same results. So for those of you that didn't try to outguess your student as we did, I want to tell you, you got a pretty good deal, and I want to apologize to Tex for not trusting him."

After the last presentation, there was much excitement and the amazed clients asked Professor A, "How did you get the students to do such a professional job? What's your secret? Can we get more research from students?"

Professor A smiled, but deferred all praise and compliments. "Thank you very much for your kind comments," he said. "But the truth is, I did very little except to organize this class and to answer my students questions. If you are happy with their work, you had better thank them, because they did it all."

The following term, Professor B conducted the course in exactly the same way. He even used the same restaurant. Everything happened exactly as it did in Professor A's class. Of course, there was no "Tex," but other clients singled out their students for praise in a similar manner. Once again, there was tremendous excitement after the presentations and similar comments and questions were asked of Professor B. However, Professor B took full credit himself, saying that he had been teaching for many years and had acquired the ability to impart knowledge to his students in a special way.

Professor B's failure to give proper recognition had several negative effects. Students attempted to avoid classes taught by this professor in the future. Why? Because what Professor B did wasn't right and it was unfair. The students had done the work. They deserved to get the recognition for their work, even if Professor B had learned some "special ways of teaching" that he thought helped the students. Moreover, what Professor B did was so demotivating that it was thought to have had a negative impact on the students' preparation for their final exam. Professor B's students scored approximately 20 percent lower on the exam on marketing research theory than did Professor A's students, though the exam was essentially identical. Conversely, what Professor A did in giving full credit to his students probably positively motivated them to study even harder.

There are important lessons for us about special ops leadership from these two professors. If we want our commandos to be continually motivated for the peak performance we demand, then we better make certain that they receive the psychological payment in the form of recognition, which they deserve when they do a good job. Besides, it's the right thing to do.

Commando Notes

Although it sounds strange or counterintuitive, you must be able to accept full responsibility *except* when you are successful. When things go wrong, hold your hand up and take the full blame. As Intel's Andy Grove implies, admitting mistakes is an important sign of good leadership. And as Joe Karbo proved, it is not only the right thing to do, but it may help you reach heights in your endeavors that you never dreamed possible. And you must hold your commandos accountable, too, since they are responsible to you. You need to do this when they fail to perform as they should. But when things are on target, let them know what a terrific job they did.

10 TAKE CHARGE!

"If the enemy leaves a door open, you must rush in."
—Sun Tzu

"Even if you are on the right track, you'll get run over if you just sit there."
—Will Rogers

CAPTAIN JASON AMERINE, a young West Pointer, led Operational Detachment Alpha 574, an "A-team" of himself plus eleven Special Forces commandos, including a U.S. Air Force combat controller. This was a part of the U.S. Army's 5th Special Forces Group in Afghanistan. The mission of his small unit was to link up with and support and protect Afghan leader Hamid Karzai, who was later elected to become first the provisional president of Afghanistan, and later president. Amerine was not only to advise Karzai on military matters, but to train his Pashtun fighters in order to assist in the destabilization of the Taliban regime in northern Afghanistan. Amerine took charge and did a lot more. Along the way to accomplishing his mission, his small commando unit led the effort that defeated a major Al Qaeda-Taliban command.

Toward the end of October 2001, Amerine with his commandos infiltrated into Oruzgan province in northern Afghanistan and made contact with Karzai. Karzai was a popular leader, but did not consider himself a military man. With little time to get acquainted, Amerine met and developed a relationship with him.

Karzai explained that the key to controlling the province was the village of Tarin Kowt. If Karzai's Pashtuns could capture it, it would be a major psychological victory. "Tarin Kowt represents the Taliban's heart," he told Amerine. "Crush that heart and we kill the Taliban."[1]

Karzai felt this wouldn't be too difficult because most of the people of Tarin Kowt were opposed to Taliban rule and would probably surrender, even to a small show of force.

However, there was one problem, and it was a big one. Tarin Kowt was in striking distance from Kandahar, a major Taliban stronghold. The Taliban and Al Qaeda had about 500 well-armed and well-trained fighters there and plenty of vehicles. Captain Amerine calculated that with his small command and a handful of untrained, poorly armed Pashtun guerillas, they could not hold the town even if they could capture it. He felt that arming as many Pashtuns as he could attract to his cause was his first priority, and getting them trained a close second. Without delay he had arms flown in.

Unfortunately, many of the villagers he armed didn't stick around. They rushed off to defend their own villages from Taliban harassment. As a result, despite his plans, Amerine never got to train anyone. Then, long before he was ready, the people of Tarin Kowt rebelled and overthrew their Taliban masters on their own. Karzai asked Captain Amerine to take his command into the city along with Karzai's thirty-man Pashtun guerilla "army," and then to defend the town against the expected counterstrike from Kandahar.

Amerine knew he was taking a great risk. However, by then it was known that Hamid Karzai would play a major role in the new Afghanistan. Amerine's orders were to protect Karzai. Amerine also knew if the Taliban retook the city now that their rule had been overthrown, there would be a bloodbath. Militarily it made no sense, and Amerine would have probably failed a classroom exercise at West Point with a solution that recommended defending the town with the force at his disposal. However, Amerine's instincts were to do it despite the odds. Moreover, he did have one ace up his sleeve: the ability to call on American airpower to help him.

Amerine wasted no time. He commandeered what vehicles he could get hold of, including touring vans, pickup trucks, and beat-up former U.N.-owned cars, and drove all night to get to Tarin Kowt with Hamid Karzai, his government officials, all their military equipment, and his eleven commandos. On arrival, Karzai was immediately hustled to a government house with Karzai to meet the Pashtun tribal leaders. As Karzai's military adviser, the young captain was invited to come along.

Amerine was relaxing, drinking the thick sweet coffee of the Middle East and enjoying Afghani hospitality, when one of the Pashtuns offhandedly mentioned that approximately a hundred Taliban vehicles with 300 to 500 fighters were on the way from Kandahar to attack Tarin Kowt! Amerine almost spilled his coffee and quickly excused himself saying, "Well, it was nice meeting all of you. I think we need to organize a force now and do what we can to defend this town."[2]

Captain Amerine identified the Taliban's most likely mountain pass approach, got his communicators on the radio calling for immediate air support, and with a group of twenty to thity of Karzai's untrained fighters, moved out on trucks to an observation point where the pass could be observed. These Pashtun fighters were willing, but they were untrained and spoke little English. Some had never even fired their weapons. The Taliban were both well trained and well armed. However, Amerine had to work with what he had.

Air support arrived almost immediately. Amerine watched their approach. As the Taliban convoy entered the valley entrance to the pass, the aircraft began their attack. Amerine's plan was to bottle the enemy up in the pass. However, while Amerine and his men were focused on directing the aircraft strikes, his untrained Pashtuns, panic stricken at the sheer numbers of the enemy relative to their own, jumped into their vehicles to flee to the town.

Not only were these vehicles critical to Amerine's mobility as the fighting progressed, but allowing the Pashtuns, untrained or not, to retreat pell-mell at the first sign of fighting would do little to maintain the confidence in either Karzai or the Americans among the villagers. So preventing their retreat assumed priority even as the enemy vehicles fought their way through the aircraft strikes.

Amerine followed his instincts again. He ordered his men into the remaining vehicles, and they tried to block the other vehicles from departing. It was to no avail. He couldn't stop the Pashtuns in their flight to return to the relative safety of the town. Amerine realized he would have no choice but to withdraw the entire force to Tarin Kowt. Arriving in town, he told Karzai what had happened and asked him to gather together all the men he could muster who could fire a weapon, or thought they could. By then, the Taliban had broken through the pass and had moved into the observation position he had just abandoned.

If the main Taliban force got into the town, their overwhelming numbers could spell the difference, so Amerine ordered his troops into a blocking perimeter in front of the town in the main direction of potential danger. There they could not only prevent Taliban troops from entering the town from this direction, but could continue to direct friendly aircraft support. The armed men Karzai collected would stay in the town to deal with any enemy vehicles that got through or somehow infiltrated from another direction.

Meanwhile, Amerine had every commando either directing aircraft or fighting. At last, the leading vehicles were stopped and some of the enemy force began to retreat. But then they heard gunfire from the town. A number of Taliban had broken through and entered the town from another direction. However, Karzai's forces, many now fighting on their home turf, were driving them off. Finally it was over. The Taliban forces retreated back toward their base, U.S. aircraft harassing them all the way. They had suffered a major defeat.

This battle broke the back of the Taliban in the area, and they never attacked again in decisive numbers. This small Special Forces team and a small number of untrained Pashtuns had won a huge victory against an experienced, well-armed, and well-trained enemy that was vastly superior in numbers. Karzai's prestige soared. Everywhere villagers tore down the Taliban flag and raised the flag of a free Afghanistan.

A few weeks later in a tragic case of "friendly fire" bombing, Jason Amerine was severely wounded and several of his Special Forces unit were killed along with twenty-seven of his guerillas, by now a far more experienced and effective force. Three days later, Kandahar surrendered.

It was ironic, but the very day Amerine's unit was struck, Kandahar was sending a delegation to negotiate surrender terms. Probably only friendly bombs prevented the entire Taliban command from surrendering to this one Special Forces officer, who given his orders and confronted with a difficult situation, took charge and not only carried them out, but led his commandos and his Pashtun allies to victory.[3]

Special ops leadership demands a leader who takes charge and gets things done. To be this kind of leader, experience in special operations shows that you must:

- Dominate the situation.

- Establish your objectives early.

- Communicate with those you lead.

- Act boldly and decisively.

- Lead by example.

- Follow your instincts.

Amerine's Actions: An Analysis

Let's look at what Captain Amerine did in exercising special ops leadership. Clearly, it was his ability to take charge that led to his success. First, he dominated a difficult situation. He may have thought that he'd have a larger number of guerrillas to work with and that they would at least have had some basic training or experience. Neither of these expectations came true. Nor were the available fighters well armed.

Tragically, some who want to lead commandos become immobilized by environmental variables over which they may have little control. The fact is, things rarely go completely as planned; not infrequently, the situation is bad through no fault of the leader. However, this is irrelevant. You must still take action, and take action at once to gain control. This is what I mean about dominating the situation.

Captain Amerine took action at once to attract more guerrillas and to arm them as his initial objectives. Even though he was not given the time to train them, or in some cases even to retain them under his own control, since they were needed to defend their own villages, his actions had a positive effect on stiffening resistance against the Taliban.

Amerine understood Karzai's need to occupy Tarin Kowt, but he also knew he would have to defend the town once it was under Karzai's control. So he successfully communicated the problems with occupying Tarin Kowt immediately, even if it could be done easily, and convinced Karzai to delay until they were better prepared to defend the town. For a twenty-seven-year-old to persuade an older man of much more experience and of national stature to take a different course of action is no small thing. To do so despite differences in language and culture speaks volumes for Amerine's training and ability in take-charge communication.

Going to Tarin Kowt under these conditions represented one big risk. Amerine may have gotten advice from others, but he was the one actually there. It was his decision. He followed his instincts, as he did later, in ordering the retreat from his initial observation position overlooking the pass when his Pashtun allies began to flee.

Amerine's final defense of Tarin Kowt was masterful. In every case he acted boldly and decisively. Moreover, he was right up front where the action was, taking the same risks as those who followed him. He did not try and lead from behind a desk or make his decisions from afar. He led by example. And this provides us with an outstanding example of how a special ops leader takes charge.

Taking Charge in a Fortune 500 Company

Xerox Corporation earned $360 million on more than $14.7 billion in revenue in 2003, while generating $1.9 billion in operating cash flow and reducing debt by $3 billion. It did even better in 2004; though revenues were still around $14.7 billion, profits increased to $859 million. It was not always so. Back in 1998, Xerox's market share was increasing, growth stock was ahead of the market, and financials were stable. A change in leadership had apparently gone smoothly. Then suddenly, in late 1999 and early 2000, the bottom fell out.

Everything happened at once. Competition increased at the same time that the economy weakened. Accounting improprieties were discovered in Xerox's Mexican operations, which led to an investigation by the Securities and Exchange Commission (SEC). Revenue and profits declined. Debt mounted while liquid cash shrunk. Old customers deserted in droves, and shareholders saw the value of their investment in Xerox stock halved and still falling.

In the midst of this mess, Anne Mulcahy, who had been president and chief operating officer of Xerox, was named CEO and chairman. She was running the whole show, and her job was to turn things around. A turnaround requires take-charge leadership and commando techniques, so what Mulcahy did is worth reviewing.

The first thing Mulcahy did was to dominate the situation. She didn't sit on her hands. The financial situation got her immediate attention. She sold $2.5 billion in noncore assets, outsourced office manufacturing, and dumped Xerox's small office/home office (SOHO) business. Simultaneously, she entered into a series of agreements to outsource the financing of Xerox's customer receivables. The idea was to focus on operational cash generation through disciplined management of inventory, receivables, and fixed capital.

Mulcahy set immediate objectives and a plan for reaching them. The plan involved three major parts:

- Focusing on cash generation for the immediate future
- Taking $1 billion out of the cost base to improve competitiveness
- Strengthening Xerox's core businesses to ensure growth in the future

She communicated with customers, employees, vendors, and consultants to find out what had gone wrong. She discovered poor response to customers and a diffusion of Xerox strength among many technologies. This meant that Xerox did so-so everywhere, but extremely well nowhere. Mulcahy spent three months just getting her employees to understand the problems. She discovered that the more obvious problems were sometimes masking more fundamental issues. Then she told all employees where they were going and gave clear direction as to how they were going to get there. Mulcahy says, "You can't communicate too much in a time of crisis."[4]

In two years, she gave twelve live television broadcasts to employees, held eighty town meetings, wrote forty letters distributed to all Xerox employees, and did hundreds of roundtable discussions. Along the way, she traveled 200,000 miles and visited Xerox employees in more than a dozen countries.[5] She earned a lot of frequent flyer miles.

These were bold, decisive moves. She didn't mess around, nor did she delegate everything, but taking charge worked. In short order, Mulcahy attained huge results, and she made them happen fast. The goal was to reduce the cost base by $1 billion. She actually reduced it by $1.3 billion. Inventory was reduced by $600 million. That was a "mere" improvement of 30 percent over the previous year. Selling, general, and administrative costs dropped 15 percent, capital spending by 50 percent. Is it any wonder that debt declined and profits quickly returned? However, while getting cash flow going in the right direction for present-day survival, this CEO didn't neglect the future. She maintained research and development investment with Xerox's partner, Fuji Photo Film, at $1.6 billion a year. Partially as a result of this action, 2004 was a major year for new products for Xerox, which introduced a third-generation color digital production publisher, new color and black-and-white office multifunction devices, and one-to-one marketing, book publishing, and print-on-demand solutions and services.

Chairman Mulcahy had plenty of help, but the decisive actions were all her calls and her initiatives. As she said later: "Get the data. Solicit opinions. Listen carefully. Be open-minded. But at the end of the day, trust your own instincts. Plays that look good on the chalkboard don't always work on the field."[6]

Anne Mulcahy's exceptional, take-charge leadership at Xerox stands with Jason Amerine's in Afghanistan as something we should all strive to emulate. Let's look at each of the elements of taking charge separately to see what we should watch for and try to do.

Dominate the Situation

I can't say it enough, but the first part of taking charge is to dominate the situation. Your goal should be to be seen everywhere at once and to be on top of the situation. Get out and make decisions. Let your commandos and others know that you are in charge, especially when things go awry.

Lieutenant Colonel J. F. Durnford-Slater was a British Army Commando leader during World War II. On December 27, 1941, he was the senior officer ashore and in immediate charge of the operations at Vaagso in southern Norway. This operation was quite significant because it was the first time all three British services combined their forces in an amphibious raid against a defended coast. As Admiral Louis Mountbatten, then combined operations adviser, told participants prior to the raid: ". . . [N]obody knows quite what is going to happen and you are the ones who are going to find out."[7]

Basically the commandos' objective was to cause as much damage as possible in a major diversionary raid. The idea was to convince the Germans of the need to allocate additional forces to Norway, thus denying their use on the Russian front. Being commandos, they knew they were going in against superior numbers. However, they also knew that they would be supported both by the Royal Navy and the Royal Air Force.

Of course, everything that can go wrong will go wrong, and this operation was no exception. The opposition was unexpectedly heavy and the battle soon developed into house-to-house fighting. Although Durnford-Slater's job was to run everything and to maintain contact with the Royal Navy's flagship, he was in the thick of it, dominating the situation. When the two shock units of his command lost five out of six officers and were stopped short of taking the town, he immediately took personal command of both units, reorganized, and attacked again until the town was totally under his control.[8]

The accomplishments of the commandos were not insignificant under Lieutenant Colonel Durnford-Slater's take-charge leadership. The commandos blew up the power station, all major coastal defenses, the radio station, several factories, and the lighthouse. In addition, 150 Germans were killed, ninety-eight Germans and four Norwegian traitors were taken prisoner, and seventy-one other Norwegians escaped with the commandos back to England. And the Germans certainly took the bait. They allocated an additional 30,000 troops for defense of the

Norwegian coast.[9] By the end of the war, this commando leader, who knew how to dominate a situation, became a brigadier general.

Establish Your Objectives Early

If you don't know where you are going, any road will take you there. That's an old saying, but it is deadly true in special operations. You want to know exactly what your objectives are, and your commandos need to know them as well, and the sooner the better. That way, when unexpected things happen or your commandos are temporarily out of contact, they can make logical decisions and, without hesitation, keep moving toward the objectives you have set.

Until you have set precise objectives, you can't do very much, and even the actions you take may be the wrong actions. So you want to decide what needs to be done and then move out and start doing it.

When long-time Democratic supporter and sudden Republican Michael Bloomberg took office as mayor in New York City on New Year's Day in 2002, the city was not in very good shape. Not only was New York still recovering from the 9/11 terrorist attack, but the stock market had collapsed. With a $5 billion budget gap that was still growing, New York's financial condition was not far from the situation that brought "the Big Apple" to near bankruptcy in 1975.

Then Bloomberg took charge. He set his objectives for a financial turnaround at once. To meet this primary objective, he didn't hesitate, but took some very unpopular moves. These included laying off 14,000 city employees, raising taxes by $3 billion, cutting spending by another $3 billion, and borrowing $2.5 billion. He even doubled the fines for parking tickets.

By early 2004 the results were clear. The city was looking at a budget surplus, and his fiscal year 2005 budget included a $400 per household property tax rebate "to thank New Yorkers for their sacrifice and assistance in getting the city through the fiscal crisis."[10] Unemployment was at a twenty month low and two bond rating agencies changed their outlook on the city's financial situation to "stable" upgraded from "negative."

However, nobody liked it, and Bloomberg's approval rating plummeted to 24 percent . . . and then fell some more. This was the lowest approval rating any mayor ever received according to *The New York Times*. So while Bloomberg's performance in setting (and meeting) his objectives can be applauded, his failing was made clear in an article in *The New Yorker* titled "The Un-Communicator."[11]

This leads us to the next very important part of taking charge, which Mayor Bloomberg, as good as he was in the task of setting his objectives early, ignored.

Communicate with Those You Lead

Somewhat overlapping in time with Michael Bloomberg's take-charge performance as mayor was another Republican with strong Democratic ties who took over in a turnaround situation as a neophyte politician. This was movie star and multiple Mr. Olympia titleholder Arnold Schwarzenegger. Schwarzenegger, who became governor of California in late 2003 after a recall election, is married to well-known broadcast journalist Maria Shriver, who is not only a Democrat, but a Kennedy.

If anything, the situation in California was worse than that of New York City. If the spending and revenues didn't change, the state would face between a $12 billion and $24 billion deficit by the middle of 2005. Virtually every financial agency lowered the state's bond rating, which was already the lowest of the fifty states. California was ranked just above junk bond status.

Like Bloomberg, Schwarzenegger took charge, set objectives at once, and took action. "The Terminator" cut budgets, laid off state workers, planned on borrowing money, and set things in motion, even invoking emergency powers so he could impose $150 million in spending cuts without the legislature's approval. "I was elected by the people of this state to lead. Since the legislative leadership refuses to act, I will act without them," he said.[12] And he threatened to take his agenda directly to the people through the media.

However, Schwarzenegger recognized that California's situation was in no small part due to Democratic-Republican deadlock in the state legislature. So he set out to communicate with everyone regarding what they needed to do: Democrats, Republicans, and most important, the people of California. The governor appeared in public promoting his objectives and strategies—in person, on television, and on giant billboard ads around the states. But he did not appear alone. Leading Democrats appeared with him helping him to promote his agenda.

It's too early to declare victory and a successful turnaround. However, there is no doubt that there is a new spirit of bipartisanship in

California and for the first time in a long time the people feel they are making progress in overcoming the crisis that threatened the state. What about Schwarzenegger's approval ratings? At mid-2004, almost 66 percent of voters approved of Schwarzenegger's job performance, according to a nonpartisan Field Poll, making him one of the most popular governors in the state's history. Of course, popularity polls rise and fall.[13] Moreover, the point isn't that fluff triumphs over substance, but that a leader who implements all parts of taking charge can have popularity too, and this may make him even more effective in achieving his objectives.

Act Boldly and Decisively

Acting boldly and decisively means taking risks. Every special ops leader knows this. He doesn't ignore the risks, but he assesses them, does what he can to make them irrelevant, and presses on with his agenda.

Mary Kay Ash planned to start a business with a $5,000 investment from her savings. She had manufacturers lined up and ready to produce her cosmetics. She contacted packagers, prepared print advertising, hired her first sales commandos, and developed her first sales training routines and procedural manuals. She knew exactly what she needed to do. She even had her cash flow budgeted and planned to use money from her husband's income for operating cash until she established a positive cash flow on her own. She was ready for everything except one thing: unexpected tragedy.

Two weeks before she was ready to launch her plan, her husband died suddenly of a heart attack. Now her plans were worthless. She had no source of operating capital while she got on her feet. She could have abandoned everything right then and there and recouped at least part of her investment. Many would have done exactly that. But that's not the commando way. Mary Kay decided after coming this far, she wasn't going to quit now. She somehow borrowed the money she needed and opened the doors to her business as planned originally. She took the risk. As a result, today Mary Kay, Inc. is a billion-dollar cosmetics firm. As the great American literary philosopher Ralph Waldo Emerson advised:

> Do not be too timid and squeamish about your actions. All life is an experiment. The more experiments you make the better. What if they

are a little coarse, and you may get your coat soiled or torn? What if you do fail, and get fairly rolled in the dirt once or twice. Up again, you shall never be so afraid of a tumble.

Lead by Example

There is a very old leadership principle that says that to be a leader, you must do everything that you demand of your followers. This is important in taking charge, in times of danger, and even in small things.

One of the worst examples of leadership I ever saw was during a welcoming lecture by a colonel to a flying course that I was about to enter. We were about a hundred recently commissioned lieutenants new to the U.S. Air Force. The colonel was welcoming us and at the same time giving us a lecture about the dos and don'ts of our expected conduct while enrolled in his school. In those days it was called "laying down the law."

The year was 1959, and it was very popular for flying officers to eschew regulation shoes in favor of Wellington boots. "As to the wear of Wellington boots," the colonel intoned, "these are strictly nonregulation and any officer wearing them will be severely reprimanded." I thought this was a little heavy-handed, but fair enough, until I glanced down at his footwear and saw that the colonel was at that moment wearing Wellingtons, and he wasn't smiling during his lecture to indicate he was joking. I'm certain that everyone who noticed felt as I did and lost respect instantly for this "leader."

Commando operations are difficult and challenging, and the more difficult and challenging, the more your commandos will expect you to lead by example. You must be willing to do and undertake everything you demand of them—and that includes small things such as dress, too.

Follow Your Instincts

You wouldn't be a leader if you hadn't developed and then demonstrated your instincts in taking the right action, even if on the surface the action appeared wrong. Too many leaders are afraid to follow their instincts. They go by the book and in this way instead of taking bold and decisive action, they attempt to avoid all risk. Never be afraid to trust your gut. If you have a gut feeling that you should do a certain thing, even though everyone recommends something else to you, listen and consider the advice, but trust your instincts and take the action that you think you should. You are the one responsible, and you are getting paid for your judgment and instincts, not for the recommendations or instincts of others.

Two authors had the idea for a new kind of book that would consist entirely of uplifting and inspiring stories. They put some sample chapters together and a formal proposal and attempted to market their concept both directly to publishers and through an agent. They couldn't find a single agent willing to represent them. Every major publisher turned down the project. They were told that this concept had been tried many times before and had never worked. They were told that no one would buy a book such as the one they wanted to produce. Every expert told them they were wasting their time. But they trusted their instincts and persisted. After more than a year, they eventually found a small publisher of mostly books in the health genre who agreed to publish their book. Not only did people buy this book, but *Chicken Soup for the Soul* by Jack Canfield and Mark Victor Hansen became a series of books—the best-selling series of all time with more than 40 million copies sold, and still selling!

As a special ops leader, be a follower in one important instance: Follow your own good instincts, no matter what others say.

Commando Notes

Special ops leaders are successful because they take charge—this time and every time. They dominate the situation right from the outset, set their objectives early in the game, communicate with their commandos, act boldly and decisively, lead by example, and follow their instincts. If you are to be a successful commando leader: Take charge!

11 REWARD EFFECTIVELY

"There must be some other stimulus, besides love for their country, to make men fond of service."
—George Washington

"If love of money were the mainspring of all American actions, the officer corps long since would have disintegrated."
—Brigadier General S.L.A. Marshall

O N E   O F   T H E   G R E A T E S T American special operations of World War II was a combined effort of the U.S. Army Air Forces and the Navy. In the spring of 1942, just months after the attack on Pearl Harbor, a U.S. Navy submariner by the name of Captain Francis Lowe proposed an unusual plan to launch U.S. Army bomber aircraft from an aircraft carrier and attack the Japanese capital of Tokyo and other major Japanese cities.[1]

The bombers would be commanded by James H. (Jimmy) Doolittle, who had a tremendous reputation as a pilot. He was the first pilot to cross the country in less than twenty-four hours, the first to perform an outside loop, and the first to take off, fly, and land an airplane using instruments alone, without being able to see outside the cockpit. He had also won the three major racing trophies: the Schneider Cup race in 1925, the Bendix Trophy in 1931, and the Thompson Trophy in 1932. He had even held the world speed record at one time. Yet he was one of the very few U.S. Army officers to possess a doctorate in aeronautical engineering. Doolittle had left active duty in the U.S. Army Air Corps to work for Shell Oil Company. He was put in charge of Shell's aviation department, but he had retained a reserve commission in the Air Corps. As war approached, he requested a return to active duty and, by 1942, was a lieutenant colonel.[2]

When the task force commander, Vice Admiral William F. Halsey, ordered the planes off on this highly secret mission, he sent this simple message:

To Col. Doolittle and His Gallant Command: Good Luck and God Bless You—Halsey[3]

The full story of Doolittle and his crew of volunteers is told in Chapter 3. At the outset of the mission (which ultimately was successful and strategically significant), Doolittle didn't have the authority to promise his crew much. He certainly couldn't reward them monetarily; say, with a big bonus package. Because his raiders weren't a permanent military organization, Doolittle wasn't in a position to promote his commandos later, either. However, Doolittle had become fairly affluent from his exploits as a civilian pilot and while working for Shell. There was no rule about spending his own money to reward whomever he pleased. So Doolittle promised his commandos that on their return, he'd throw them the biggest, most lavish party they had ever seen. And he kept his promise. Doolittle and his raiders were also decorated for heroism by the military, and many were promoted. Before his death at the age of ninety-six, Doolittle was the only reserve officer who was ever awarded the four stars of a full general. Doolittle and his command were stunningly effective, and they deservedly were rewarded effectively in turn.

Rewards Can Come in Many Forms

While most people will take all the material goods you are ready to give them, this is not necessarily the best way to reward people because compensation may not be the whole reason, or even the main reason, that people perform at the highest levels (or even at any level at all). It is a strange but true fact that in the 1880s, right in the middle of the Indian wars, Congress failed to appropriate pay for officers, including those in combat on the frontiers. Yet most officers continued to serve throughout this period without pay. For almost two years, they and their families subsisted on army rations and living quarters that the army provided.

Or consider Clarence "Kelly" Johnson. Johnson was the aeronautical innovator who founded Lockheed Aircraft's super-secret "Skunk Works," a gathering of top Lockheed designers and engineers. There,

Johnson and his group designed more than forty aircraft, including the world's fastest and highest-flying aircraft, the SR-71 Blackbird, and developed a satellite, the Agena D, that became our nation's workhorse in space. Johnson was a magnificent engineer and manager, but he challenged his people to challenge him. If they disagreed with him, they had to put up a quarter bet. If he was right, the dissenter lost a quarter. Johnson didn't lose many of these bets, but he said he definitely lost some. The reward for being right obviously wasn't the twenty-five cents, *it was winning it from the boss.* This story is a clear demonstration that you can have a very effective reward system for contributing without it costing the organization much in terms of cash.[4]

Fred Smith, founder and CEO of FedEx Corporation and a former U.S. Marine Corps officer, does the same with "Bravo Zulu." To marines, that means "Well done!" (although it actually comes from the U.S. Navy signal book). Frankly, its origins are unimportant. What is important is that it's a reward and doesn't cost FedEx anything—but it's very special and important to employees.[5]

Let's look at some other examples of how successful leaders reward effectively, and how you should, too. Rewards are significant for two reasons. First, your commandos deserve it. Second, it will help motivate them and others in your organization for future projects or tasks.

The Compensation Trap

In Chapter 1, we noted that high pay, in and of itself, wasn't necessarily a top motivator for commandos or any other "workers," according to one major study. But recognition for good work was. In fact, recognition for good work was one of the top-three motivators. This is probably the only way that high pay (or a cash bonus) enters the picture. High pay could be considered part of recognition for good work; it is one way to reward effectively. However, unless you have an unlimited supply of money, high pay shouldn't be the only, or even the primary, means of motivating or rewarding lavishly.

That's the trap that American industry got itself into. It started rewarding successful executives primarily through compensation increases. Eventually, if top executives couldn't get sky-high compensation from one company, they felt unappreciated and unrecognized and went somewhere else where they could. To be competitive and to keep the top management talent they needed, companies were forced to pay ever-increasing amounts. As a result, top American executives are paid many times the salary of those who actually do the work. For example, CEOs in many other countries are paid five to ten times the salary of their most junior workers. In the United States, top executives of many major corporations are paid 100 times (or more) the salary of their most junior employees.

I'm not so sure this is really necessary to attract and keep top executives. It is far more than the ratio paid in the country even twenty years ago. Our top military men—generals and admirals with responsibilities for people, equipment, and money that in many cases far exceed those of top executives in industry—are paid at a ratio similar to most executives abroad: five to ten times that of the lowest-level employee in the organization.

Now you may think high compensation for executives is a good thing. Better think again. It forces all salaries upward. It becomes a major inflationary factor to our economy, and it works against your own bottom line. Also, this siphoning off of funds for executives unnecessarily cheats shareholders. Moreover, it is a major source of dissatisfaction among those hundreds of other business commandos you need to motivate and lead to their greatest productivity. It isn't right, and your employees know it.

This inequality of pay has been recognized for a long time. Thirty years ago, Robert Townsend was president of Avis Rent-A-Car. He came up with the "We Try Harder" concept. He turned things around at Avis, which wasn't number two, but number four or five in its market when he took over. At one board meeting, he refused to leave even after the chairman requested that he do so. His reason? "If I do, you'll raise my salary and that would be improper. I'm making a fair amount now. Raise it and you'll be destroying everything I'm trying to build in the spirit of all workers at Avis." Some ethical CEOs are refusing compensation for unwarranted salary increases today, and they should. It's not only ethical, it makes sense.

Enlightened business commando leaders have recognized fair compensation for a long time. So have leaders of "biblical proportions." The bible notes its importance in Numbers 16:15. When Moses's leadership was challenged by another, he defended himself not on the basis of having successfully negotiated the Israelites out of Egypt, or his successful military campaigns, or even the authority given him by God, all of which was true. Rather, his defense was that he didn't take more than he was worth, although he had the power to do so.[6]

It's pure rationalization to say that excessive monetary reward acts as a motivator for higher executive performance or as a motivator to work harder for promotion for those commandos currently at the lower levels. Study after study shows that top executives in this country get their high salaries whether they perform well or not. And don't think your people are stupid. They know that organizations are structured like a pyramid, with fewer and fewer positions as one approaches the top. They know that for the vast majority, these princely monetary rewards will never be theirs. So why should they break their necks? Sure, no one held a gun to anyone's head to get them to work for you. However, that misses the point. Does high executive compensation motivate others or demotivate them? That and fairness should be the question.

Characteristics of Effective Rewards

Commandos in battle put their lives on the line not for money, but for other reasons, and depending on the circumstance, other lavish rewards can be considered more important than "the almighty buck." That's true in battle, and it's true in business. To be effective, rewards should be:

- Timely
- Fair
- Tied to specifics
- Important

  Let's examine each of these characteristics more closely.

Effective Rewards Are Timely

To be effective, a reward needs to be given as closely as possible in time to when the work that earned the award was performed. In battle, smart commanders give this a high priority, and whenever possible, they make the award personally, within a few days of it being earned.

However, did you ever consider making the award before the event? Don't laugh. No less a figure than General Douglas MacArthur did it, and it was grandly effective. Here's the story.

During World War I, General MacArthur was a thirty-eight-year-old brigadier general. He had been "over there" for several months, but had just assumed command of a new brigade in France. After ordering an important attack against a German position, he went forward and waited in the trenches with the battalion that was going to lead the way and make the attack. To his surprise, he learned this battalion had never been in battle before. The battalion's young commander was nervous and MacArthur could see it.

He summoned the commander out of hearing of his men and said: "Major, I know you are wondering how your battalion will perform in battle and whether they will really follow your orders when the chips are down. I've been here for awhile, so let me tell you something I've learned. When the signal comes to go 'over the top,' if you go first, and get in front of your men, they will follow. Moreover, they will never doubt your courage and they will always follow you in the future."

Now usually, a battalion commander was not supposed to lead an attack from the front. The military tactics manuals said that a battalion commander should be somewhat behind his leading company. That way, he was not as vulnerable and could better control the attack as it unfolded. But MacArthur knew that there were times when the rules must be violated, and this was one of those times.

"Of course, I will not order you to do this," continued MacArthur. "In that position at the front of your battalion, you will be a clear target for the Germans. It will be very dangerous and require a great deal of courage. However, if you do it, you will earn the Distinguished Service Cross and I will see that you get it."

In those days, soldiers wore the combat awards that they had earned on their battle uniforms. MacArthur himself had been awarded this decoration and wore it proudly on his tunic. He stepped back and looked the major over for several long moments. Then he stepped forward again. "I see you are going to do it. So, you will have the Distinguished Service Cross now."

Then, MacArthur unpinned the decoration from his own uniform and pinned it on the uniform of the major.

What do you think happened when the signal came to go over the top and attack? Well, you know as well as I do. The major, proudly wearing a Distinguished Service Cross, which he had not yet actually earned, charged out in front of his troops. And as MacArthur had predicted, the major's troops followed behind him. As a result, they were successful in securing their objective and, as MacArthur promised, the young commander led his men with great confidence in the future.[7]

How a Medal Acted as a Demotivator

I wish I could say that military commanders always behaved in this manner to give rewards a top priority and to ensure that their men got the awards they had earned and deserved in a timely fashion. Unfortunately, sometimes it was just the opposite.

More than ten years ago I received a new assignment and took over an organization that I had once served in. Several days before a conference, I was informed that one of my lieutenant colonels had been awarded a medal for contributing to the development of an advanced guidance system. The conference would be an excellent opportunity to present the award in an official ceremony with photographers, so I gave the orders to set it up. Then I received a telephone call informing me that this lieutenant colonel was declining the medal. I was amazed and called the officer myself.

He told me that the work he had done to earn the medal had been done more than two years earlier. He had never asked for the award for which his immediate supervisor had recommended him, but was pleased that his supervisor had done so. Several months after his supervisor had forwarded the paperwork for approval, his supervisor was informed that the award of the medal had been rejected by the Award and Decorations Board. They sent the recommendation back stating that there was insufficient justification for award of the medal. So the supervisor prepared additional documents and forwarded the recommendation again.

At this point, the supervisor was reassigned and my lieutenant colonel got a new boss, and the process had continued, sometimes for truly stupid reasons, such as a typographical error. There was additional correspondence and work as the original supervisor, no longer in the same location, was contacted for his concurrence each time.

When the medal was finally approved, two years had passed. Although the awardee was glad that he had made a significant contribution and that the whole process was finally over, he was sorry that his supervisor ever recommended him for the medal. He had spent more time providing input to justify the award to the board than he had in performing the duty that had earned him the recommendation in the first place! As he told me, he was thoroughly disgusted and didn't want the medal. I didn't blame him. Do you think the award of this medal represented an effective reward? You know it didn't.

Fortunately, with the help of his wife, we were able to persuade him to go through the ceremony and accept the medal, despite his bad and completely undeserved experience over the preceding two years.

Last winter, I was happy to be present when this officer, now somewhat older, was promoted to the rank of major general. So good will win out, despite what some folks seem determined to do to screw things up.

Interestingly, in earlier years, I once heard a presentation by a colonel from headquarters who headed up the board that reviewed the awards at the command level. He explained an amazing concept behind the board's policies and practices. And, I'm afraid, many who decide on awards, in and out of uniform, think the same way. Basically, the thinking was that few accomplishments or achievements were really good enough for the award for which they were submitted. Therefore the board's primary purpose was to protect "the integrity of the award." He told us outright that by policy, his board rejected every single high award at least once to make sure that the individual who recommended it really felt strongly about his recommendation. Now, I don't think that every single award that someone thinks someone else should receive is necessarily warranted. However, to reject recommendations for an award as a policy has got to be a brilliant way to waste time and irritate and discourage people. Fortunately, later I was able to rectify some of these misguided, dysfunctional ways of operating. Don't let this kind of thing happen to your commandos!

Effective Awards Are Fair

If you want to destroy morale and the effectiveness of any reward you can give your commandos, then hand the rewards out unfairly. Leaders don't intentionally hand out rewards unfairly (although I've seen this happen, too), but they sometimes dispense rewards on what they think is a fair basis, only it isn't.

A friend of mine was director of research and development for a company developing and manufacturing aviation equipment for the government. He led a half-dozen project engineers with similar responsibilities. Just before the Christmas holidays, his boss, who was the president of the company, told him about their bonus system. Bonuses were based on the company's previous year's profits and individual performance during the year.

My friend was told to give the president his recommendations about how bonuses should be distributed among his project engineers. He looked over the past performance of his group and determined what percentage each project engineer would receive. He justified each with specifics as to what each individual had accomplished and forwarded this information to the company president.

Not long after, a representative of the finance office dropped off sealed envelopes with the bonuses for each engineer. My friend was a little uncomfortable with this procedure, since he would not know how much each engineer had received and if a mistake had been made regarding the percentages. He called the president and received permission to open the envelopes. To his amazement, he discovered that his top project engineer received the smallest bonus among his engineers, half the size of the others. On questioning, it turned out that the vice president of finance had disregarded my friend's recommendations because this project engineer had a three-year technical degree, rather than a full engineering degree. He had therefore given this engineer the same bonus as a secretary, rather than the higher bonuses given to managers and professionals.

Fortunately my friend caught and questioned this bad decision, and a new check was made out before the bonuses were disbursed. However, it points out how the effectiveness of rewards can be destroyed through unfairness.

To ensure fairness, you should:

■ Explain the criteria you intend to use for rewards to subordinate managers, and get feedback to ensure that your criteria make sense. Do this before the rewards are to be made, not afterward.

■ Never make the decision about a particular award entirely by yourself. Get recommendations from supervisors. Then, if you decide against using a recommendation, get back to the supervisor and explain why.

■ Accept input from other managers or staff people, but never use this information as the primary rationale for a reward without talking to the supervisor. In the final analysis, if you are making the award, it's your decision.

■ Require specifics for justifying special rewards.

■ Make absolutely certain that you are rewarding the right person when rewards are made for an event or series of events. Unfortunately, some people are all too ready to take credit for the work of others.

■ Watch for personality or other conflicts. If a supervisor specifically does not want an individual to be rewarded, you've got a problem. Normally, you must back your subordinate managers. However, in these cases, you'll want to investigate the situation thoroughly and think long and hard. It is a mistake, and probably even unethical, to withhold an earned reward, even if the supervisor has a real problem with the commando for other reasons. As my father, who was an Air Force JAG (judge advocate general), once said: "You'd be surprised at the number of individuals that get decorated for bravery and court-martialed in the same month." An individual may be rewarded for one thing he did and "court-martialed" for an entirely different reason.

Effective Rewards Are Tied to Specifics Whenever Possible

Linking rewards with specific accomplishments helps to ensure fairness and is motivating, too. That way, everyone knows exactly what they need to do to earn a particular reward. (Of course, group rewards, such as the party that General Doolittle threw for his fliers, may not lend themselves to specifics.) Sales organizations, for example, know how to do this very well. They reward at one scale for beginning-level sales accomplishments and then offer greater rewards (e.g., trophies, vacations, etc.) on top of that for higher levels.

The key is that all sales awards are tied to very specific, numerical, levels of accomplishment. The same type of reward system can apply to other areas of business as well: finance, marketing, human resources, you name it. Sure, it's tough working out some of these details, but that's what makes it worthwhile, and the result is that we would have a much more effective commando leadership. It's just plain wrong and demotivating to have different commandos accomplish identical feats and to be rewarded differently.

Effective Rewards Are Important

"Important" is a relative term, because what is important to one group of people may be unimportant to another group, and vice versa. Doolittle's party was important to his raiders. To those who attend lavish parties on a routine basis, it may not be so important.

If you want to reward your commandos effectively, you must establish or develop a reward that is important to them. For example, titles are important to many people. Titles cost nothing, yet I have seen companies that are very stingy with handing them out either as a reward for performance or even in their own interest.

One company I know hired a senior executive to represent its interests in a foreign country. As a former national of that country, he had the contacts and knew what he had to do to be effective. Unfortunately, this man was given a job title that was too low-level to make him credible in the eyes of those he needed to influence. Yet his company told him that a higher-level title was "against policy," even though it cost nothing and he needed the title to do his job effectively.

It's a fact that many corporations organize using their salespeople as individual contractors rather than employees. They award only low-level titles at first. However, one company gave each new salesperson the title of CEO right from the beginning. Since each salesperson was an independent contractor, the title was descriptively correct and it was definitely important to the salespeople.

I'm not saying you need to do the same thing. There are an infinite number of ways to reward your employees. If the simple words "Bravo Zulu" are so important to FedEx employees, surely you can come up with rewards that are important to your commandos. One method is to establish your own medals (or other awards). Here are two good examples, from the past and the present, to get your creative juices flowing.

■ *Medals of Merit.* During the Civil War, George Armstrong Custer became disgusted with the time it took for medals to be approved, so he established his own award in gold at his own expense, the "Custer Gold Medal for Bravery."

It's illegal to wear officially unauthorized medals on military uniforms today. However, I got pretty frustrated with the slowness in rewarding my "commandos," too. So, taking a leaf from General Custer's actions, I established a special medal of merit. It was pretty big and flashy and was hung by a red, white, and blue ribbon. The recipient got the medal with his name engraved on the back during a ceremony.

At the ceremony I announced that wearing this medal on the uniform was unauthorized, so anyone who showed up at our annual "dining out" wearing it would be sent to "the Grog Bowl." The dining-out is an annual formal affair with much military tradition. I think we borrowed it from the British. At these affairs, we wear our most formal uniforms and follow strict ceremonial protocol. Miscreants or those doing something contrary to good behavior, real or imagined, are sent to "the Grog Bowl," which contains a drinkable but unpleasant mixture of various liquids, once (but no longer) alcoholic. There, they were required to drink a full tankard of this grog. Naturally, awardees of the unauthorized medals of merit took great pride in wearing their medals and being sent to "the Grog Bowl" to do penance for wearing them at that unique event.

Where does it say that nonmilitary organizations can't reward with medals as well? Sports organizations, right on up to the Olympics, award medals with great success.

- *Other Nonmonetary Rewards.* I talked about Mary Kay Cosmetics in Chapter 1 and Chapter 3. Few organizations are better tuned in to what is important to their own people than this organization. Mary Kay had herself been a sales employee of another firm before she founded her own company. Maybe that's why she knew exactly what was important to women. Her company was one of the few that offered women an opportunity to earn money (at the time the company was founded, there were few jobs open to women), and fewer yet that rewarded successful women with some type of managerial positions, which Mary Kay was quick to do.

With nonmonetary rewards, Mary Kay really excelled. In fact, one reward was probably worth millions of dollars in promoting the Mary Kay name, the pink Cadillacs awarded to top performers. Pay attention here. Are there rewards you can give your commandos that can lead to national publicity? Probably. Nor were pink Cadillacs the only rewards Mary Kay initiated that her salespeople found important. They also included white mink coats and diamond-studded bumblebee pins.

The bumblebee pins had some symbolism, which is another aspect you should consider when establishing your rewards. A bumblebee's body is too heavy for the lifting power of its wings. But it flies anyway. Mary Kay took that as a symbol of successful salesmanship. Educational background, age, or the fact that the salesperson was a woman was unimportant—you could be fabulously successful anyway. All of these very effective means of rewarding Mary Kay's saleswomen helped build a billion-dollar business.

Commando Notes

To encourage your commandos to perform at their absolute maximum best, give them effective rewards for their efforts. Rewards and recognition for a good job can come in many forms. However, rewards, even if small, are not a small thing. Rewards, of whatever size or form, are a big thing. Therefore the rewards you give should be timely, fair, tied to specifics, and important to the people who are to receive them. Don't be afraid to use your imagination, either, the way General Custer or Mary Kay did for their organizations. Remember that the idea is to give deserved recognition for performance to encourage not only the awardee, but other commandos as well.

MAKE THE MOST OF WHAT YOU HAVE

"Do what you can, with what you have, where you are."
—Theodore Roosevelt

"I rate the skillful tactician above the skillful strategist, especially him who plays the bad cards well."
—Field Marshal Sir Archibald Wavell

GREGORY ''PAPPY'' BOYINGTON had been a U.S. Marine Corps pilot before World War II, a volunteer with Chennault's Flying Tigers in China (where he shot down six enemy planes), and then an administrative officer commanding nonoperational squadrons back with the U.S. Marines in the Pacific. Despite his best efforts, he couldn't get a flying position in an active combat squadron.

In August 1943, Boyington noted that there were late-model Corsair fighter planes available just sitting on the runway, but they weren't being flown in combat against the Japanese. The problem was administrative. The combat squadrons had all the planes they needed. Logistically, they couldn't absorb more. There were also pilots available to fly these planes, but they weren't being utilized in combat either, because they were in a replacement pool. New squadrons were on the way to the theater by ship that would fly the unflown airplanes, but they wouldn't arrive for some time. So a strange situation existed: In the middle of a desperately fought war, there were both planes and pilots on the American side that weren't being used.

The pilots in the replacement pool were a mixed lot. A few were experienced fighter pilots chomping at the bit to get back into action. Some were brand-new from the states and hadn't been checked out as qualified to fly the new Corsairs; some were pilots of nonfighter air-craft, bombers, and transports and such. The pilots in this group may have been willing, but they had not been trained to fly fighters and it wasn't clear that they possessed the necessary skills.

A few of the pilots in the group had been "grounded" because they were in one kind of trouble or another. Boyington could relate, because he had been in trouble of one sort or another throughout his military career, which was probably one reason that he wasn't made commander of one of the operational Marine fighter squadrons, despite his consid-erable experience and earlier success as a fighter pilot.

In any case, Boyington suggested that neither planes nor pilots be wasted for the war effort. Why not form a temporary squadron from this mixed lot of misfits? That way, not only would the Marine Air Wing receive a boost in its fighting potential against the Japanese, but these replacements would be trained, combat-experienced, and ready to go when needed to join permanent squadrons. Of course, Boyington himself would be happy to take on the duty of commanding this tempo-rary combat squadron of airmen.

Some visionary or friend saw the wisdom of Boyington's proposal, and he was named squadron commander of a temporary combat squad-ron of flying misfits. For administrative purposes, the squadron was given an official U.S. Marine Corps designation: VMF-214, later known as the "Black Sheep Squadron" because of its origins.

As Boyington wrote: "I hadn't approached any of the pool pilots yet, and not every pilot in the pool happened to be a fighter pilot. But I knew that most pilots wanted to be fighter pilots, if they were dumb enough."[1]

One of the bomber pilots, Bob McClurg, begged to join the squad-ron, although at first Boyington didn't want to take him. Boyington had flown with him and didn't believe he had fighter pilot skills. Finally, Boyington, admiring McClurg's courage and persistence, relented.[2] It was good that he did. Bob McClurg became the third highest ranking VMF-214 ace, with seven confirmed kills.

The squadron never gave up its misfit replacements. Over the next eighty-four days, Boyington's Black Sheep became the leading Marine fighter squadron in the Pacific, having piled up a record 197 enemy planes damaged or destroyed, and VMF-214 was made a permanent U.S. Marine Corps squadron.[3] Eventually Boyington was shot down and spent the remainder of the war as a prisoner, but not before he destroyed twenty-six enemy aircraft himself and won the Congressional

Medal of Honor. He survived his captivity and retired from the Marine Corps as a colonel, despite his personal "bad boy" reputation.

Working with What You Have

Chapter 2 examined how to create commandos from scratch—to get the very best from the beginning and to essentially build on excellence. Unfortunately, you don't always have that luxury. There are times when you must work with the material that you have, even when that raw material may not look all that good. But as Pappy Boyington demonstrated, you can do incredible things, even with so-called misfits, if you know how. In this chapter we're going to look at how special ops leaders go about building successful commando organizations even when they don't have "the very best" to begin with.

Lest you think that Pappy Boyington's efforts were an exception to the rule, let me assure you that this is not the case. What Boyington did is rare and difficult, but still doable—and it is doable not only in a combat aviation unit, but in business and other organizational environments as well.

A Coach Who Built a Commando Soccer Team

Arthur Resnick was a high school athletic coach in Scarsdale, New York. In a six-year period, Coach Resnick's high school soccer team set a record for 109 consecutive soccer matches without a loss and only two ties.[4] No soccer team in the nation equaled Scarsdale's record. Of course, Scarsdale won the regional title every year. I know what you're thinking. This is one of those schools that trains professional athletes and every student is a "jock." Not quite. Moreover, Resnick's team wasn't even male. It was the girl's soccer team. And no other team at Scarsdale did as well as Resnick's, male or female.

Yet Resnick created this amazing string of unbroken victories, unequaled before or since. How did he do it? He worked with the material he had and made them better than their opponents. His girls trained year-round even though soccer season was only in the spring. And the training wasn't easy. There wasn't a girl on the team that couldn't do a hundred sit-ups or thirty-five push-ups. That's more sit-ups and push-ups than many, if not most, men athletes can do. Moreover, Resnick sought every edge. The girls got special vitamins and iron, physiological training, and even attention by a podiatrist for their feet.[5]

How a West Point Coach Won with Little Raw Material

I have some personal experience with this sort of thing in athletics. When I was a cadet at West Point, gymnastics was considered a minor sport. Whereas the major sports—football, basketball, and baseball—got considerable support for recruiting, gymnastics received none. At the time of my tenure as a cadet, in twenty-seven years of coaching at West Point, Coach Tom Maloney's teams won 161 gymnastic meets and tied nine. This record included numerous Eastern Intercollegiate Championships. Army hadn't lost to its traditional rival, Navy, in eleven years. Moreover, in addition to developing champion teams, Maloney developed numerous individual champions. Most had never participated in gymnastics until they arrived at West Point.

With other colleges actively recruiting outstanding high school gymnasts, how did Coach Maloney find gymnasts to fill his ranks, much less to successfully win out over all competitors and compile such a record? His first step was simple.

To qualify physically for West Point, all candidates had to take a rigorous physical fitness test that included doing an established minimum repetition of exercises that included pull-ups, push-ups, and sit-ups. These three exercises are particularly important as a measurement of upper body strength. Gymnastics requires a lot of upper body strength, but not body weight. So Maloney would go through each new class's entry records and find candidates who had significant upper body strength as demonstrated by the results of these three exercises, but who were not heavy. During new cadet basic training, beginning in early July and ending in late August, these cadets were invited to a gymnastics screening during which their upper body strength was further tested with parallel-bar body dips and additional exercises. Those that excelled in this strength were invited to compete for a position on West Point's gymnastics team. Then, like Coach Resnick thirty years later, Coach Maloney insisted that gymnasts train every day, both on season and off.

I was one of these gymnasts who had never before participated in the sport of gymnastics. I passed the screening and went out for the team. There were six gymnastic events in which it was possible to engage in those days: tumbling, horse, high bar, parallel bars, flying rings, and rope climb. I decided that the high bar looked the most promising. However, Coach Maloney soon discovered that while I had upper body strength, my coordination left much to be desired.

Maloney didn't give up easily. "Why not try the rope climb?" he suggested. Rope climbing was an event that required much more body strength than I possessed then, but that strength-endurance could be developed. Rope climbing held a major advantage for someone like me because coordination was much less important. The event was simplicity in itself. You sat on the floor with your arms stretched up over your head, grasping the rope. When you felt so moved you heaved your body off the floor in an explosive movement and then, without hesitation, reached out and pulled yourself up with one arm as fast and far as you could. At the same time you leaned back and kicked upward with the opposite leg. You did not grasp the rope with your legs. That would slow you down. You kept the momentum going by reaching up with alternating arm and leg movements as you progressed upward. In this fashion you climbed straight up until you reached a black pan at the end of the twenty-foot rope. You lunged upward and struck the pan with one hand. It was coated with a black charcoal substance. The black residue on your fingers proved you had actually made it to the top and touched it, in case the sound of striking the pan could not be heard. Your time was from the time you left the floor until you touched the pan.

Coach Maloney told me that a few years earlier the climbing distance and length of the rope had been twenty-five feet, so in only having to climb the twenty-foot rope I was getting a good deal.

You could come down the rope any way you wanted at any speed you chose. I guess you could have dropped if you were so inclined. "Best of all," an upper-classman rope climber told me, "it was really an easy way to be a gymnast because the whole process took less than ten seconds." You wouldn't even break a sweat, or so he said.

Coach Maloney told me that if I could make it to the top without using my legs, I had the makings of a rope climber. Motivated by the thought that this was an easy way to become an Army gymnast, I sat myself down and climbed. It was tough, but I made it to the top. It took me about eight seconds. "How fast do I have to go to make the first team?" I asked. "Five seconds," he answered. Wow! That was only three seconds difference, I thought.

No one told me the thousands of times I'd have to climb that twenty-foot rope, as well as the old twenty-five-foot rope, sometimes wearing a forty-pound weight belt, or the number of one-armed pull-ups I needed to do, all in practice, to get to that five-second goal. To get to the point where I could climb to the top in five seconds or less and thus represent the U.S. Army in competition took me two years. Still, it was worth it, and my senior year at West Point I tied the West Point and Intercollegiate rope climb records. In fact, by actual time, I beat these records, but the Amateur Athletic Union rules said you needed to beat the record by a whole second. My time was only 0.5 second better than the record—3.35 seconds to get from the floor to the twenty-foot pan. However, bear in mind that the world record in those days (which still stands today) was 2.8 seconds. I'm not sure that even a couple years of tough training would have got me that seven-tenths of a second I needed to break that record.

About thirty years later, I was at West Point for our older son's Plebe-Parents weekend, something that didn't exist when I was a cadet. Rope climbing was no longer a gymnastic event, and I had not climbed a rope since my own graduation. Still, I was attending the Industrial College of the Armed Forces in Washington, D.C. and had been engaged in training for a physical fitness competition for several months, so I was in pretty good shape. While I couldn't do one-armed pull-ups anymore, I was still capable of doing forty pull-ups with both arms.

I insisted on returning to the scene of my boyhood trials and found a deserted twenty-foot rope ready and waiting for me. I handed my camera to my wife and asked her to take a picture of my triumphal comeback. It was a hundred times harder than I remembered. With great difficulty, I made it up the twenty feet of rope and lunged and managed to touch the pan. I thanked the gods that no one had a stop-watch, because I doubt if I broke eight seconds on that day.

On the way down the rope, I noticed a flash. When I was back on terra firma and had caught my breath, I asked my wife: "Did you take two pictures?" "No, just one," she answered, "I took it on the way down." "You're supposed to take it on the way up," I admonished. "No problem," she replied, "just do it again." I decided that discretion was the better part of valor. So I have pictures of myself, while a cadet, going up, and one as a middle-aged colonel coming down.

Maybe that's a long story to make a short point, but sometimes you must build your commandos from what you have, and that is entirely possible. Were Coach Maloney still there, I'm sure he could have trained me to do it again, despite being "a little older."

A Commando Who Worked His Magic in Education

Steve Barr is a leader in education without any background in education to speak of, although he did graduate from college. However, Barr is an activist, and a special ops leader. Several years ago he became upset with what was happening in high school education in one of the poorer Latino neighborhoods of Los Angeles, where a very high percentage of students were dropping out.

Committing his own life savings of $100,000, Barr convinced state authorities to fund his school system as a charter school. The charter system was set up in California to encourage innovative methods of education. Barr's concept was not to educate the best and the brightest, but to get average students, 140 in a class, into his classrooms and get them to graduate. Barr's school district opposed his proposal, despite its own less-than-sterling record in education. Nevertheless, he got approval to open a charter school called the Animo Leadership Charter High School. "Animo" means spirit. He would get the same operating budget as other schools in his district that were already well established with capital equipment, buildings, etc. So he leased space and a building and forged ahead with no sports or clubs or any other frills.

For teachers, he hired the young and inexperienced, mostly under age thirty. Unlike other schools in his district, most of his teachers aren't credentialed. Students didn't get in by academic excellence. Anyone who wanted to enter his school entered a lottery. Why did they bother? According to one freshman whose two siblings had dropped out of other high schools in the area, maybe Animo would work.

Barr's first class just graduated. Guess what? Every single graduating student is going to college or a trade school. Sixty percent are going to four-year colleges, including the University of California Berkeley, UCLA, the University of Southern California, and Pomona College— some of the best schools in California. Some students have full scholarships. Another measurement of Barr's success can be seen in the scores Animo's students made on the California Academic Performance Index. Animo scored in the middle of all California high schools. Other schools in Animo's district, drawing from the same demographics, with 94 percent qualifying for free lunches, scored far less; two were even among the bottom schools in the state.

How did Barr get both inexperienced teachers and average students from low-income families to perform so brilliantly? The same way as Boyington, and Coaches Resnick and Maloney—by demanding a lot of extra hard work on everybody's part. Animo's story appeared in the *Los Angeles Times*. The newspaper attempted to contact school district officials to get their side of the story, but they couldn't be reached for comment. Meanwhile, Barr has started more charter schools of the same type.[6]

Working with Other Organization's Castoffs

Pappy Boyington's dilemma required him to use the raw human material on hand. Another, similar situation might be that while you are assigned a commando-size task, you are given other organizations' castoffs. Maybe people are assigned to you simply because they are available or can be spared. Or you could be assigned good people, but people who are untrained, inexperienced, or otherwise unqualified or unprepared for the job at hand. When that happens, you should think about Bob McClurg, former bomber pilot and later Black Sheep Squadron ace.

Or maybe you need to do more with less. That's what happened to the 1st Special Service Force. This was a joint American-Canadian unit that was the forerunner of many commando units today.

They called themselves "the Forcemen." On February 2, 1944, after engaging in considerable combat elsewhere, the Forcemen were sent into the Anzio beachhead in Italy. Despite being 40 percent under strength, they were assigned almost two miles of front. They held this front for ninety-nine consecutive days while continually penetrating and raiding the German lines. It was at Anzio that the Forcemen earned their famous nickname, the "Devil's Brigade." You may remember the movie about them of the same title. It wasn't perfectly accurate, but the basic concept was true. The name came from their fierce fighting style and the fact that they attacked with blackened faces. Moreover, they left "death cards" written in German behind: "Das Dicke Ende Kommt Noch," meaning "the worst is yet to come."[7] An entry from a diary found on the body of one German officer read, "The Black Devils are all around us every time we come into line, and we never hear them."

There may be any number of reasons why you may have to work with what you have, but unless you consider the accomplishment of your mission impossible without specific expertise that is being denied you, don't despair. Remember what others have done and start planning how you are going to do it.

Building Commandos Out of What You Have

Every successful team of commandos has four major characteristics:

- *Cohesion.* By sticking together, team members put the interests of the group over their own interests.

- *Teamwork.* Team members work together in order to maximize the strengths of individuals in the group and minimize their weaknesses.

- *High Morale.* Morale is an inner feeling of well-being that is independent of external factors.

- *Esprit de Corps.* This French term refers to the morale (common spirit) of the organization as a unit.

Developing Cohesion

Cohesion is known in the military as a combat force multiplier. That is, the mere existence of strong cohesion in an organization can multiply the effectiveness of the unit in competition with others or, in the case of a commando organization, in combat. Through strong cohesion, a smaller organization with fewer resources can overcome one that is larger with many more resources. This isn't just theory. It has been demonstrated with hard research, mostly done by the military.

For example, Lieutenant Colonel Jon W. Blades, a former U.S. Army officer at the National Defense University with a doctorate, investigated cohesion among training platoons taking army basic training. He investigated both individual and group performance in rifle marksmanship, physical fitness, drill and ceremonies, and individual soldier skill tests. Blades observed significantly better average individual and group (platoon) performance scores in each of these four major training areas when cohesion was at a higher level.

Analyzing the reasons, Blades found that cohesion produced good working relationships among the members of the group; consequently, they made more efficient use of group assets, including individual ability, time, and other resources that were available. One example was that in the more cohesive platoons, the more talented soldiers voluntarily spent their free time teaching and coaching those who were less talented.[8]

Research into cohesion hasn't received the attention it deserves outside of the military. However, some important work should be noted. One study of 575 members of more than a hundred different German software teams listed cohesion as one of six facets of quality affecting performance.[9] Another study examined what led to successful long-term alliances in the hospital industry. The answer? Strong cohesion among partners.[10]

If you want to develop strong cohesion in your organization, start by developing pride in membership of the organization. To feel pride, your group must believe that they are in the best organization of its type, anywhere. That is true regardless of the type of organization. I guarantee you that it didn't take long before VMF-214 thought it was the best fighter squadron, long before the statistics proved it to be so. I would wager the same was true of Resnick's soccer team and all other organizations demonstrating high levels of cohesion. They either believe they are the best, or they believe that they are well on the way to becoming the best. For example, when former CEO and president of Southwest Airlines, Howard Putnam, took over he said, "I couldn't understand when I first got there why we didn't have any complaints. The employment group worked with the mentality that we hire people who have fun. When I spoke to new employees I'd tell them, 'You've chosen Southwest Airlines and you're going to work harder than at any other airline. You're going to get paid about 30 percent less, but in the long run, when we make this thing work, with your profit sharing you'll be far ahead of anybody else.'" Notice how Putnam spoke about "having fun." That's always been a hallmark of Southwest Airlines.

With what other airline are you likely to open an overhead luggage rack to reveal a smiling live stewardess who climbed up and squeezed herself into the rack just to surprise you? So first, clearly define the position of your organization in the scheme of things. You cannot be everything to everybody. You must decide exactly what you are, what sets your organization apart from all others, and in Peter Drucker's words, you need to decide what business you are in. If you look at any successful commando organization in or out of business, every single one had a clearly defined niche at which it excelled. Boyington didn't claim his squadron was the best at everything . . . only that it was the best fighter squadron around.

Once you know exactly what your mission in life is, you can articulate your vision and use many of the techniques in Chapter 9 (especially those having to do with promotion) to inspire others to follow your vision. Then do everything possible to prove your organization's worth.

There is little question that you can improve group cohesion by establishing the worth of the organization and its values. The more good stories that you can uncover illustrating your organization's worth, the better. Everyone likes to be associated with winners and winning organizations. No one wants to be in a losing organization. So if you can establish your group as a winner based on accomplishments in its past, you are heading in the right direction toward a strong, cohesive unit.

If your organization is a new one, try and find a previous organization within or even outside of your corporation with which you can identify. This is a way to acquire instant traditions. When the modern U.S. Army Rangers were created during World War II, their leader, Colonel William O. Darby, immediately identified his unit with Roger's Rangers of the eighteenth century, which was actually part of the British Army. As noted above, the very term *commando,* used by Winston Churchill during World War II, was based on the commando Boer units in South Africa that he had fought against as a young man!

Developing Teamwork

Peter Drucker found an interesting phenomenon in investigating the procedures in a well-run hospital. Doctors, nurses, X-ray technicians, pharmacologists, pathologists, and other health care practitioners all worked together to accomplish a single objective. Frequently he saw several working on the same patient under emergency conditions. Seconds counted. Even a minor slip could prove fatal. Yet, with a minimum amount of conscious command or control by any one individual, these medical teams worked together toward a common end and followed a common plan of action under the overall direction of a doctor.[11] Many studies done in and out of the military have confirmed Drucker's observations and discovered even more. The quality of performance is far less influenced by the individual abilities of a group's members than it is by the amount of time these individuals have worked together.

The problem is, if working together is a prime factor in quality of performance, what can you do about it? Given enough time together, your commando team will improve. However, what if you don't have "enough" time? You need top performance right from the start. How can you get it—or can you?

Fortunately, through training together, you can. If you are engaged in a work activity where training together is possible, it is a worthwhile activity. That's what commandos do. As covered in Chapter 7, the unit, the team, and teamwork are everything. They practice together again and again. And this practice doesn't stop once they have successful battles behind them, either. It is ongoing. Before every raid, they practice that raid. They get better and better as time goes on. Musicians, athletic teams, and actors train and practice continuously as well. Any team that wants to operate as commandos do should train and practice together, too.

Now I know that to some organizations, training together for the actual work is pretty close to impossible. When the type of work you do doesn't lend itself to training, you've got to have some other way of accomplishing the same thing. With a little thought, you can come up with some kind of substitute training for all organizations of any type, from scientists to stockbrokers, so that people can learn more about each other as individuals, rather than simply how their technical tools fit. People need to learn that some individuals have certain strengths, so they learn to rely on them. People who make many contributions also have weaknesses, but they learn how, as a team, they can make these weaknesses irrelevant. That's why companies offering group activities in the wilderness or in various types of physical challenges claim that these activities increase group productivity. They do, because they help build teamwork and cohesion. But you don't need to take your commandos out into the wilderness to foster teamwork. Playing team sports like baseball or softball together does the same thing. Playing together in this fashion is an advanced form of collegiality and, in this sense, can substitute for formal training.

Arthur Wellesley, the Duke of Wellington, Napoleon's conqueror at Waterloo, said: "The Battle of Waterloo was won on the playing fields of Eton." MacArthur rephrased this sentiment when he was superintendent at West Point with the words: "On the fields of friendly strife are sown the seeds that, on other fields and other days, will bear the fruits of victory."

Developing High Morale

Remember Colonel John Mosby, the Gray Ghost? He knew the value of high morale. He wrote in his memoirs: "Men who go into a fight under the influence of such feelings are next to invincible, and are generally victors before it begins."[12]

General George Patton not only knew the value of high morale, but he knew it could be developed, too. Moreover, contrary to many management experts, high morale isn't necessary developed over a long period of time. It can be developed very rapidly. Patton understood this. Patton wrote, "In a week's time, I can spur any outfit into a high state of morale."[13]

How could General Patton "spur any outfit into a high state of morale"? Many factors go into establishing a feeling of personal well-being and invincibleness that constitutes morale. I have seen many organizations, both in and out of uniform, dramatically change from low morale to high morale simply because of what the leader does. It isn't a question of making "nice-nice" with one's commandos; rather, it is about giving them confidence that, as the leader in charge, you are going to lead them to success, take care of them to the best of your ability, and allow them to have an important part to play in the oncoming success.

One of Patton's early successes was after the Battle of Kasserine Pass in North Africa. The Germans had handed the inexperienced American troops of U.S. Army II Corps a major defeat with heavy casualties. The commander of II Corps was relieved. II Corps was completely demoralized. There was even talk about dismantling it. Patton was promoted to lieutenant general and sent in to take command.

Patton took over II Corps like a cyclone. He didn't hesitate. He exuded self-confidence. He told the troops what they needed to do to win and he said they would win. He was hard, but fair, and as a result he was both liked and respected by his troops. Morale instantly turned around. He made his troops feel important. Listen to how he speaks to the first African-American troops, the 741st Black Panther Tank Battalion, to join his command later in the war:

> Men, . . . I would never have asked for you if you were not good. I have nothing but the best in my army. I don't care what color you are as long as you go up there and kill those Kraut sons-of-bitches. Everyone has their eyes on you [and] are expecting great things from you. Most of all, your race is looking forward to your success. Don't let them down, and, damn you, don't let me down! If you want me you can always find me in the lead tank.[14]

Only two weeks later at El Guettar in North Africa, these same troops faced the Germans again on March 23, 1943. At El Guettar, Patton's II Corps gained the first major victory over the Germans at this battle. After the war, Nazi generals admitted that of all American field commanders, Patton was the one they most feared. Patton knew what he was doing and knew how to gain high morale. If we analyze Patton's methods of morale boosting, we can see that it is based on many principles we have discussed previously, including displaying confidence, being hard but fair, setting a personal example from "the lead tank, if necessary," and promoting your principles and your vision. Simple, but not easy. But if you do it, as Patton said, it doesn't take long.

Developing Esprit de Corps

Individual morale is linked with group morale, and here, too, there are actions the special ops leader should take. After World War I, General James Harbord, a senior U.S. Army leader, commented on his experiences in France:

> Discipline and morale influence the inarticulate vote that is constantly taken by masses of men when the order comes to move forward—a variant of the crowd psychology that inclines it to follow a leader. But the army does not move forward until the motion has carried. "Unanimous consent" only follows cooperation between the individual men in ranks.[15]

What Harbord was saying is that there is a group spirit that you must reach in order to motivate groups of people to do things . . . even in the military, and despite the effect of orders. His comments were probably based not only on what he saw in France, but on a book on group psychology by a Frenchman, Gustave Le Bon, written around 1895. The book was said to have had a major impact on Hitler and Mussolini.[16]

Esprit de corps is built on three elements: your personal integrity, mutual confidence, and a focus on contribution rather personal gain. All three are linked together.

Personal integrity is a primary driver in trust between followers and leaders. Those that follow special ops leaders in battle trust them with their lives and well-being. Those that follow business leaders trust them with their careers and their well-being. This demonstrates that to be effective over time and when time is short, those who follow you must be able to believe what you say and that what you tell them is true. Sure, you can get away with fluff, exaggeration, and lies over the short term. But if you plan on great exploits over the long term, be careful what you say. Or, put another way, say what you mean and mean what you say. If you make a promise, keep it. Watch every word. You can make mistakes, even big mistakes, and your commandos will still follow. Look at Patton. Although he once slapped a soldier (an incident over which he later apologized publicly), his soldiers followed him all the way to the collapse of the Third Reich. Patton was human and could err big time, but he didn't lie and his soldiers trusted him.

Well-being is something important in both military and business operations. This must be a personal concern and a personal responsibility. You must look out for the best interests of your commandos, most certainly before your own. As a twenty-nine-year-old colonel during World War I, Patton demonstrated real concern for the lives of his men. On being given command of the first American tank unit by General John Pershing, he said, "Sir, I accept my new command with particular enthusiasm because with the eight tanks, I believe I can inflict the greatest number of casualties on the enemy with the smallest expenditure of American life."[17]

Finally, think contribution rather than exploitation. Your commandos will always do their utmost and work together for a greater common cause. However, if what you are exhorting them to do is for your own personal benefit or aggrandizement, your own ego, or something other than a common cause, don't expect much, because you won't get much.

Commando Notes

There are times when you must make do with the human resources you have. You may take over an organization and be told that you must work with the existing staff. You may be given the castoffs from other organizations, or you may be assigned responsibilities with limited personnel resources to accomplish a mission they were not trained for. You will find that any man or woman can be turned into a valuable member of a commando team if the leader knows how to work the raw material at hand. As a leader, you can accomplish such a transformation by focusing on certain primary tasks. Build cohesion by focusing on organizational pride. Build teamwork by having your team members work, train, and play together as much as possible. Build morale by working with your commandos and being out in front. Build esprit de corps by thinking contribution, not exploitation.

13 | NEVER GIVE UP

"Victory belongs to the most persevering."
—Napoleon

"Great works are performed not by strength, but by perseverance."
—Samuel Johnson

I N 1 9 4 1 , the British had managed to sink the German battleship *Bismarck*. But a little over six months later, the Germans completed construction of the Bismarck's sister ship, the *Tirpitz*. It was equally powerful. They managed to get it launched and sailed it north to Trondheim on the Norwegian coast. Here it presented a severe threat. If it could break out into the North Atlantic, it would endanger the British fleet in the North Atlantic. In fact, all Atlantic convoys would be in jeopardy. Winston Churchill wrote that the entire strategy of the war at that period depended on destroying this one German ship.

Four times the English planes attacked the *Tirpitz* from the air, but the ship was too well defended, resulting in no damage to the ship and the loss of twelve British aircraft. The British admiralty looked at the situation again and devised a plan involving a commando raid that was eventually approved by Admiral Mountbatten, the head of combined operations, and by the prime minister himself.

The plan observed that there was only a single port on the European continent that could service the *Tirpitz* and that would allow it to operate effectively in the North Atlantic. That port was Saint Nazaire on the French coast. Unfortunately for Allied interests, the port was arguably the most heavily defended area along the whole of the German-occupied Atlantic coast. Air attacks against the port proper would be ineffective and probably suicidal. Even a commando raid from the sea would not be easy due to the magnitude of German defenses.

However, there was a weak point that might be exploited if it could be reached. If the lock gate at the port could be destroyed, it would deny the Germans use of the dry-dock. Without a dry-dock, the port was useless for the *Tirpitz*. Thus, if a way could be found to destroy this one lock gate, the British could neutralize the threat the *Tirpitz* posed and get on with the war with their own offensive plans in the North Atlantic.

The problem was, how to get to the lock gate. After considerable study, planners thought that they had found a way. Although the Germans had fortified most of Saint Nazaire, they did not expect an attack over the mud flats and shoals. Such an attack did not appear feasible because only shallow draft boats could use this approach over very specific times when the tides were in. Consequently, the shoals were less heavily defended.

Carefully analyzing tides, winds, and maps, some of which were more than a hundred years old, the British admiralty came up with a plan. A destroyer of shallow draft would be especially modified. In theory, this ship could sail over the shoals and go straight for the outer lock gate during certain hours. Once over the shoals, it would pick up speed and ram the lock gate head-on. Then it would be sunk in place. Moreover, this destroyer would have two cargoes. The human cargo of commandos would immediately disembark. The second cargo was equally deadly. The destroyer would be packed with explosives. Another 150 commandos would be in accompanying shallow draft motor launches. The commandos would defend the scuttled ship against the vastly superior numbers of enemy troops anticipated during the time it took to set the demolitions. Unfortunately, the commandos were not given much of a chance at a successful withdrawal. However, in order to incapacitate the port at Saint Nazaire, the whole force was considered expendable.

Once the explosives were set, the commandos would reembark on the launches to two other destroyers and, if possible, escape. The operation would be helped by a simultaneous diversionary air raid against military targets in the nearby town that, it was hoped, would cause defenders to remain in their bunkers at least during the initial assault and possibly while the demolitions were being set.

The commando fleet departed Falmouth, England during the afternoon of March 26, 1942. Royal Navy Captain Robert Ryder was in overall command of the combined operation, with Lieutenant Commander Stephen Beattie commanding the destroyer to be grounded at the lock and blown up. Army Lieutenant Colonel Augustus Newman was in command of Number 2 Commando, which would do the ground fighting.

Of course, things rarely go as planned. The small fleet immediately ran into trouble, first encountering a German submarine. They damaged the submarine and, knowing that their position would be reported, altered course to deceive the submarine as to their direction and intentions. However, Ryder continued with the mission. As it turned out, this deception worked. The Germans launched five torpedo boats to engage the small fleet, but they headed in the wrong direction and didn't participate in the upcoming engagement. The Germans had no idea that they were headed to Saint Nazaire.

Next, the fleet ran into French trawlers. Vichy French and Germans manned them. Ryder sank the trawlers and took the crews prisoner on board one of the escort destroyers. Ryder ordered the fleet on its mission.

Then, a motor launch carrying part of the commando force reported engine trouble. They abandoned it, with its crew and commandos transferring to another commando vessel. The attack force moved on.

Around midnight, the diversionary air raid started and the commandos saw the tracers and the bombs in the distance. However, because of low cloud cover, the bombing was ineffective, with many bombers not attacking under the poor visibility to minimize civilian casualties. Instead of creating the diversion intended and lessening the defenses, it put the Germans on their guard. Moreover, because the aircraft did not bomb, the air raid lasted much shorter than intended. This was no fault of the aircrews. For security reasons, the bomber crews were not told about the commando raid. Their instructions were that they weren't to bomb unless they could see what they were aiming at. Ryder knew that without the air raid diversion, the job would be much more difficult, but he and his commando fleet pressed on.

Finally, the fleet approached the estuary. The destroyer crept through it at only five knots. That's about six miles per hour. Lieutenant Commander Beattie kept constant watch and consulted his ancient charts. Still, he ran aground twice. Remaining undeterred, he continued onward toward his objective.

By 01:20, the approach of the attackers could no longer be concealed. The Germans turned on floodlights and illuminated the attackers. Due to some subterfuge signaling by the British ships, the enemy hesitated for a short period. Nevertheless, during the final fifteen-minute run-in by the destroyer, accompanying launches, and motor torpedo boats, the defenders opened fire on the attackers with everything they had. Half the raiders in the motor launches were killed or wounded. Nevertheless, the commandos persisted. They didn't stop.

At 01:34, the destroyer cleared the estuary, increased to flank speed, and drove itself into the dry-dock lock at its maximum speed of eighteen knots. Commander Beattie gave the order to set the explosives and to scuttle the ship. The commandos disembarked. Meanwhile, the motor torpedo boats fired torpedoes with delayed explosive charges into the dry-dock's foundation. The commandos deployed and kept the Germans at bay, despite massive and intense effort on the part of their adversaries. Captain Ryder himself came ashore during this firestorm of battle to inspect the ship to ensure that it was both scuttled and embedded in the dry-dock's lock. It was now 02:30, and Ryder's force was taking heavy casualties, so he ordered the withdrawal to begin. Of the eighteen coastal craft employed in the operation, only four survived.

Lieutenant Colonel Newman and No. 2 Commando continued to fight to cover the withdrawal of the others and to prevent the Germans from discovering the now-ticking explosives. He and his commandos continued to fight until they were completely out of ammunition, then surrendered.

Unable to escape because so many launches were destroyed, Lieutenant Commander Beattie was also captured. It is said that an interrogator berated him saying, "Surely, you didn't think that ramming your silly little boat into the lock would destroy it?" At that moment, the explosive charge went off with a thundering noise and a tremendous fireball. It instantly killed 200 or more of the enemy that were milling on and around the scuttled ship. Without missing a beat, Beattie answered his interrogator's question: "No, we didn't."[1]

On the evening of March 29, the delayed torpedoes exploded causing further damage and German casualties. The dry-dock gates were completely destroyed and not repaired until after the war.

However, of the 241 British commandos who took part in the raid, fifty-nine were killed or missing and 109 were captured. Also, eighty-five Royal Navy personnel were killed or missing, and a further twenty were captured. Many more of both commandos and navy men were wounded. Five of those listed as missing managed to escape over land and returned to England through Spain.

The *Tirpitz* was trapped in Norwegian waters for lack of a port. The threat it posed was removed. Combined-operations historians still consider this the greatest commando raid. It was successful because three commando leaders and their commandos didn't stop until they won. All three leaders received the Victoria Cross, Britain's highest decoration for bravery.[2]

Many times, the only difference between success and failure is that special operations people simply don't quit. You, and those you lead, need to understand this in your gut. You are simply going to keep going until you get there. If you are a commando, it is assumed that you are unstoppable. This is both an attitude and a fact.

Ray Kroc Succeeded Because He Kept Going

There aren't many entrepreneurs who can claim to have actually changed the American way of life. If you look at nontechnical areas, there are even fewer. Ray Kroc is one of those very few. He's the leader responsible for "the Golden Arches," the man who built McDonald's.

Kroc revolutionized American buying habits. He created such concepts as food service automation, franchising, and shared national training and advertising and made them work. He was a fifty-two-year-old mixer salesman when he first became involved with McDonald's. From a single outlet started by the McDonald brothers in San Bernardino, California, Kroc built a business whose annual sales today are counted in the billions of dollars.

Ray Kroc did an awful lot right. But, as he himself contended, his biggest secret was simply that he continued toward his goal no matter what happened. In fact, the very title of the book that he wrote telling the story of McDonald's founding and development expresses this fact. It's called *Grinding It Out*. In this book, Kroc states that the key element in the success of McDonald's could be found in his favorite quotation. It comes from the former president, Calvin Coolidge:

> Press-On: Nothing in the world can take the place of persistence. Talent will not; nothing is more common than unsuccessful men with talent. Genius will not; unrewarded genius is almost a proverb. Education will not; the world is full of educated derelicts. Persistence and determination alone are omnipotent.[3]

Three Qualities of Determined Commandos

To get your organization to adopt Kroc's philosophy, to press on with persistence and determination and not quit, demands three qualities in special ops leaders and their commandos:

■ A tough mental attitude

■ Flexibility

■ Determination in the face of adversity

A Tough Mental Attitude

We might well consider adopting Winston Churchill's tough mental attitude for our commandos and ourselves. On October 29, 1941, Churchill was visiting Harrow School that he had attended as a youth. Asked to speak, his words included those that are so-oft quoted: "Never give in! Never give in. Never, never, never, never—on nothing, great or small, large or petty—never give in except to convictions of honor and good sense."

Clearly, he had the actions of the ongoing war in mind, since things had not always been going so well for England. However, his tough mental attitude, clearly embodied in these words, filtered down to his commandos—including those who made the Saint Nazaire raid.

This Man Couldn't Read, but Founded Kinko's Anyway

Paul Orfalea had, and still has, dyslexia. As a result, Orfalea hated school and was frequently expelled. He flunked the second grade and spent time in a school for students with learning disabilities. He finally graduated from high school, eighth from the bottom, out of a class of 1,200.[4] He was a self-described "woodshop major" with a solid D average.

Maybe having to overcome limitations is what gave Orfalea his mental toughness. He decided he would go to college, despite his dyslexia and despite his academic performance in high school. It wasn't easy, but he used what he had: his personality, his brains, and his ability to persuade. He got to a junior college and, through sheer guts, determination, and an unbelievably tough mental attitude, took the courses he needed. He was later able to transfer to, and eventually graduate from, the University of Southern California.[5]

But how does a man who can't read get a job? Not easily, so Orfalea created his own job. Recognizing the need that college students had for copying, in 1970 he borrowed $5,000 and opened a small store near the University of California, Santa Barbara campus. The copier he bought wouldn't fit in the store, so it was positioned out on the sidewalk. Inside he sold paper, pens, and other school material. He called the store "Kinko's" after a nickname given him to describe his fuzzy hair.

Orfalea knew that the keys to his success were his employees, the care and motivation he provided to them, and the service they provided to his customers. He took care of both: employees and customers. He couldn't read well, but he could inspire, and he inspired his employees with the same tough mental attitude that he had acquired. He built a following among the students by offering services that other shops didn't, including twenty-four-hour word processing and copying services.

His mental toughness was not an insignificant asset, because he knew in his gut he could handle every obstacle that appeared—and he did. As personal computers and campus copy shops became more common, many competitors went out of business. Orfalea went upscale with higher-quality color printers; he introduced new services for binding student reports and duplicating articles ordered by professors for classes. Again, it was his tough mental attitude that got him through. He knew that he could hold customers by serving them well. He opened many stores and flourished.

However, everything threatened to tumble down in the early 1990s, when Kinko's and Paul Orfalea and his business commandos faced one of their greatest challenges. By then, faculty members across the country had become accustomed to using Kinko's stores to print and sell copies of articles they wanted their students to read. It had become a big part of the business. Several academic publishers launched a lawsuit challenging this practice. The company's lawyers argued that this type of duplicating for small groups such as school classrooms was included in the fair-use doctrine. However, the court disagreed. Overnight, a major source of revenue disappeared.[6] Some predicted Kinko's demise. Orfalea disagreed

He shifted his company strategy again, this time focusing on business firms and offering new and greater services, including KinkoNet. With this service, business executives could work on their sales presentations until the very last minute and then zap it straight from their personal computers to Kinko's. Not only that, they didn't need to go to a local store to pick up anything. They could arrange to have professionally bound color copies waiting for them in almost any city on their arrival for a scheduled meeting.

At the time of Orfalea's retirement as chairman in 2000, Kinko's had become the world's leading provider of visual communications services and document copying. It had a global network of more than 1,000 digitally connected locations and offered twenty-four-hour access to technology for high-volume color printing, documents on demand, and electronic file submission. Paul Orfalea, the man with the tough mental attitude, may not have been able to read well, but he had built a $1.8 billion business with 25,000 employees (a business that was purchased by Federal Express in 2004) and made major contributions to companies and industries throughout the world using his products and services.

Flexibility

Many people keep doing things in the same old way they have been taught. They don't change no matter what. As a result, they are certain to fail eventually. If the plan calls for certain actions, they will carry them out to the letter. This approach is fine, as long as nothing happens in the environment to deviate from the plan. But as we have said before, no plan is perfect once you start to implement it. Unfortunately, some people will keep doing the planned thing even when conditions have changed and this action is clearly the wrong one to take. They are not commandos.

Commandos know all about things not going as planned. They expect problems and are flexible. They may change their strategy, but they keep moving toward their objective. They try something else and follow the dictates of Roger's Rangers: If everything else fails, disregard the rules and go ahead anyway. They keep focused on their objective, make changes as necessary, and keep moving in the right direction regardless. But could any commando organization be so flexible as to operate when assigned varied assignments, on different continents in different theaters of war, with none of these assignments having to do with the original mission, or even located in the same country for which the commandos were organized? One did.

The Most Flexible Commandos

The 1st Special Service Force (introduced in Chapter 12) was recruited for a special project that never took place. It was formed to conduct winter hit-and-run raids against Nazi forces occupying Norway and Rumania, to blow up hydroelectric plants, power stations, and the like. The scheme was built on snow. For nearly half of the year 1944, much of Europe was covered in snow. A British eccentric by the name of Geoffrey Pyke theorized that whatever country mastered the snow would control Europe. He devised the Plough Project, which was a plan for parachuting men into snow-covered areas so they would destroy important strategic Axis targets.[7]

Commando recruiters looked for Americans and Canadians who had been forest rangers, hunters, lumberjacks, and game wardens. The recruits were carefully selected under the recruiting motto, "Vigorous Training, Hazardous Duty: For Those Who Measure Up, Get into the War Quick."[8]

However, further analyses showed that the anticipated raids would require the considerable diversion of other resources to support them. Military planners decided that their original plans for destroying such targets through bombing was still best, so the operation was abandoned.

However, the Forcemen, as they called themselves—173 officers and 2,194 commandos under the command of Colonel Robert T. Frederick—had already been recruited and trained. In fact, they were among the most highly trained commandos of any army during World War II.[9] Now it was a highly trained force without a mission. But the First Special Service Force was flexible. They were given a new mission. Invade Kiska in the Aleutian Islands and seize it from the Japanese. The commando brigade carried out its orders. However, the landing was unopposed, the Japanese having abandoned Kiska before the assault, so the Forcemen were disappointed.

From the cold of Kiska and northern Alaska, the Forcemen were sent to Italy. There they were given the mission of securing the 3,000-foot Monte la Difensa, an important component of German defenses. Senior commanders thought the job would take at least three days. A German panzer grenadier division, well entrenched along the slopes of the two masses, had already thrown back repeated Allied attempts to gain control of the heights. But the Forcemen scaled a 200-foot cliff in the rear and got behind the German defenses. They completed the job in two hours.

After further combat, at the price of significant losses, the Force-men were fortified with 250 Rangers and sent to Anzio. Because of their actions at Anzio (described in Chapter 12), they acquired their nickname: the Devil's Brigade. After this battle, they were withdrawn from combat and refitted, then participated in the assault that took Rome. The unit was the first into Rome, and its assignment was to capture seven key bridges before they could be blown up by the Germans, a mission the Forcemen accomplished successfully.[10]

Withdrawn and refitted again, the Forcemen participated in the amphibious landings in southern France. They were given the mission of destroying German artillery located on various small islets on the flank of the invasion force. They landed by rubber boats and captured the islets from the astonished German defenders in two days. They then joined the 1st Airborne Task Force on the mainland and fought eight battles in three weeks. Afterward, they fought their way northward to the border area between Italy and France. It was their swan song. The 1st Special Service Force, which had fought so bravely under so many varied conditions as to almost impossibly test the limits of flexibility, was inactivated in 1945.

Determination in the Face of Adversity

Let's face it. The whole idea of employing commandos is to overcome adversity. That's true both on the battlefield and in the boardroom. Your commandos must have the determination to see things through to the end, come what may . . . and sometimes the "what may" can be pretty horrific.

Night Stalkers Don't Quit

The 160th Special Operations Aviation Regiment was formed in October 1981 to support U.S. Army special operations missions. Because of their unique night capabilities, they were known as "the Night Stalkers." Their primary mission included clandestinely infiltrating, supporting, and retrieving special operations forces from behind enemy lines and rescuing personnel in hostile environments, as well as carrying out routine combat patrols.

On October 21, 1983, the unit received a short notice order to plan for what became known as Operation Urgent Fury in Grenada. Two days earlier, Grenadian Prime Minister Maurice Bishop and a number of his top aides were murdered by a Marxist revolutionary council in a power struggle. If that weren't enough, 600 militarily trained Cuban workers and other advisers were present, and a 10,000-foot runway capable of handling military transports was under construction. These facts, coupled with concern for the safety of several hundred American medical students on the island, caused President Ronald Reagan to act.

In a major miscalculation, the commandos were briefed to expect little, if any, opposition. Based on this intelligence briefing, the crews were armed only with .38-caliber pistols and six rounds of ammunition. There was even talk of leaving their gunships back at their base. Fortunately, they didn't.

The 160th was trained for clandestine infiltration and exfiltration of special ops personnel in hostile locations. The unit's objectives during Operation Urgent Fury were to infiltrate the radio/TV station, the governor's mansion, and the Richmond Hill prison. Senior members of the revolutionary Marxist council were living at the prison, and various civil servants arrested by the council were imprisoned there as well. Grenada's governor general, Sir Paul Scoon, was a known target, and protecting him was the reason for the infiltration planned for his residence. Taking over the radio/TV station was a primary objective for the entire operation.

Two of the three objectives would be successfully accomplished through Night Stalker efforts, and it wasn't through lack of trying that the third objective wasn't accomplished.

The plan at the prison was for six helicopters to hover while the assault force "fast roped" to the ground to capture the Marxist council members and free the prisoners. Three other helicopters assigned to the missions at the other localities would simultaneously break off and proceed on their assignments.

The first thing to go wrong is that the assault should have been made at night—in fact, that was the original plan. However, due to various high-level administrative screw-ups, the commandos got off the ground from their staging area in Barbados five hours late. So they made their approach during daylight with the rising sun and with little surprise, since it was already several hours after Operation Urgent Fury began. Still, intelligence had reported they would encounter only lightly armed prison guards who were unlikely to fire, so the force hoped for the best.

That hope didn't last long. En route they picked up a local radio report from Grenada alerting listeners to attend to their weapons and to shoot down incoming American aircraft. Rounding a hill south of the prison, the helicopters came under a massive barrage of antiaircraft fire. As they attempted to hover to disgorge the Delta Force and Ranger commandos, the enemy fire became so intense that it was clear that their planned method of disembarking their commandos wouldn't work. They withdrew to regroup and then approached the prison to try something else. This time the antiaircraft fire was even more intense. Every single helicopter was hit and damaged and had wounded aircrew and commandos.

The assault force, now incapable of carrying out their mission, headed out to sea in the hopes of locating an American warship. However, before they could even leave the coast, one of the damaged helicopters crashed. The remaining seven located a ship, and once onboard, their wounded were removed and treated. With minimal crews the damaged helicopters took off again for Salinas airfield, located on the southern tip of Grenada. It was still in enemy hands, and the helicopters came under fire again. However, Rangers parachuting from U.S. Air Force transports only minutes later captured the airfield and all seven badly damaged Blackhawks were repaired sufficiently to return to Barbados, landing with minimum fuel.

Meanwhile, two of the original force of nine helicopters had proceeded to the governor's mansion. These helicopters also immediately came under fire: from the mansion, the prison, and the city proper. They withdrew briefly and went in again. On the second attempt, one helicopter was successful in disembarking its commandos at the front of the mansion. The commandos drove the enemy force out of the building, but not before the enemy hit the second helicopter that was landing its commando passengers. Ultimately, both helicopters were able to recover at sea after completing their mission. Only the helicopter assaulting the radio/TV station was able to accomplish its mission without sustaining casualties.

Richmond Hill prison wasn't taken until the morning of the third day by a combined force of U.S. Marines and Rangers, with heavy air support that had been unavailable when the 160th attacked in the early morning of the first day.

Operation Urgent Fury was probably one of the worst failures of American intelligence of the period. There were many other lessons learned from this operation. Yet, despite flying against a heavily armed and totally unexpected Cuban and Grenada force, the 160th Special

Operations Aviation Regiment completed its mission and earned the motto "Night Stalkers Don't Quit," which it still proudly proclaims.[11]

Mary Kay Ash, that incredible commando leader who built the billion dollar Mary Kay Cosmetics Company used to exhort her commandos to greater things by reminding them that those who were successful did everything required "and then some." It was the "and then some" that made all the difference.

Commando Notes

The key to successful special operations is not quitting, no matter what. That is, you must keep going until you win. You can change your strategy; you can be adaptable; you can do what you want. But what you cannot do is stop or give up. Perseverance makes all the difference in performance. You can get high levels of performance if you imbue your commandos with mental toughness, warn them away from rigidity in their thinking, and lead them by demonstrating your own determination to see things through, regardless of adversity.

14 FIGHT TO WIN

"Victories that are cheap, are cheap. Those only are worth having which come as a result of hard fighting."
—Henry Ward Beecher

"Whoever wants to keep alive must aim at victory. It is the winners who do the killing and the losers who get killed."
—Xenophon, 431–352 B.C.

K N U T E   R O C K N E was the greatest of Notre Dame coaches, but in the 1928 season he was desperate. His team had been decimated by injuries. It had already lost two of its first six games. Contests against three teams, all powerhouses, lay ahead. Army was the first of these three, and Army had had an undefeated season up to that point. Army was the out-and-out favorite. On top of this disturbing situation, stories were going around that Rockne had "lost it"—that he was no longer the coach he once was. Rockne knew that if his Irish could upset Army, this notion would be largely dispelled. Moreover, the wily old coach had a plan. What happened wasn't an accident. We know this because despite the odds against it, he actually told his neighbor that Notre Dame would win the game with Army before the game was played. Considering the known facts, that was quite a prediction.

How could Rockne make such a prediction? What was his plan? Notre Dame might not be able to win on talent, but Rockne knew that other things that can't be defined usually count for a lot more. Rockne played to win. To win, he would deliver what would later become known as the most famous inspirational talk in sports history.

The game was played at Yankee Stadium before 85,000 fans. Some same it was before the game that the event occurred. Others say it was at half-time. It really doesn't make that much difference when it happened. That it did happen is what is important. Rockne huddled his players in the locker room. It is said that they sat on the cold cement floor on old army blankets, surplus from World War I. The blankets were uncomfortable and barely retarded the chill from the cement floor. Rockne waited patiently until the room was silent and then began to speak slowly and softly. This was pretty unusual and captured immediate attention, because Rockne was known for his fiery half-time speeches. He began talking about George Gipp, a player who had played for Notre Dame eight years earlier. Gipp had died during his senior year at Notre Dame.

Gipp had an incredible four-year, thirty-two-game college football career. Known as "the Gipper," he had scored twenty-one touchdowns during which the Fighting Irish had won twenty-seven, lost two, and tied three games. On defense, Gipp was equally outstanding. Some called him invincible. Not a single pass was completed in his protective zone during his entire four years of play. During Gipp's final twenty games, Notre Dame's record was 19-0-1, with the team scoring an incredible 560 points to their opponents' miserable 97.

Gipp was Notre Dame's first all-American, the greatest player of his time, and Rockne's present team knew all about him. Unfortunately, during his senior year Gipp contracted a strep infection. In his last game, Notre Dame trailed Northwestern. Rockne kept Gipp out of the game because of the throat infection. Notre Dame fans demanded that their hero enter the fray. They chanted "Gipp! Gipp!" over and over again. Gipp begged to be put into the game. Rockne finally relented and let the pleading Gipp onto the field, despite his throat ailment and a painful shoulder injury that he had also incurred. Without fanfare, Gipp immediately made a touchdown. He remained in the game, probably in great pain, until the Notre Dame victory was certain. Only then did he take himself out. But his throat infection was worse than Rockne or anyone else imagined. Two weeks later he was forced to enter the hospital. The infection was now coupled with pneumonia.

From there, it was all downhill. Doctors tried everything, but they could do nothing. The mighty Gipp was failing. Rockne had been frequently at Gipp's bedside. Rockne told his team that he had kept Gipp's last words to himself, but now was the time for him to tell them the story.

"The day before he died, George Gipp asked me to wait until the situation seemed hopeless—then ask a Notre Dame team to go out and beat Army for him. This is the day, and you are the team." Then he said, "These were Gipp's last words to me: 'I've got to go, Rock. It's all right. I'm not afraid. Sometime, Rock, when the team is up against it, when things are wrong and the breaks are beating the boys—tell them to go in there with all they've got and win just one for the Gipper. I don't know where I'll be then, Rock. But I'll know about it, and I'll be happy.'"

Line coach Ed Healey said later, "There was no one in the room that wasn't crying. There was a moment of silence, and then all of a sudden those players ran out of the dressing room and almost tore the hinges off the door. They were all ready to kill someone."

Notre Dame was behind by six points when Notre Dame player Jack Chevigny made a one-yard plunge over Army's goal line to tie the score at 6-6. He immediately shook off the Army players who had tried to stop him and shouted so that everyone could hear: "That's one for the Gipper!"

In the fourth period Chevigny was spearheading Notre Dame's drive to the game-winning score when he was tackled so hard that he was badly injured and had to be taken out of the game. Even so, he refused to leave the field. He huddled on the bench. Now things were even more difficult for the Irish. They were at the Cadet's 32-yard line when left halfback Butch Niemiec took the ball and threw a pass over an Army defender. It wasn't a great pass, but he managed to put it in range of his receiver, Johnny O'Brien. O'Brien plucked the ball from the air on Army's 10-yard line and, without stopping, clutched the ball to his chest. He miraculously snaked past two Army tacklers and dove into the end zone. It was a clean touchdown.

O'Brien had never been and never became a starter in his entire football career. He was not on the first team. He was not a great player. Rockne put him in when Chevigny was injured because there was no one else. It didn't make any difference. Notre Dame now led Army 12-6. But the Cadets hadn't suddenly become pushovers. They were still a top-ranked team and they played to win, too. Could Notre Dame hold onto its lead?

With less than two minutes to go, the West Point cadets charged through the Notre Dame defense, after a spectacular 55-yard kickoff return by Army all-American Chris Cagle. Cagle, who had played the entire game, collapsed at the 10-yard line from the effort. He had given it his all and was carried from the field in a semiconscious state due to extreme exhaustion. This was a story of two teams, one the top-ranked team in the nation, the other, much less talented but playing on sheer emotion. But both teams were fighting with every ounce of strength they possessed.

Cagle's teammate Dick Hutchinson, who later became an Air Force colonel, took the ball and got it first to the Irish four and then, on a second play, to the Notre Dame one-yard line. But the clock was ticking, and it was over. Time ran out before the Cadets could run another play. Notre Dame fulfilled Rockne's pregame prediction. Against all odds and sober calculations, it had "won one for the Gipper."[1]

Don't Fool Around—Play to Win!

It makes little sense to spend the effort to incorporate any of the special ops leadership methods we have discussed in the previous chapters if you do not intend to win. There is absolutely no other reason for even reading this book unless you intend to apply the concepts to be successful in whatever projects you anticipate or are currently involved in. Rockne won, and his team won, because they intended to do so, no matter what. They were determined to "win one for the Gipper." They fought to win.

One thing that should be clear is that all commandos, business or military—all of them that you read about in the previous chapters—fought to win. They did not hold back. They put everything they had into whatever their enterprise. They risked all. Not just financial resources, but time, effort, physical blood, and emotional response. Each and every commando leader poured his soul into his enterprise. There was no other way of becoming successful and winning. There was no such thing as coming in second. They either ended up in first place or they perished, or if in business, they failed.

Let's be absolutely clear about this. If you intend to build a commando organization, you must fight to win. I will positively guarantee you that it will not be easy. You are going to encounter obstacles along the way that you never even dreamed of. At times you are going to wish you had never even speculated about adopting commando ideas to your business. You are going to get tired; you are going to wonder whether it is really worth it. You are going to long for the old, easy times. You are going to doubt yourself, your abilities, and your commandos. You are going to wonder whether anyone can succeed under the difficulties you face. You will be tempted to quit and go back to the old, easier ways.

I can't guarantee that you will always succeed. No one can do that. But I can guarantee this: If you follow the concepts laid out in the previous chapters and apply them, you will have given yourself the best possible chances at success, regardless of the task or project and the odds against your succeeding. But when things get tough, as they always will, there are things that we can do to help restore and boost our confidence, faith, and fighting spirit. When the team is up against it, when things are wrong and the breaks are "beating the boys," it is the fighting spirit of your commandos that will see you through every time. The great Knute Rockne knew that there are some things of the spirit and psyche that are more important than mere facts. Like Rockne, there are actions that you can take to give yourself the opportunity to overcome all difficulties and go on to victory. Like Notre Dame in the 1928 Army game, you can fight to win and you can win, too, and I don't care about the odds.

Here is another story of commandos who fought to win and thereby changed history.

At Thermopylae, the Spartans Fought to Win

Ancient Sparta was a city-state. It was smaller than many other Greek city-states, maybe a few thousand citizens and a large village of mud huts. However, there was one thing absolutely unique about the Spartans. They valued their independence above all else. Consequently, they were willing to do anything to ensure it. That meant maintaining an unbeatable military force. Unlike other Greek city-states, every able-bodied male served in Sparta's standing army, and they trained all year around. The training was unbelievably tough and brutal, with injuries common and almost universal. No one was exempt from the army or this continual training. Even the Spartan king fought and served. Spartan mothers told their sons that in battle they must either return victorious with their shields or dead on them. Sparta had the acknowledged best army in Greece, and any aggressor, within or without, had to consider this fact.

Nor could just anybody claim Spartan citizenship and become a Spartan. Unlike Athens and other Greek city-states, you couldn't acquire Spartan citizenship with its heavy demands—you had to be born a Spartan. You might live in Sparta, and you could, say, run a business.

However, you couldn't serve in her army. This hard service was only entrusted to citizens.

For some years, Xerxes I, king of Persia, had been preparing to continue the war against the Greeks started by his father Darius. Darius was king of Persia at the famous Battle of Marathon, which Greece won. Marathon is famous because of the legend that a Greek soldier, Pheidippides, sacrificed his life to run from Marathon to Athens with news of the victory. However, the Battle of Marathon was a fleabite for the Persians. They weren't done, not by a long shot, and they had no intention of this minor defeat stopping them. Darius was later killed elsewhere, but his son Xerxes hadn't given up the idea of conquering Greece. Persia had already conquered a good deal of the ancient world by then. It was the largest empire in the known world.

In 484 B.C., Xerxes's army and navy arrived in Asia Minor to invade Greece. To cross the Bosphorus strait, the Persians built a bridge of boats lashed together over a mile long. His army was immense. Several contemporaries claimed that it numbered in the millions. That hardly seems possible. Most historians today estimate that Xerxes's army probably numbered around 200,000, maybe 250,000 tops. Still, the number of Greeks under arms didn't even come close.[2]

The major Greek city-states formed an alliance, led by Sparta under King Leonidas. Leonidas championed the idea of blocking the Persian advance at the narrow pass of Thermopylae in northern Greece. If the Persians could be held at the pass long enough for the Greeks to mobilize, form a viable army, and reconstitute the Athenian navy, it was thought that the Greeks stood a chance in first relieving the force sent to block the pass and then defeating the Persians as they had at Marathon.

The Greeks were able to assemble several thousand men. These troops were spearheaded by a commando-like force of 300 Spartans under King Leonidas himself. First, it was a race as to whether the Greeks or Persians would get to the pass first. The Greeks won this part of the battle by arriving first, in early August of 480 B.C.

When Xerxes arrived at the scene, he was stunned that such a small force would dare oppose him. He offered to negotiate with Leonidas. Persia had many subject states. They were treated well. Why not Greece? All Leonidas had to do was withdraw and nobody would get hurt. He gave Leonidas five days to retreat and open the pass. A Persian negotiator told Leonidas that even with Xerxes's "artillery" (i.e., bowmen) alone, his numbers were such that the Persian arrows would blot out the sun. Leonidas refused to budge. Tradition says that he retorted, "Good, then we'll have our fight in the shade."

Xerxes next sent forth a herald offering very simple terms: "Lay down your weapons and you will be allowed to live." King Leonidas responded with the only answer a free citizen and a commando leader fighting to win, regardless of the odds, can give to an offer like that: "Molon Habe." That's ancient Greek for "Come and get us."[3]

Xerxes still waited patiently for five days, disbelieving that the Greeks would really fight against such odds. He sent for Demaratus, a Spartan King who had been exiled. Xerxes wanted to know whether the Spartans would really fight against such odds as his army represented. Demaratus told him that "one-against-one, they are as good as anyone in the world. But when they fight together, they are the best of all. For though they are free men, they are not entirely free. They accept the Law as their master. And they respect this master more than your subjects respect you. Whatever the Law commands, they do. And this command never changes: It forbids them to flee in battle, whatever the number of their foes. He requires them to stand firm—to conquer or die."[4]

When the Greeks did not withdraw, as expected, Xerxes attacked. However, because of the narrowness of the pass, only a limited number of his soldiers could enter at one time. He launched wave after wave, but each wave of soldiers, even his vaunted "immortals," was defeated in turn by the Greeks led by the indomitable Spartans. Leonidas took advantage of weaponry best suited for the mission of defending the pass, too. Persian standard-issue short spears were at a disadvantage because they could not easily break through the long spears of the Greek hoplites. The first day of battle ended with the death of thousands of Persians and their allies and very few Greeks. The second day of battle was a repeat of the first.

At this point a traitor named Ephialtes defected to the Persians and told Xerxes of a little-known path around the Thermopylae pass. The alternate route was guarded, but by Phocians, not Spartans, and these troops were unprepared. If attacked, they were supposed to hold until they could warn Leonidas. When the Persians attacked, the Phocians offered a brief resistance and then fled without giving the required warning. As a result, the way was open and the Persians poured through this pathway unopposed.

When Leonidas finally learned of the Persian breakthrough, it was too late. He recognized that his orginal plan of holding the pass until the Greek alliance could send a relieving force was no longer possible. He ordered all Greeks to withdraw to fight another day—except his 300 Spartan commandos. A small contingent of Thespians volunteered to stay as well. Their objective now was to delay the Persians to allow the bulk of the Greek force to escape. They were fighting not to win a battle, but a war, and all recognized that the price of achieving their objective was to be their lives.

The Spartans killed many Persians, including two of Xerxes's brothers. Persian casualties were estimated by historians at more than 20,000. The last Spartans were killed as they went forward to recover the body of King Leonidas. He had been in the forefront of the fighting when he was killed, along with all 300 of his Spartans.

Except for the Spartans, the bulk of the Greek force at Thermopylae escaped. The determination of the Spartan commandos, at the cost of their lives, gave the Greek alliance time to organize and build. The Persians advanced into central Greece and captured Athens, but the Greeks had already withdrawn to the city of Salamis on an island off the coast. It was here that the new Athenian navy stood ready. The stand made by Leonidas and the Spartan commandos encouraged the Greeks to fight against superior numbers, and it simultaneously disheartened the Persians. The Battle of Salamis was a tremedous Greek victory, the equivalent of the Greeks "winning one for the Gipper." The battle was so decisive that Xerxes left his army in place and sailed home. Greece remained independent. All we know of democracy and more that has affected Western civilization is a gift from those 300 Spartan commandos and their leader King Leonidas, bought and paid for in 480 B.C. with their lives.[5]

At the site of the battle, Simonides, one of Greece's greatest ancient poets, wrote this epigram to the Spartans:

> Go and tell the Spartans, stranger passing by,
> That here, obedient to their laws, we lie.[6]

The Spartans fought to win.

Business Commandos Build an Airplane

In the early 1970s, I spent three years in Israel and got a good look at both the country and Israel Aircraft Industries, or IAI. IAI was founded in 1953 by an American, Al Schwimmer, to assist the fledgling Israeli

Air Force with aircraft maintenance and parts manufacture at a time when, greatly outnumbered in men and material, Israel was at war with seven Arab states. The United States and Russia claimed neutrality, but maintained an embargo on war material, as did many other countries. Until 1957, Great Britain supplied Israel's enemies. Schwimmer's operation was all Israel had in the way of support for its air force.

By the early 1960s, IAI was the largest company in Israel. Israel was still at war with its Arab neighbors, but it was now the Soviet Union that was lending military support to Israel's adversaries. Now the British and the United States were neutral, but Israel had gained a major ally in France. France had sold Israel seventy-eight first-line Mirage III fighter jets to oppose the Russian MIG-21s and MIG-23s flown by Egypt, Syria, and Iraq. Because of the disproportionate military equipment sent from the Soviet Union to the Arab countries, President John F. Kennedy lifted the total embargo of war materials to Israel and sold it Hawk antiaircraft missiles, but no airplanes.

In 1967, using her Mirage fighters, Israel successfully fought the Six-Day War against superior numbers of aircraft from Egypt, Syria, Iraq, and Jordan. France had also developed an advanced model of the Mirage, designated the Mirage V, with Israeli input and help. Israel had paid for fifty of these new aircraft, which were manufactured in France but had not yet been delivered. Meanwhile, as France withdrew from Algeria, French foreign policy had shifted. Probably to make its change of position clear, France eventually sent these fifty aircraft to Libya's dictator, Muammar Gaddafi. About this time, President Lyndon Johnson made the decision to sell a U.S. aircraft for the first time. This was the F-4 fighter. Nevertheless, Israel decided that it shouldn't depend on the goodwill of another country, but must do something on its own.

The decision to build an Israeli fighter did not come lightly to the Israeli government. Although IAI had earlier manufactured a French military training plane under license, it had never designed a first-line fighter. The investment would be tremendous, and experts weren't even certain IAI could pull it off. As an interim measure, the decision was made to modernize Israel's aging Mirage IIIs.

The Mirage had a well-designed airframe, but its Atar 9 engine produced only 9,500 pounds of thrust, so the airplane was underpowered. Because of the U.S. sale of American planes, the Israeli Air Force was flying U.S. F-4s powered by General Electric J-79 engines. Each J-79 produced about 11,000 pounds of thrust. If a J-79 engine were mated to the Mirage III, the Mirage's performance could be significantly enhanced. Of course, the structural problems had to be solved. The Atar 9 engine was longer and the airframe would have to be modified. The cockpit and its layout would also have to be modified, and a new ejection seat would need to be developed and installed. Along the way, why not fit the airplane with the latest avionics, rather than continue to use those that were now more than ten years old? Even this modification would not be an easy task.

A young thirty-year-old engineer by the name of Ya'acov Ben Bassat was selected to lead the commando team. Ben Bassat had been born in Turkey, but immigrated to Israel as a boy. He had an engineering degree from Technion, the Israel Institute of Technology, and had spent four years as an engineer in the Israeli Air Force before coming to IAI. He was known as a man that could get things done. He selected his commando team, about a dozen engineers, and they went to work. Ben Bassat chose the right commandos, and he motivated them to fight to win. Knowing that their country's future depended on their efforts, they outdid themselves to perform, making mistakes, but not being afraid to take risks or to make quick decisions. They put in the overtime hours without pay and did everything else they could to succeed. When the modified airplane began flying and it became clear that there was no way these commandos were going to lose, the Israeli government made the decision to go one step further and authorize a completely homegrown fighter based on the Mirage V design.

Now Ben Bassat had two major aircraft development programs going at once. Amazingly, his small commando team completed both successfully. Their efforts resulted in the world-famous Kfir (Lion Cub) aircraft, adopted not only by the Israeli Air Force but other countries as well. This is extraordinary for several reasons. First, it was the very first fighter produced by a tiny country the size of New Jersey with a much smaller engineer base than the United States, the Soviet Union, England, France, Spain, Germany, and other countries that produced aircraft. Moreover, as a small country at war with far more powerful oil-producing states, Israel had relatively few countries willing to adopt such a conspicuous military product without political repercussions to the potential buyer. In addition, because the plane uses the J-79 engine, which is an American product, the United States had to grant Israel an export license for each foreign country Israel sold to. As a result, although Colombia and Ecuador bought the aircraft, they had to wait years for U.S. approval. Other countries that wanted to buy the Kfir were denied permission by the United States. Few countries wanting to buy first-line military aircraft were willing to await U.S. approval or risk being turned down. However, the U.S. Navy and Marine Corps also bought twenty-five Kfir aircraft, giving them the designation F-21A. Clearly, commandos that fight to win succeed in doing just that despite the obstacles.

Commando Notes

I've seen the insides of hundreds of businesses in every industry you can think of, and when they are commando-run, you can tell the difference. There's a look in the eyes of every employee, a determination to overcome all obstacles, an eagerness to take risks and get the job done that you just don't find in other organizations.

Commandos play, fight, and do business to win. This doesn't mean that they act unethically or without integrity. True commandos do not lie, cheat, or steal in their quest for victory. As that great football coach Vince Lombardi, once a line coach at West Point long before he became the legendary coach of the Green Bay Packers, is quoted as saying: "Winning isn't everything. It is the only thing." Commandos fight to win.

15 FINAL THOUGHTS ON SPECIAL OPS LEADERSHIP

"Whatsoever things are true, whatsoever things are honest, whatsoever things are just, whatsoever things are pure, whatsoever things are lovely, whatsoever things are of good report; if there be any virtue, and if there be any praise, think on these things."
—Philippians 4:8

"A man should never stop learning, even on his last day."
—Maimonides

SOME IMPORTANT POINTS about special ops leadership don't fit neatly into any of the fourteen practices/strategies covered in previous chapters. None require so much explanation that they deserve chapters of their own. Yet these ideas are sufficiently important that they should not be omitted. Therefore, these thoughts and concepts are covered in this final chapter.

Leadership Isn't About Talking Tough

Over the years I have read a number of books written by former commandos and others regarding special operations leadership applied to business. Perhaps to dramatize the commando concept, some of these authors express their ideas in the most warlike terms possible. They speak of killing and winning at any cost. Frankly, killing and winning at any cost is not necessarily true even in every single battle situation. The misleading idea you get is that if you want to apply special ops leadership practices to your business organization, you need to express yourself as if you were some sort of god of war. This is a major fallacy.

First, any leader should adjust her manner and speaking to the audience being addressed. It's okay to talk tough and to be tough when circumstances require it. General George Patton actually practiced looking tough in front of a mirror every day to optimize what he called "his war face." (We know this for a fact because he wrote his wife Bea and told her so.) His profanity and tough talk could be pretty effective in leading his men in combat or in preparing them when they were about to go into battle. However, Patton got himself fired by General Dwight D. Eisenhower when he used this tough and profane language when making a speech to a group of Gold Star mothers who had lost their sons in the war. Patton knew better, but he let himself get carried away with the tough image he had developed and used with his troops.

That's probably an extreme example, but you don't need to talk tough to lead commandos, or others, even in battle. Although many combat leaders I have known did display a tough persona, some of the best did not talk so tough; they let actions speak for themselves.

This hasn't been just my experience. One of my colleagues at Touro University, where I hold an appointment as a professor, is a retired colonel from the Israeli Army by the name of Mickey Shachar. Mickey wasn't a commando, but as a combat officer in tanks, he clearly practiced what I call special ops leadership. This characteristic of his probably came, in part, from his father, who saw combat in World War II as a British commando. In one operation his father was severely wounded and lost both legs. Mickey and his brothers all fought as armor officers in Israel's wars. In two wars, Mickey was severely wounded, once escaping from the field hospital to return to his command. One brother was killed in action. Mickey and his brother were both decorated for valor in different actions. "War is hell," Mickey said. "Within the battlefield's canon roars confusion, uncertainty, on one hand—and personal emotions and fears stretched to the limits of human endurance. And, on the other, what the soldiers truly cherished was their leader's *quiet* calming voice and *sound* judgment in the eye of the maelstrom. This does not necessarily need to be 'packaged' in a Herculean frame and carry a bass voice."

In a recent discussion regarding one of the articles I wrote for *The Journal of Leadership Applications*,[1] Mickey said that some of the best combat leaders he ever met were not of the shouting, tough-talking variety. In fact, he was always suspicious of the tough talkers because he felt that some were just trying to cover up their own insecurities. So the point here is that you don't have to be some sort of a hard-talking, hard-drinking, go-for-the-throat wild man to be an outstanding business commando leader. More than likely you are fine just the way you are.

Integrity First

All leaders, especially special ops leaders, need to practice absolute integrity at all times. The first sentence of The Code of the Air Commando says, "I will never forget that I am an American fighting man, placing duty, honor, country, above all else." Honor and integrity means doing what you believe to be right, no matter what.

Major Clay McCutchan was an air commando and pilot of an AC-130 gunship in the U.S. Air Force Reserve. The AC-130 is a descendent of earlier prop-driven aircraft developed primarily to attack traffic on the Ho Chi Minh Trail during the Vietnam War. The basic C-130 is a transport aircraft. Extensively modified with side firing guns and the latest acquisition electronics, the AC-130 became a formidable flying gunship. It could loiter for long periods of time until it was needed. When called upon, the AC-130 could provide unparalleled firepower to destroy most targets in areas where the ground defenses were not too heavy.

In late December 1989, Clay McCutchan and his crew were one of two U.S. Air Force Reserve crews volunteering to relieve an active-duty AC-130 crew assigned to Panama during the Christmas holidays. They had relieved active-duty crews in Panama three times before. There had been an ongoing problem with Manuel Noriega, the Panamanian dictator. But few realized how rapidly the United States was approaching war at this time . . . certainly not Clay McCutchan and his crew.

What McCutchan and others didn't know is that the decision to invade Panama and capture Noriega had already been made a few days earlier by President George H. W. Bush. The invasion, called Operation Just Cause, was set for the nights of December 19–20, 1989. As luck would have it, this was only two days after McCutchan's arrival.

The objectives of Operation Just Cause were to oust Noriega, take him into custody, and return him to the United States to stand trial on drug charges. As you probably know, that was the end result of the campaign. As in Iraq today, the United States hoped that a new, more democratic government in Panama would result. Air Force Special Operations were to spearhead the invasion. Active-duty gunship crews had practiced for months in firing at and destroying mock-ups of certain predesignated targets. Since McCutchan's crew hadn't prepared for this mission or received special training, they were given a different task. McCutchan's crew was put on standby alert to guard Howard Air Force Base, the American air base in the Canal Zone, and the Panama Canal itself, in case it came under attack. Some hours into the operation, when it became clear that the base wasn't going to be attacked, McCutchan's crew was ordered into the air to respond on call for help to friendly troops fighting on the ground.

However, there was considerable confusion in communications with friendly forces during this operation. As a result, for some time they flew around over the base without receiving an assignment. Finally, they were sent to aid a group of civilians at another airfield immobilized by a sniper. A few rounds from their 40-millimeter guns easily took care of that problem. Then they orbited the area again waiting for a new assignment. Hours went by. No one seemed to need them.

With only about an hour's fuel remaining, they were finally sent to a fortified area known as Fort Amador, where there was a large fight in progress. When they got there, they couldn't tell the good guys from the bad guys. They couldn't even establish radio contact. Without radio contact, they couldn't get instructions or permission to fire. Communications were made more difficult because they were given three different call signs to use depending on whom they were talking to. Even worse, McCutchan, flying at only 4,500 feet, was the lowest of a number of other AC-130s orbiting at different altitudes and only under marginal control of anyone on the ground. When another unseen AC-130 at a higher altitude opened fire right through their flight orbit and almost hit them, McCutchan decided it was time to get out of the way. He altered course to take his AC-130 out of the area.

Just as they flew away from the ground fighting, McCutchan's crew was ordered to attack three enemy armored cars spotted on the Fort Amador causeway. They tried calling a controller on the ground on a prebriefed radio frequency. This time they made radio contact with the forward air controller (FAC) on the ground right away. The FAC's job is to control all friendly air strikes in his assigned area.

The FAC was confident the armored cars targeted were unfriendly because the vehicles were not of a type used by our forces. "They're not friendly, you can open fire on them," advised the voice of the FAC on the ground.

McCutchan planned to start with 40-millimeter armor-piercing ammunition and then use high-explosive ammunition to finish off the armored cars. As McCutchan prepared to fire, his sensor operator and fire-control officer (FCO) spotted thirty to forty troops coming out of the jungle.

McCutchan's FCO called the controller on the ground and told him about the arrival of these new forces. "Take them out, they're not ours," shouted the controller. In the AC-130A that McCutchan flew, the pilot fired the guns using a thumb trigger. As his thumb began to itch in readiness, his crew studied the ground situation more closely using infrared and television sensors.[2] The more they looked, the more worried they became. They became convinced that these troops and their vehicles were Americans. McCutchan had just rolled his airplane in to attack when one of his crew stopped him with a sudden warning: "Don't fire, they may be friendly!"

McCutchan took his thumb off the trigger. After talking it over with his crew, he spoke to the FAC on the ground again and told him that they had identified the troops with the vehicles as possibly American.

"Negative, negative, they are not friendlies. They are enemy, and you are cleared to fire," the controller responded, his frustration clear in his voice. By now the FAC was excited. "Shoot, shoot, shoot," he repeated.

McCutchan called his command post back at Howard Air Force Base and briefed them on the situation. He asked for positive confirmation of their enemy identity. After several minutes the command post duty officer came back with a decision made by McCutchan's commander. "These are confirmed enemy. You are ordered to fire."

Now, McCutchan's actions were no longer discretionary. His commander had given him a direct order. He had also been handed the supreme test of integrity. He and his crew believed that these were friendly troops with the enemy vehicles. Usually the FAC on the ground had a much better picture of what was going on. But with their sophisticated equipment, McCutchan's crew might be in a better position to judge whether the troops were friendly or enemy in this instance. Our forces were not being fired on by these vehicles or these troops, and they were not an immediate threat to anyone, reasoned McCutchan. If they were enemy and they lived, it would make little difference to the war. But if they were friendly and he attacked, we could never bring them back to life.

Clay McCutchan told the controller he was leaving the area to return to base. He was not going to fire. "I was convinced I was going to get court-martialed because three times I disobeyed a direct order to fire," McCutchan told me when I interviewed him in 1997.

Their commander met them as they landed at dawn. "You're either a hero or in a lot of trouble," he told McCutchan.

McCutchan spent a sleepless morning despite his fatigue. He had been up all night and in the air almost six hours. By noon, the whole story came down from higher headquarters. Contact had been made with the troops surrounding the vehicles. McCutchan and his crew had been right. The troops were American commandos who had captured the enemy armored vehicles. They had been unsuccessful in contacting anyone by radio to identify themselves. McCutchan and the others on his crew were awarded medals for having the moral courage . . . the integrity . . . not to fire, even when ordered to do so. This was the exception to the rule of absolute obedience—when you know you must do what is right, even if it means the end of employment!

Typical of an outstanding leader of integrity, McCutchan gave full credit to those he led. "My crew was very experienced. I was only an average pilot, but my copilot had 1,500 hours of combat in Vietnam. All of my officers and noncommissioned officers were very experienced and absolutely top-notch. It was my sole responsibility to make this decision, but I could not have made the decision I did if I did not trust them completely."[3]

McCutchan may or may not have been an average pilot. But for certain, the U.S. Air Force recognized that he was a far above average leader. In 2001, I was invited to speak on leadership at Air War College. My escort officer was a full colonel: Clay McCutchan! Several months later, McCutchan was promoted and became a general. I was not surprised. General McCutchan had demonstrated emphatically that he was a commando who put integrity first. He did not practice an attitude of "winning at any cost," which in this instance would have meant the death of fellow-American special forces troops.

A Leader Should Always Have a Full "Bag of Tricks"

Leaders come in all shapes and sizes and styles of leadership. My first piece of advice is that you should not try to be something you are not. If you are a "hard ass" by nature, be one. If you are the friendly type, keep doing that. There are lots of styles of leadership and they all can work equally well.

The commander of coalition forces during the first Gulf War against Iraq was General H. Norman Schwarzkopf. General Schwarzkopf was known as a tough cookie. He was especially tough on his senior subordinates. It worked very well for him and he was a highly successful commander.

The commander in the second Gulf War, including for the invasion of Iraq, was General Tommy Franks. General Franks had an entirely different style of dealing with his senior commanders. He was far more easygoing and forgiving. That style worked for him and he was very successful also. So accept whatever style you have developed. If you try to be something you are not, your commandos will instantly recognize your phoniness and you are likely to fail.

However, while you want to keep one style, you want to vary the leadership tactics you use according to the situation. I have identified some tactics that are part of any leader's "bag of tricks." A good commando leader may use any or all of them, depending on the situation. Some of these tactics may sound pretty lame to you—after all, aren't you "the boss"? Yes, but sometimes your authority is very limited or temporary. Others you lead may have as much or more power than you do. Under different situations, different approaches may be necessary.

The eight major tactics are:

1. Direction—Giving orders

2. Persuasion—Giving reasons and convincing

3. Negotiation—Offering something in exchange for obedience

4. Involvement—Interesting others in the task

5. Indirection—Making desires obvious, but not mentioning them

6. Enlistment—Requesting obedience as a favor

7. Redirection—Focusing on something else more acceptable which if done, will achieve your aim

8. Repudiation—Disclaiming your own power to do the contrary of what you want

Any of these tactics may be appropriate, or equally inappropriate, depending on the situation. One particularly useful "trick" is the tactic of direction. As noted previously, on the reality TV program *The Apprentice,* a leader is chosen or appointed to lead a team competing with another team in accomplishing a business project every week. Someone is "fired" each week from the losing team and no longer has the opportunity to become Donald Trump's "apprentice" for one year at a salary of $200,000. Meanwhile, the winning team receives some kind of reward.

For several weeks during the second season, one team had lost repeatedly. Trump selected a top-performing member of the team that had been winning and switched her to the other team. He made her leader of this team for the following week. This woman took charge in a no-nonsense way and, using the direction tactic, began issuing rapid-fire orders to her new teammates. Although she was obeyed, her direction tactics were bitterly resented by her new teammates. When again this team lost the competition, everyone on the team blamed her. In the boardroom, where Trump made the decision as to who gets fired, every team member stated that the loss was due to her poor leadership. In the end, saying he had no choice, Trump fired her. Without question, her inappropriate adoption of the direction tactic in this instance was the reason for her elimination as an apprentice candidate.

Contrast this with the following leadership situation that my oldest son Barak observed when he went through U.S. Army Ranger School. In this example, the direction tactic was absolutely appropriate. In Ranger School, different battlefield missions requiring extended time in the field are assigned. These missions fall into four different phases lasting about eight weeks and involve urban, jungle, desert, and mountain commando warfare. An instructor accompanies each team of Ranger trainees. He assigns leadership roles on a rotating basis and grades the students. While in the field, Ranger trainees get little food and are sleep-deprived. The physical exertion, stress, and real danger are all significant. The elimination rate is usually 60 percent or higher for the course.

In the mountain (cold weather) phase, my son's team included a number of his West Point classmates. After several days in the field, one of his classmates was leading. He observed that another Ranger student, who was also a West Pointer, seemed to be faltering and actually fell in the snow. The student team leader went to the fallen student, yanked him to his feet roughly, and spoke to him in a threatening manner.

My son was standing next to the instructor, who did not hear what was said. The instructor beckoned to the team leader to approach him. "What did you say to that guy?" he asked. "I said that if he didn't get his act together I was going to beat the living shit out of him," answered the team leader. My son told me that the instructor nodded affirmably and said, "That's the way to do it."

Barak knew that I don't normally recommend this very physical style of leadership and wanted to know what I thought. I told him that I agreed with the instructor. Under these circumstances, where everyone was tired, hungry, and greatly stressed, one or more of the other leadership tactics were unlikely to be effective, especially since both the team leader and the trainee who fell were both West Point classmates and presumably knew each before entering Ranger training.

According to my son, this approach did work, and the faltering classmate was able to complete the mission. I told my son that while he would be ill-advised to use this direction style on a routine basis, it was one more method that he could call upon from his leadership "bag of tricks"—provided the situation needed it and he had the authority to pull it off. In this instance, the selection of the direction tactic was exactly right.

Ready, Aim, Fire

These three basic sequential commands are given to direct accurately aimed fire, in the minimum time, against a target that has been identified as important by a military leader in battle. The commands are short and the sequence involves no wasted effort or time. Yet these commands are intended not only for efficiency, but also for effectiveness.

When time is crucial and maximum firepower must be brought against a real live enemy who has the capacity to do your own organization great harm, all available force must be concentrated against the target in the shortest time possible. This action ensures the greatest shock power and probability of succeeding in overcoming or eliminating the threat, before the adversary can act first. You will recall that part of the theory of commando operations involves concentrating superior resources at a specific time and place. When combined with surprise, this tactic can make up for the fact that the commando force can be relatively small in numbers.

Even though accuracy is required, the "Ready, aim, fire" commands preceded the availability of accurate weaponry. When the weapons used in battle were highly inaccurate smoothbore muskets, similar commands were still employed to concentrate the firepower of those individual muskets available against a selected target. Individually, musket fire was inaccurate, but concentrated in this way, it was not only accurate, it was deadly. Before the advent of firearms, firepower from longbows, crossbows, and thrown spears was concentrated using the same model in almost the identical fashion. So the model has a long history of successful usage.

The Importance of Ready, Aim, Fire as a Model

Why did these commands evolve in just this way? Early battlefield commanders soon realized that simply launching a huge number of missiles in the general direction of an enemy had only a limited effect on the outcome of a particular action, despite their lethality. To be effective, missiles had to be directed against a target. When concentrated in this fashion, a target could be neutralized or destroyed. Once this had been accomplished, the commander could then direct fire against a new target and repeat the process. This process could be continued indefinitely as long as the commander had the resources to maintain the momentum.

If we look at this simple "Ready, aim, fire" model more closely, it becomes apparent that it is useful in the application of strategy to a number of different human endeavors besides battle commando operations.

The first two elements are strategic. For example, the command "Ready" assumes the identification and selection of the target. Consider a target market for a new product or service. We might select a market because of its size, growth or profit potential, the state of the competition at this particular time, the organization's fit or match with the market, our goal or objectives, or some other factor (or factors) important to us.

The "Aim" command is also strategic. Whereas during the "Ready" phase organizational fit is an important concern, now we must fit the product or service the organization offers to best satisfy the target market. In fact, it is our ability to construct this fit that defines the difference between marketing and selling. In selling, the product or service is largely fixed; the basic task of the seller is to persuade the target market to buy what already exists. In marketing, we attempt to uncover what the target market needs or wants first, and then design our product or service to fulfill the needs or wants we have identified before we ever approach a potential buyer or attempt to sell. World-famous management thinker, Peter Drucker, makes the point that if marketing were done perfectly, "selling" would be unnecessary since the seller would possess something that would already be highly desired by prospects; then, all that would be necessary would be to make the prospect aware that the product was available.

So, during the phase initiated by the command "Aim," we must make certain that we have the right product/service for this particular market and that the product/service we intend to offer has the correct attributes. That is, we want to offer exactly what this particular market wants at this particular time. During the Aim phase, we may also further define our target market to identify a segment (or segments) of the overall target market that is particularly interested or desirous of our offering.

You might note how universal this "Ready, aim, fire" model is. In this example, we're talking about the introduction of a new product. However, the same is true when seeking a new job or developing a career in your present industry, or in starting a new business. It is also necessary for effective special ops leadership in all situations. You can't be everything to everybody, but you can define a target—or understand those you desire to lead—and continue to develop yourself to best satisfy the demands of the target market you have chosen or the uniqueness of the followers you must influence and lead.

The "Fire" Phase Is Tactical

Although "Fire" is a tactical command, we must still pay attention. Those who teach marksmanship caution neophytes not to jerk the weapon while pulling the trigger to fire, because if the trigger isn't pulled smoothly, the aim is spoiled. At the moment of firing, the weapon is no longer on target. Therefore, despite all the good strategic work that has gone before in "Ready" and "Aim," you will still not hit the target.

In the example of a new product or service, the tactical variables may include the distribution system, advertising, the sales force and its methods, training, compensation, the pricing model, or sales promotional methods. None of these things can be ignored.

Yet contrary to the belief of some people, no matter how good your performance in the tactical phase, it cannot overcome the preparation that must go before. If the first two phases—"Ready, Aim"—are done poorly, your "Fire" phase will be less than optimal, no matter how good a salesperson you are or how brilliant a copywriter for advertisements. Though your firing may be perfect, you may be firing at the wrong target, or with the wrong weapon to be fully effective. Therefore, all three phases must be done correctly to be successful.

The three sequential commands originate from observations over the millennia. They are not complex or difficult to understand or to implement. However, these simple words are extremely powerful. The commands represent a model that is effective both in the application of a strategy and in leading commando organizations.

Commando Notes

Good special ops leadership requires good thinking, not martinet execution. Take the knowledge of what makes commando operations unique and leadership particularly effective and apply it to your situation. Remember that there are always limitations to its application. However, as you apply the concepts and ideas from this chapter, plus the main strategies described throughout this entire book, you will discover new opportunities to make use of the material and will be able to optimize these concepts uniquely for your organization.

Good luck, commando!

NOTES

Why Are Special Ops Special?

1. United States Special Operations Posture Statement, www.socom.mil, p. 39, accessed March 16, 2005.
2. Linda Robinson, "The View from the Inside," *U.S. News and World Report* (October 18, 2004), pp. 48–49.
3. Ira Stoll, "The Apprentice," *The New York Sun* (December 20, 2004), Editorial and Opinion, p. 1.
4. W. John Hutt, "Skills that Translate," in Brace E. Barber, *No Excuse Leadership: Lessons from the U.S. Army's Elite Rangers,* (Hoboken, NJ: Wiley, 2003) p. 218.

The Principles of Special Ops Leadership

1. Rob Landley, "How a Start-Up Evolves," *The Motley Fool* (July 31, 2000); available at http://www.fool.com/news/foth/2000/foth000731.htm (accessed June 4, 2004).
2. "Ranger History," available at http://www.globalsecurity.org/military/library/policy/army/fm/7-85/appf.htm (accessed March 22, 2004).
3. "The King Philip War," available at AOL Hometown at http://members.aol.com/Lynnash911/war.html (accessed March 22, 2004).
4. "The Battle of Lexington and Concord," *Kisport Reference Library;* available at http://www.kidport.com/RefLib/UsaHistory/AmericanRevolution/LexingtonBattle.htm#BattleLexingtonConcord (accessed October 22, 2004).
5. John S. Mosby, *The Memoirs of Colonel John S. Mosby* (Nashville: J. S. Sanders & Company, 1917), p. 181.
6. William H. McRaven, *Spec Ops: Case Studies in Special Operations Warfare in Theory and Practice* (Novato, CA: Presidio Press, 1995), p. 1.
7. McRaven, *Spec Ops,* pp. 4–23.
8. William A. Cohen, *The Art of the Strategist: 10 Essential Principles for Leading Your Company to Victory* (New York: AMACOM, 2004).

9. Peter F. Drucker, *Management: Tasks, Responsibilities, Practices* (New York: Harper & Row, Publishers, 1973), p. 77.

10. "The Ton Say Raid," available at http://www.psywarrior.com/sontay.html (accessed March 16, 2004); and Michael Nikiperenko, "The Son Tay Raid, Blue Boy Element," available at http://www.sfalx.com/h_son_tay_raid_blue_boy.htm (accessed March 16, 2004).

11. "Rogers Rangers Revenge," from Henry H. Saunderson, *History of Charlestown, NH*, Chapter V, p. 79; available at http://users.rcn.com/smartin.java net/revenge.htm (accessed March 16, 2004).

12. "Lofoton Islands Raid—3/4 March 1941," available at http://combinedops .com/Lofoten_Islands_Raid.htm (accessed March 15, 2004).

13. "The Raid on Dieppe: August 19, 1942," available at http://users.pandor a.be/dave.depickere/Text/dieppe.html (accessed March 15, 2004).

Chapter 1

1. "Bataan Rescue," from *PBS American Experience*; available at http://www .pbs.org/wgbh/amex/bataan/peopleevents/e_raid.html (accessed October 28, 2004).

2. John Richardson, quoted in "Bataan Rescue," from *PBS American Experience*; available at http://www.pbs.org/wgbh/amex/bataan/peopleevents/ p_mucci.html (accessed October 28, 2004).

3. Max De Pree, *Leadership Is an Art* (New York: Dell Publishing, 1989), p. 28.

4. John Naisbitt and Patricia Aburdene, *Reinventing the Corporation* (New York: Warner Books, 1985), pp. 85–86.

5. Ron Yeaw, quoted in Orr Kelly, *Never Fight Fair!* (New York: Pocket Books, 1995), p. 3.

6. Don Ericson and John L. Rotundo, *Charlie Rangers* (New York: Ivy Books, 1989), p. 8.

7. William A. Cohen, "Undiscovered Gold in Your Organization," *The Journal of Leadership Applications* Vol. 3, No. 2 (2004); available at http://www .stuffofheroes.com/Vol.%203,%20No.2.htm (accessed October 28, 2004).

Chapter 2

1. I consulted several sources for the description of the Entebbe rescue, including "What is the story of the IDF's operation to release the hostages from Entebbe in July 1976?" *Palestine Facts: Israel 1967–1991 Entebbe*, available at http://www.palestinefacts.org/pf_1967to1991_entebbe.php (accessed March 21, 2004), and the Israeli Defense Force's own release, translated into English at http://www.idf.il/english/organization/iaf/iaf7 .stm. I also spoke with participants. This particular action had more than

passing interest for me because when I lived in Israel and flew in the
Israeli Air Force during the Yom Kippur War of 1973, my squadron—
Squadron 120—had been assigned C-97 aircraft. The C-97 was a very old
American transport from the 1950 era. The Israeli Air Force used it for
transport, electronic countermeasures, and command-and-control work.
The squadron also owned two more modern C-130H model aircraft pur-
chased from the United States in 1972. In the middle of the Yom Kippur
War, the U.S. donated about a dozen C-130E aircraft. Squadron 120 immediately split into an additional squadron, Squadron 131, to fly the
C-130. Two years after the war, new Boeing 707s, especially modified by
Israel Aircraft Industries, Ltd. to Israeli Air Force specifications, finally
replaced the old C-97s. Squadron 120 with its 707s and Squadron 131
with its C-130s supported the assault commandos in the Entebbe raid. Of
course, by then I had left Israel and was actively seeking to be recommis-
sioned in the USAF. Nevertheless, the descendants of my old squadron
from earlier years were among those who "dared to do the impossible."

2. Virginia Cowles, *Who Dares Wins* (New York: Ballantine Books, 1958),
   p. 5.

3. Reported in *The Mammoth Book of Elite Forces* edited by Jon E. Lewis (New
   York: Carroll & Graf Publishers, 2001), p. 1.

4. Ben R. Rich, "Clarence Leonard (Kelly) Johnson," National Academy of
   Sciences Biographical Memoirs, available at http://www.nap.edu/html/
   biomems/cjohnson.html (accessed April 15, 2004).

5. "The Flying Tigers," available at the Flying Tiger Web site at http://www
   .flyingtigersavg.com/tiger1.htm (accessed October 26 2004).

6. Claire L. Chennault, *Way of the Fighter* (New York: G. P. Putnam's Sons,
   1949).

7. Charles Garfield, *Peak Performers: The New Heroes of American Business*
   (New York: Avon Books, 1986), p. 26.

8. Donna Fern, "The Lord of Discipline," *INC.* (November 1985), pp. 82–85,
   88, 95.

Chapter 3

1. Ian Padden, *U.S. Air Commando* (New York: Bantam Books, 1985), pp.
   4–18.

2. "The BluBlocker Story," available at http://www.blublocker.com/gallery/
   history.html (accessed February 9, 2004).

3. Robert Todd Carroll, "Bridey Murphy," *The Skeptic's Dictionary,* available
   at http://skepdic.com/bridey.html (accessed February 12, 2004).

4. A. C. Ping, "From Vineyard To Vat—Encouraging Innovation and Creativity" (May 1998), available at http://www.insight-works.com/Articles/

Innovation_&_Creativity/VineyardtoVat.htm (accessed February 17, 2004).

5. Mary Bellis, "Inventors: Silly Putty," available at http://inventors.about.com/library/inventors/blsillyputty.htm (accessed February 25, 2004); "Silly Putty," available at http://www.chem.umn.edu/outreach/Sillyput ty.html (accessed February 25, 2004); and Gianfranco Origliato, "Silly Putty: 50 Years," *Toy Collecting*, http://toycollecting.about.com/library/weekly/aa051800a.htm (accessed February 25, 2004).

6. James A. Lovell, "Houston, We've Had a Problem," Chapter 13.1 in *Apollo Expeditions to the Moon SP-350*, edited by Edgar M. Cortright (Washington, D.C.: Scientific and Technical Information Office, National Aeronautics and Space Administration, 1975), available at http://www.hq.nasa.gov/office/pao/History/SP-350/ch-13-1.html (accessed February 25, 2004).

7. Linda Stradley, "History of the Ice Cream Cone," available at http://www.whatscookingamerica.net/History/IceCream/IceCreamCone.htm (accessed February 27, 2004).

8. "Doolittle Raid on Japan, April 18, 1942," Department of the Navy Historical Center Online Library of Selected Images, available at http://www.history.navy.mil/photos/events/wwii-pac/misc-42/dooltl.htm (accessed February 27, 2004).

Chapter 4

1. Edwin P. Hoyt, *SEALs at War* (New York: Dell Publishing, 1993), pp. 171–172; and Congressional Medal of Honor Society, "Kerrey, Joseph R. 14 April 1969, Republic of Vietnam," available at http://www.cmohs.com/recipients/photo-citations/pcit-Kerrey-Joseph-R.htm (accessed March 12, 2004).

2. Edward O. Welles, "Captain Marvel," *INC.* (January 1, 1992); available at http://www.inc.com/magazine/19920101/3870.html (accessed March 23, 2004).

3. Ben McConnell, "The Wild, Flying Turkey with Wings" (September 1, 2001), available at http://www.creatingcustomerevangelists.com/resources/evangelists/herb_kelleh er.asp.

4. Herb Kelleher, "Commitment," *Leader to Leader* No. 4 (Spring 1997), available at http://www.pfdf.org/leaderbooks/L2L/spring97/kelleher.html (accessed March 23, 2004).

5. Michael Lyga, "Ralph S. Klimek, United States Army: Merrill's Marauders," available at the "Small Town Goes to War" Web site at http://www.indeeve terans.com/WWII/RalphKlimek.htm (accessed March 22, 2004).

6. Greg Way, *Fallschirmjäger 1936–1945*, "The rescue of Mussolini from the Gran Sasso: 12th September 1943," available at http://www.eagle19.free serve.co.uk/gransasso.htm (accessed March 22, 2004).

7. Tom Terez, "The Soft Side of a Steel Company," *BetterWorkplaceNow.com,* available at http://www.22keys.com/iverson.html (accessed March 24, 2004).

8. "About Nucor," *Nucor Website,* http://www.nucor.com/aboutus.htm, accessed March 25, 2004.

9. Ken Iverson quoted during a telephone interview with the author, October 30, 1997.

Chapter 5

1. D. Fite, "Horatius Cocles" (2001); available at http://www.dl.ket.org/latin lit/historia/people/heroes/horatius01.htm (accessed March 27, 2004); and "Roman Bridges—The Pons Sublicius," available at http://www.mmdtkw .org/VBridgesSublicius.html (accessed March 27, 2004).

2. Jim Collins, *Good to Great* (New York: Harper Business, 2001).

3. Shabtai Teveth, *Moshe Dayan* (New York: Dell Publishing Co, 1972), pp. 207–208.

4. Leigh Buchanan, "Managing One on One," *INC.* (October 2001), available at http://www.inc.com/magazine/20011001/23479.html (accessed April 2, 2004).

5. Susan Greco, "Little Big Company," *INC.* (November 15, 2001), available at http://www.inc.com/magazine/20011115/23526.html (accessed April 5, 2004).

6. "Survey: Committed Employees Lack Committed Employers," study done by Wirthlin Worldwide, McLean, Virginia, compiled by Michael A. Verespej, IndustryWeek.com (April 5, 2001); available at http://www.industry week.com/DailyPage/newsitem.asp?id=3009 (accessed April 5, 2004).

7. "Cockleshell Heroes," Royal Marines Regimental (2002), available at http://www.royalmarinesregimental.co.uk/histcockintro.html (accessed March 30, 2004).

8. Ibid.

9. Ibid.

10. Ibid.

11. Ibid.

12. Herb Kelleher, "A Culture of Commitment," *Leader to Leader* No. 4 (Spring 1997); available at http://www.pfdf.org/leaderbooks/l2l/spring97/ kelleher.html (accessed April 8, 2004).

Chapter 6

1. The Apprentice Season One Web site, available at http://www.nbc.com/ nbc/The_Apprentice/ (accessed April 17, 2004); and Mike DeGeorge, "The Apprentice on Larry King Live: A Recap" *Reality News Online* (April 23, 2004), available at http://www.realitynewsonline.com/cgi-bin/ae.

pl?mode = 1&article = article4412. art&page = 1 (accessed April 23, 2004).

2. Craig Dunn Enterprises, "George Day Wagner," Civil War-Indiana Web site, available at http://www.civilwarindiana.com/biographies/wagner _george_day.html (accessed November 1, 2004).

3. John J. Lumpkin, "Former NFL Player Killed in Afghanistan," Top Stories AP (April 23, 2004), http://story.news.yahoo.com/news?tmpl = story& cid = 514&e = 3&u = /ap/20040423 /ap_on_sp_fo_ne/ fbn_afghan_nfl_player_1, accessed April 23, 2004.

4. J. D. Hayworth, quoted in Billy House and Judd Slivka, "Pat Tillman Killed in Afghanistan," *The Arizona Republic* (April 23, 2004), available at http:// www.azcentral.com/sports/cardinals/tillman/0423Tillman23-ON.html (accessed April 23, 2004).

Chapter 7

1. Jane Resture, "About Evans Carlson and the Carlson's Raiders," Jane's Oceanic Home Page, available at http://www.janeresture.com/carlson _about/ (accessed April 28, 2004).

2. Dick Gaines, "Carlson of the Raider Marines," Gunny G's Marines Web sites, available at http://www.angelfire.com/ca/dickg/carlson.html (accessed April 28, 2004).

3. This information was presented verbally during a class in military psychology and leadership conducted in 1957 at the United States Military Academy (USMC) at West Point. USMC exchange officer, Lt. Colonel F. C. Caldwell, stated that while Carlson's leadership techniques had been effective in combat, marines reassigned after service in Carlson's unit had great difficulty in adjusting to the more formalized relationships required between officers and other ranks in regular marine units. In today's parlance, there was a cultural mismatch.

4. Seymour M. Hersh, "Annals of National Security: Escape and Evasion," *The New Yorker* (November 12, 2001), available at http://www.newyorker. com/fact/content/?011112fa_FACT (accessed May 19, 2004).

5. Bob Tutt, "World War II Remembered: Guerrilla-Like Carlson's Raiders Rode to the Sound of the Guns," *Houston Chronicle* (June 30, 1995), available at http://www.chron.com/content/chronicle/world/95/07/01/raiders .html (accessed April 28, 2004).

6. Edward C. Whitman, "Submarine Commandos: Carlson's Raiders at Makin," *Undersea Warfare* Vol. 3, No. 2 (Winter 2001), available at http:// www.chinfo.navy.mil/navpalib/cno/n87/usw/issue_10/ submarine_command os.html (accessed April 28, 2004). Although a remarkable tactical success, the Makin Atoll raid is considered a failure by

many because it revealed some of the marines' capabilities to the enemy and caused the Japanese to reinforce other island garrisons that might otherwise have proved easier to capture later.

7. "The Long Patrol," U.S. Marine Raider Association, available at http://www.usmarineraiders.org/longpatrol.html (accessed April 28, 2004).

8. Joel M. Hutchins, *Swimmers Among the Trees: SEALs in the Vietnam War* (Novato, CA: Presidio Press, 1996), p. 13.

9. Tom Peters, *Thriving on Chaos* (New York: Knopf, 1987), p. 306.

10. Jeffrey R. Dichter, "Teamwork and Hospital Medicine: A Vision for the Future," *Critical Care Nurse* (June 2003), p. 8.

11. Alan Chapman, "Bruce Tuckman's 1965 Forming, Storming, Norming, Performing Team-Development Model," available at http://www.business balls.com/tuckmanformingstormingnormingperforming.htm (accessed November 2, 2004).

12. F. Petrock, "Team Dynamics: A Workshop for Effective Team Building," Presentation at the University of Michigan Management of Managers Program, 1997.

Chapter 8

1. "Col. John Mosby and the Southern Code of Honor," available at http://xroads.virginia.edu/~class/am483_97/Projects/anderson/intro.html (accessed May 2, 2004).

2. "Physical Appearance and the Code of Honor," available at http://xroads .virginia.edu/~CLASS/am483_97/projects/anderson/body.html (accessed May 3, 2004).

3. "The War in the Shenandoah Valley: Colonel John S. Mosby," available at http://www.angelfire.com/va3/valleywar/people/mosby.html (accessed May 3, 2004).

4. "Colonel John Singleton Mosby, 43rd Battalion Virginia Cavalry," *Confederate Military History*, Vol. III, pp. 1057–1059; available on The Virginia Civil War Page at http://members.aol.com/jweaver300/grayson/mosby.htm (accessed May 2, 2004).

5. Geri Smith and Stephanie Forrest, "Slim's New World: Mexico's Richest Man Is Betting Big on U.S. Computer Retailing," *Business Week* (March 6, 2000), p. 161.

6. Ibid.

7. Colonel Andrew Summers Rowan, "How I Carried the Message to Garcia," available at http://hermstrom.tripod.com/rowan.html (accessed May 12, 2004).

8. John Sculley, *Odyssey* (New York: Harper & Row Publishers, 1987), p. 90.

9. Charles J. Schwahn and William G. Spady, "Why Change Doesn't Happen

and How to Make Sure It Does," *Educational Leadership* Vol. 55, No. 7 (April. 1998) pp. 45–47.

10. Sally Love, "It's 8 A.M.—Do You Know Where You Are Heading?" *PaperAge* (July 2000), available at http://www.paperage.com/07_2000love.html (accessed May 12, 2004).

11. When I became a general officer, I directed that a challenge coin be minted on which our organization's vision was inscribed. The coin debuted at our organization's annual dinner party. It occurred to me that rather than just hand out these coins, it would be nice to have someone read the history of the challenge coin. At the time, despite the best efforts of some of the finest researchers at Air University in Alabama, we could never find a confirmed and documented true history. So, based on hearsay and anecdotal evidence, I wrote "The History of the Challenge Coin" and had it printed and distributed, along with the coin, to the dinner's 300 participants. This was in 1992. Much to my chagrin, I've since learned that any Internet search will now bring up many versions of my original words as the absolute and unvarnished story of how the challenge coin came about. Be careful of what you write or say, even in a relatively closed setting. It may become history.

12. "Vietnam War Congressional Medal of Honor Recipient Captain Humbert Roque 'Rocky' Versace," The Medal of Honor Web site, available at http://www.medalofhonor.com/RockyVersaceBiography.htm (accessed May 14, 2004).

Chapter 9

1. "The Battle of Gettysburg: July 1–3, 1863," available at http://www.ameri cancivilwar.com/getty.html (accessed May 16, 2004).

2. "The Gettysburg Campaign," from Steven E. Woodworth, Kenneth J. Winkle, and James M. McPherson's *The Atlas of the Civil War* (Oxford University Press), available at http://www.civilwarhome.com/gettyscampaign .htm (accessed May 16, 2004).

3. "Battle of Gettysburg," The History Place, available at http://www.history place.com/civilwar/battle.htm (accessed May 16, 2004).

4. Jim Schmidt and Curtis Fears, "Lee to the Rear," The Battle of the Wilderness: A Virtual Tour (July 12, 2000), available at http://hallowed-ground. home.att.net/lee_to_rear.html (accessed May 17, 2004).

5. Andrew S. Grove, *One-on-One with Andy Grove* (New York: G. P. Putnam's Sons, 1987), p. 60.

6. Michael Shaara, *The Killer Angels* (New York: Ballantine Books, 1974), pp. 265–266.

7. Naval Special Warfare Public Affairs, "Navy SEAL Leader Receives German

Award for Afghanistan Operations," *Navy Newstand* (August 24, 2002), available at http://www.news.navy.mil/search/display.asp?story_id=3260 (accessed May 20, 2002).

Chapter 10

1. John Hendren and Richard T. Cooper, "Fragile Forces in a Hostile Land," *Los Angeles Times* (May 5, 2002) available at http://www.why-war.com/news/2002/05/05/fragilea.html (accessed May 22, 2004).

2. "Interview with Captain Jason Amerine," *PBS Front Line* (July 9 and 12, 2002), available at http://www.pbs.org/wgbh/pages/frontline/shows/cam paign/interviews/amerine.html (accessed May 22, 2004).

3. Ibid.

4. Anne M Mulcahy, "Success Is Management: CEO's Taking Responsibility," Vital Speeches of the Day Vol. 69, No. 2 (November 1, 2002), p. 45.

5. Ibid, p. 46.

6. Ibid.

7. "Op. Archery—Vaagso and Malloy—27th December 1941," Combined Operations Web site, available at http://www.combinedops.com/vaagso .htm (accessed June 1, 2004).

8. "No. 3 Commando," available at http://www26.brinkster.com/yvonneml/History/details.asp?name=Durnford-Slater (accessed June 1, 2004).

9. "Op. Archery—Vaagso and Malloy—27th December 1941," http://www .combinedops.com/vaagso.htm (accessed June 1, 2004).

10. "Mayor Michael R. Bloomberg Presents $45.7 Billion FY 2005 Preliminary Budget," *News from the Blue Room* (January 15, 2004), available at http://home.nyc.gov (accessed June 2, 2004).

11. Elizabeth Kolbert, "The Un-Communicator," *The New Yorker* (March 1, 2004) available at http://www.newyorker.com/fact/content/?040301fa _fact (accessed June 2, 2004).

12. "Schwarzenegger Declares a Financial Crisis," Asia.News.Yahoo (December 11, 2003) available at http://asia.news.yahoo.com/031219/ap/d7vh76 781.html (accessed June 2, 2004).

13. Alexas H. Bruth, "Governor's Popularity Keeps Rising," *Sacramento Bee* (May 27, 2004), available at http://www.sacbee.com/content/politics/ca/story/9441157p-10365310c.html (accessed June 2, 2004).

Chapter 11

1. "Doolittle's Tokyo Raid," Air Force Museum, available at http://www .wpafb.af.mil/museum/features/trvideo.htm (accessed June 4, 2004).

2. "Jimmy Doolittle," Wikipedia, the Free Encyclopedia, available at http://en.wikipedia.org/wiki/Jimmy_Doolittle (accessed June 4, 2004); and Pam-

ela Feltus, "Jimmy Doolittle—Aviation Star," U.S. Centennial of Flight Commission, available at http://www.1903to2003.gov/essay/Air_Power/doolittle/AP17.htm (accessed June 4, 2004).

3. "The Doolittle Raid," *U.S. Enterprise CV-6: The Most Decorated Ship of the Second World War*, available at http://www.cv6.org/1942/doolittle/doolittle.htm (accessed June 4, 2004).

4. Ben R. Rich, "Clarence Leonard (Kelly) Johnson," National Academy of Sciences Biographical Memoirs, available at http://www.nap.edu/html/bio mems/cjohnson.html (accessed June 10, 2004).

5. "Bravo Zulu," Department of the Navy—Naval Historical Center, available at http://www.history.navy.mil/faqs/faq101-2.htm (accessed June 11, 2004).

6. "Executive Salaries," Jewish Association for Business Ethics, available at http://www.jabe.org/ethical-dilemmas/executive_salaries/ (accessed June 5, 2004).

7. Douglas MacArthur, *Reminiscences* (New York: McGraw-Hill Book Co., 1964), p. 70.

Chapter 12

1. Gregory "Pappy" Boyington, *Baa Baa Black Sheep* (New York: Bantam Books, 1977), p. 123.

2. Ibid, pp. 124–125.

3. "Major Gregory 'Pappy' Boyington," American Aces of World War II, available at http://www.acepilots.com/usmc_boyington.html (accessed June 14, 2004).

4. Thomas Rogers, "Scouting," *The New York Times* (May 17, 1984), p. D26.

5. "Scarsdale Soccer Fitness Routine Pays Off in an 83-Game Streak," *The New York Times* (October 23, 1983), p. S12.

6. Jean Merl, "Teenagers' Graduation Proves Activist's Vision," *Los Angeles Times* (June 18, 2004), pp. B1, 8.

7. "A Brief History," www.TheBlackDevils.com, available at http://www .theblackdevils.com/Brief%20History.htm (accessed June 16, 2004).

8. Jon W. Blades, *Rules for Leadership* (Washington, D.C: National Defense University, 1986), pp. 76–78.

9. Martin Hoegl and Hans Gemuenden, "Teamwork Quality and the Success of Innovative Projects: A Theoretical Concept and Empirical Evidence," *Organization Science* Vol. 12 No. 4 (July/August 2001), p. 435.

10. Robert Frankel and Judith Whipple, "Testing a Model of Long-Term Alliance Success," *Hospital Material Management Quarterly* Vol. 20, No. 4 (May 1999), p. 55.

11. Peter F. Drucker, *The Effective Executive* (New York: Harper and Row, 1967), pp. 68–69.

12. Robert Debs Heinl, Jr., *Dictionary of Military and Naval Quotations* (Annapolis, MD: United States Naval Institute, 1966), p. 196.

13. Edgar F. Puryear, Jr., *19 Stars* (Novato, CA: Presidio Press, 1981), p. 233.

14. Steven R. Ginley, "Principles of Public Speaking (SPE 101) Internet," available at http://usingyourspeechpower.com/kick_rear_end.shtml (accessed June 16, 2004).

15. *The Armed Forces Officer* (Washington, D.C.: U.S. Government Printing Office, 1959), p. 159.

16. Gustave Le Bon's book has been translated into English and published as *The Crowd: A Study of the Popular Mind* (Minneola, NY: Dover Publications, Inc., 2002).

17. Puryear, *19 Stars,* p. 326

Chapter 13

1. William H. McRaven, *Spec Ops* (Novato, CA: Presidio Press, 1995), p. 142.

2. "St. Nazaire—Operation Chariot—28 March 1942," CombinedOperations.com, available at http://www.combinedops.com/St%20Nazaire.htm (accessed June 21, 2004).

3. Ray Kroc, with Robert Anderson, *Grinding It Out: The Making of McDonald's* (New York: St. Martin's Press, 1987), p. 201.

4. Andrew L. Carney, "Learn by Looking: See the Obvious, Ask Questions, Find Answers" (February 5, 2003), available at http://www.uic.edu/classes/neuros/neurosvascular1/publications/kinko-orfalea.pdf (accessed June 22, 2004).

5. Paul Seaburn, "Paul Orfalea: Duplicating Success," *Y&E* (Summer 2000), available at http://ye.entreworld.org/5-2000/bio_orfalea.cfm (accessed June 22, 2004).

6. David Smith and Frieda Gehlen, "GBR Conversation with Paul Orfalea," *Graziadio Business Report* Issue 4 (2002), available at http://gbr.pepperdine.edu/024/print_conversation.html (assessed June 22, 2004).

7. Patrick O'Donnell, "America's Elite Troops in World War II: The Force," World War II History Information, available at http://worldwar2history.info/Army/elite/Special-Forces.html (accessed June 22, 2004).

8. "History: First Special Service Force," available at http://www.groups.sfahq.com/fssf/history.htm (accessed June 23, 2004).

9. Lance Zedric and Michael Dilley, *Elite Warriors: 300 Years of America's Best Fighting Troops* (Ventura, CA: Pathfinder Publications, 1996), p. 158.

10. "The Devil's Brigade," Wikipedia, the Free Encyclopedia, at http://en.wik ipedia.org/wiki/Devil's_Brigade (accessed June 22, 2004).

11. "Operation Urgent Fury (October 198s)," Night Stalkers Web Site, available at http://www.nightstalkers.com/history/2.html (accessed June 22, 2004); "Urgent Fury," *Night Stalker History*, at http://www.nightstalkers .com/urgent_fury/ (accessed June 22, 2004) and Thomas Hunter, "Fort Rupert and Richmond Hill Prison," Special Operations Command, available at http://www.specialoperations.com/Operations/richmond.html (accessed June 22, 2004).

Chapter 14

1. "Win One for the Gipper," available at http://home.no.net/birgerro/gipp win.htm (accessed June 24, 2004); and "George Gipp," available at http:// www.clk.k12.mi.us/chs/laurium/gipp/gipphist.htm (accessed June 24, 2004). "Win One for the Gipper:1928 Notre Dame vs Army," at www .2cuz.com/features/nd-army1928.html (accessed June 24, 2004).

2. "The Battle of Thermopylae," available at http:// joseph_berrigan.tripod.com/ancientbabylon/id28.html (accessed June 28, 2004).

3. "Molon Labe: A Response to Tyranny," available at http://www.thefiring line.com/HCI/Tam_Essay.htm (accessed June 28, 2004).

4. "Thermopylae," available at http://www.greyhawkes.com/blacksword/ Spartan%20Combat%20Arts%202001/1-Pages/Hi story/Thermopylae.htm (accessed June 28, 2004).

5. Ellis Knox, "The Battle of Platea and After," *The Persian Wars*, Boise State Web site, available at http://history.boisestate.edu/westciv/persian/23.htm (accessed June 28, 2004).

6. "The Battle of Thermopylae," Wikipedia, the Free Enclycopedia, available at http://en.wikipedia.org/wiki/Battle_of_Thermopylae (accessed June 28, 2004).

Chapter 15

1. *The Journal of Leadership Applications* is an e-journal edited and published by this book's author, William A. Cohen; to sign-up for a free subscription, go to www.StuffofHeroes.com.

2. Orr Kelly, *From a Dark Sky: The Story of U.S. Air Force Special Operations* (New York: Pocket Books, 1996), p. 280.

3. Clay McCutchan, telephone conversation with the author (October 1, 1997).

INDEX